I Must
HAVE THAT
RECIPE

I Must Have That Recipe

S.P.I. BOOKS

A division of Shapolsky Publishers, Inc.

Previously published by the Westchester Chapter—National Women's Division—of Albert Einstein College of Medicine of Yeshiva University, 1300 Morris Park Avenue, Suite B-802, Bronx, New York 10481

For any additional information, contact:

S.P.I. BOOKS/Shapolsky Publishers, Inc.
136 West 22nd Street
New York, NY 10011
(212) 633-2022
FAX (212) 633-2123

ISBN: 1-56171-166-7

10 9 8 7 6 5 4 3 2 1

Printed and bound in the United States of America

INTRODUCTION

For those who love food, there are certain special moments–at a restaurant, a dinner party, or just dining informally with friends–when a beautifully prepared dish delights us and we suddenly think, "I must have that recipe." For those fine recipes which can be collected after such an experience, everyone has a special fondness. We know they represent "the best;" family secrets lovingly passed down through generations, or created by inspired cooks, or those culinary masterpieces incorporating the trade secrets of highly skilled professionals. These are the recipes we invariably desire when we want to treat our family and friends with special care and affection.

It is just such a collection that the Westchester Chapter of the National Women's Division of the Albert Einstein College of Medicine presents in this volume. Since the proceeds from the sale of this book will help support one of the best known and most distinguished biomedical institutions in this country, many sources normally closed to others were available to us. Restaurateurs, spa nutritionists, entertainers and manufacturers of kitchen equipment have generously contributed to our collection. As word of our project spread, we received recipes from almost every region of the country, as well as from abroad, reflecting a diversity of backgrounds and tastes.

Whether you are trying the *Caviar Pie*, the savory *Roast Rack of Lamb*, an elegant poached fish, or that piéce de resistánce, *Death by Chocolate*, we know you will find these recipes a pleasure to cook with and a means of pleasing those you love.

Proceeds from the sale of "I Must Have That Recipe" will benefit research in cardiology, cancer, neuroscience and metabolic diseases which are the ongoing projects of the Einstein Women's Division. We hope you, our reader, will gain satisfaction from knowing that as you expand your culinary experiences you are simultaneously helping to support researchers at the Albert Einstein College of Medicine of Yeshiva University in their continuing efforts to enhance life for all mankind.

The Albert Einstein College of Medicine is a graduate school of Yeshiva University, therefore, all our recipes are consistent with Dietary Laws. Rabbinic Certification is available, where needed, for all products included in these recipes.

Hope K. Hirschhorn
Chairwoman

Corrine Katz
Editor

Cookbook Committee

CHAIRWOMAN	Hope Hirschhorn
EDITOR	Corrine Katz
ASSISTANT EDITOR	Len Feiman
MARKETING	Renee Geller
	Charlotte Gold
	Irene Lippert
TREASURER	Linda Altman
COVER & SECTION DIVIDERS DESIGNED BY	Dana Sloan

Adele Bagg
Susan Berenson
Maureen Berkman
Joanne Bross
Phyllis Fass
Roxene Feinberg
Sondra Feinberg
Rona Feuer
Carol Goldstone
Diane Hallenbeck
Micki Hoffman
Madeline Klein
Marge Lewin
Paula Lustbader
Gail Marcus
Ilana Nowick
Patricia Patent
Helen Peck
Rita Rosen
Susan Sandelman
Elaine Satuloff
Estelle Silverstone
Debbie Simon
Lila Stillman
Elaine Strauss
Gloria Svirsky
Lucille Wagner
Penny Weill
Frances Weisman
Helene Wolloch

Credits

The Westchester Chapter of the National Women's Division of the Albert Einstein College of Medicine of Yeshiva University wishes to express our gratitude to the following for their generous contributions:

Dennis Gottlieb/Photographer
Richmond B. Ellis/Food Stylist
Nancy Mernit/Prop Stylist
China courtesy of/Hutschen Reuther/Bernardaud/Villeroy + Boch

Acknowledgement

We are especially grateful to all the talented cooks who submitted their recipes. Without them, this fabulous collection would not have been possible. Unfortunately, we did not have the space to include all the many wonderful recipes that we received and for that we are truly sorry. Our warm thanks to our contributors whose names are listed below.

Susan Abrams
Ruth Abromowitz
Ruth Alpert
Linda Altman
Mary Barnhard
Susan Berenson
Terry Berger
Linda Berk
Maureen Berkman
Janet Bernstein
Fritzi Bertuch
Marianne Beyl
Judy Bianco
Fern Bindelglass
Barbara Blau
Lilly Block
Ellen Bloom
Carol Bockner
Fae Boczko
Joanne Bross
Sandy Butwin
Serita Butwin
Helen Campbell
Vicki Capin
Joan Carroll
Marylyn Castros
Evelyn Colton
Rona Cutler
Carolyn Davis
Flora Dominus
Daisy Dwyer
Eve Ebenhart
Sondra Eichel
Reba Etra
Phyllis Fass
Goldie Feigert
Len Feiman
Betty Feinberg
Roxene Feinberg
Sondra Feinberg
Pearl Firestone
Al Fields
Marilyn Fields
Susan Fischer
Wendy Friedrich
Sarah Jane Fuchs
Lois Gallant
Rita Glanzer
Robert Gold, M.D.
Myra Goldberg
Mildred Goldberger
Gail Goldey
Lee Goldman
Carol A. Goldstone
Shirley Goller
Stephanie Green
Florence Greenberg
Ruth Greer
Arnold Gross
Blanche Gutstein
Diane Hallenbeck
Ethel Halpern
Grace Heller
Gloria Hendler
Marcia Hendler
Hope Hirschhorn
Mark Hirschhorn
Roger Hirschhorn
Gail Hoffman
Micki Hoffman
Cynthia Hogan
Taubene Hoppenstein
Paulette Howard
Ann Jacobson
Kim and Spencer Joyce
Dorothy Kagon
Aileen Karp
Susan Kaskel
Corrine Katz
Jeffrey Katz
Lisa Katz
Marilyn Katz
Mark Katz
Sally Katz
Susan Katz
Alice Kent
Joy Klebanoff
Maria Kokinakis
Doe Koppana
Denise Korngold
Dorothy Kramer
Annette Kranich
Amy Berk Kurtzman
Betty Laboz
Emily Landau
Michelle Lattman
Eve Lefes
Myrna Lehr
Amy Satuloff Lemle
Audré Lemler

Beryl Levitt
Sherry Lieb
Paula Lustbader
Duffy Lyon
Audrey Mann
Philip Martino
Harriet Mattikow
Yvonne Maxwell
Morton Metzger
Harriet Meyers
Hilda Milton
Anita Newman
Renee Nussbaum
Sylvia Orenstein
Blanche Orlofsky
Grace Oshin
Judi Paseltiner
Helen Peck
Beverly Picker
Ann Pochapin
Marsha Pollack
Sugs Pulitzer
Jeanne Quinn
Rose Rabbino
Judy Resnick
Pearl Resnick
Meri Ritter
Nataly Ritter
Anita Roe
Judy Rosenberg
Mary Rosenblatt
Marcia Rosenthal
Ruth Rosenthal
Margo Ruddy
Joan Safir
Elaine Satuloff
Lucille Scheer
Barbara Schlein
Ellie Schwartz
Rita Schwartz
Rose Segal
Wendy Shemer
Marilyn Sherman
Menucha Shrier
Brenda Sichel
Margot Sider
Brenda Siegler
Estelle Silverstone
Debbie Simon
Fredya Simon
Amy Singer
Marcia Singer
Elinore Skalit
Joanne Skemer
Rita Sloan
Bobbie Sloate
Pearl Smith
Carol Solomon
Lotty Stein
Ellie Stengel
Elaine Strauss
Sharon Strongin
Gloria Svirsky
Judy Tallarico
Judy Tauber
Nancy Thompson
Amy Townsend
B. Terri Trieger
Ruth Turim
Gen Vergari
Lucille Wagner
Pat Wagner
Zilota Walters
Elizabeth Waymire
Gregory Weill
Penny Weill
Eleanor Weiner
Sylvia Weinsier
Elaine Weiser
Fran Weisman
Audrey Wiley
Marilyn Wilkes
Aileen Wolff
Cuisinarts

Restaurants & Celebrities
Abigail Kirsch
America
Auberge Maxime
Brae Burn Country Club
The Cafe Budapest
Charley's Crab
Charley's 517
"Empress Subaru"
Enzo's
Ernie's
Famous Sammy's Restaurant
Suzanne Farrel
Fenway Golf—Club
Diane Von Furstenberg
Gregory's
Hay Day
Jillyflower's
Jorge's Uptown Enchilada Bar, Inc.
La Recólte
Marion & Robert Merrill
Michelangelo
Old Drovers Inn
Roberta Peters
Prunelle
Restaurant Laurent
Scarlatti
Tavern On the Green
Teacher's
The Point
The Saloon
Tony's
The "21" Club
Umberto
Vanessa
Vista International Hotel
Vivolo
Shelley Winters

Spas
Bonaventure® Resort & Spa
Canyon Ranch®
Doral Saturnia International Spa Resort
Elizabeth Arden's Maine Chance
Spa Food by Edward J. Safdie
Woodrow Weigh of Life

PERTINENT PARTICULARS

- Read all recipes thoroughly before starting for optimum success.
- Have all utensils and ingredients out and ready before beginning a recipe.
- Follow directions exactly as given.
- Use size of pan suggested in recipe.
- Try to always use fresh available ingredients.
- Rinse saucepan with cold water, before boiling milk to prevent scorching.
- To cut dates and other sticky fruits, use a wet scissor dipped in water occasionally.
- Adding salt to water while boiling eggs will prevent shell from cracking.
- When sautéeing, add a little oil to butter or margarine to prevent burning.
- Pour fresh lemon and lime juice in freezer ice trays. When frozen, remove from trays and put into plastic bags. You will have them on hand for any recipe requiring fresh lemon or lime juice.
- To release juice from lemons or limes, have at room temperature. With the palm of your hand roll them on the counter top, back and forth a few times. Cut in half and squeeze the juice from each half.
- Grate fresh lemon and lime rind on wax paper or in a bowl. Put into a plastic container and store in freezer or cover with vodka and refrigerate.

Table of Contents

Weights and Measures

3 teaspoons	equal	1 tablespoon
2 tablespoons	equal	1 ounce
4 tablespoons	equal	¼ cup
5⅓ tablespoons	equal	⅓ cup
8 tablespoons	equal	½ cup
16 tablespoons or 8 fluid ounces	equal	1 cup
1 cup	equal	½ pint
2 cups	equal	1 pint
4 cups	equal	1 quart
4 quarts	equal	1 gallon
2 tablespoons butter	equal	1 ounce
½ cup butter	equal	¼ pound
1 cup whipping cream	equal	2 cups whipped
2¼ cups granulated sugar	equal	1 pound
2¼ cups firmly packed brown sugar	equal	1 pound
3½ cups sifted confectioners' sugar	equal	1 pound
4 cups sifted all-purpose flour	equal	1 pound
2 cups barley flour	equal	1 pound
4½ cups sifted cake flour	equal	1 pound
4½ cups rye flour	equal	1 pound
8-10 egg whites	equal	1 cup
10-14 egg yolks	equal	1 cup
4-6 whole eggs	equal	1 cup
10 average eggs without shells	equal	1 pound
7-8 large eggs with shells	equal	1 pound
9-10 medium eggs with shells	equal	1 pound
11-12 small eggs with shells	equal	1 pound
1 pound medium ground coffee	equal	45 cups
1 pound tea	equal	60 cups
1 teaspoon of any dried herb	equal	1 tablespoon fresh
1 square chocolate	equal	1 ounce
1 cup chopped nuts	equal	¼ pound
Juice of one lemon	equal	2 tablespoons bottled lemon juice

Hors D'Oeuvres & Appetizers

PERTINENT PARTICULARS

- When using phyllo dough spread work surface with waxed paper, and always work as quickly as possible. To prevent sheets from drying out, cover loosely with plastic wrap.

ARTICHOKE CHILI CHEESE DIP

A sure hit with your guests.

Yield: 2½ cups

1 (8½-ounce) can artichoke hearts, packed in water, drained
1 (6-ounce) jar marinated artichoke hearts, drained
1 (4-ounce) can diced green chilies
6 tablespoons mayonnaise
1½ to 2 cups Cheddar cheese, shredded
Tortilla chips

- Preheat oven to 350 degrees. Generously grease a shallow 2 quart baking dish.
- Chop artichokes together and distribute evenly over bottom of baking dish. Scatter chilies on top. Carefully spread mayonnaise over all. Sprinkle with the cheese.
- Bake covered for 15 minutes or until hot and bubbly.
- Serve with tortilla chips.

Note: If prepared ahead, cover and refrigerate until ready to bake. Bake for 30 minutes.

Barbara Schlein
Ryebrook, New York

ARTICHOKE HORS D'OEUVRE

Serves: 8

1 (8½-ounce) can artichoke hearts (not marinated)
1 large onion, chopped fine
1 cup mayonnaise
1 cup grated Parmesan cheese
Dash (2 to 3 drops) Worcestershire sauce
Juice of ½ lemon or 1 tablespoon frozen concentrate, defrosted
Dash salt and pepper
Italian flavored bread crumbs for topping
Toasted pita bread

- Preheat oven to 350 degrees. Drain artichokes, using a strainer, then dry on paper towels.
- In a food processor, chop onion and artichokes fine. Remove to a bowl and stir in mayonnaise. Add Parmesan cheese, Worcestershire sauce, lemon and seasonings.
- Pour mixture into a lightly greased au gratin dish and top with Italian bread crumbs. Bake for 1 hour. Serve with toasted pita cut into sections.

Marcia Singer
Harrison, New York

BABA GHANOUJ

Serves: 8

1 medium-size eggplant
Juice of 1 lemon
¼ cup tahini (canned sesame paste), drained
1 small onion, minced, optional
1 clove garlic, minced, optional

- Preheat oven to 450 degrees. Cut off the blossom end of eggplant and place eggplant in a pie plate or on aluminum foil. Bake for 1 hour. When cool enough to handle, peel the skin from the eggplant.
- Put all the ingredients in a blender or food processor and blend for 1 minute.
- Serve cold with rye toast triangles, bagel chips or toasted pita bread.

Note: Can be used as a vegetable dip.

Betty Feinberg
Short Hills, New Jersey

Editors Note: Found the eggplant was baked in 30 to 40 minutes.

BAKED BRIE IN PHYLLO

A creative touch.

Serves: 32

Prepare ahead

¼ cup apricot preserves (optional)
1 (2-pound) wheel of Brie
½ pound frozen phyllo dough (10 to 12 sheets) thawed
½ cup butter, melted

- Use a cookie sheet.
- Spread preserves on top of Brie. Wrap Brie in thawed phyllo leaves, 2 sheets at a time. Brush with melted butter. Turn cheese over, wrap with phyllo, brush with butter. Turn cheese over, repeat using all the phyllo sheets. Cover, brush with butter and refrigerate for 1 hour or up to 24 hours.
- Place on cookie sheet and bake in 425 degree oven for 8 to 12 minutes or until golden brown. Let stand 10 minutes before serving.

Shirley S. Goller
Mission, Kansas

BASIC FISH MOUSSE FOR FOOD PROCESSOR

An attractive company dish.

Serves: 8 to 10

1¼ pounds skinless, boneless, white fish (bass, flounder, fluke or sole)
2 large eggs
Salt and pepper to taste
⅛ teaspoon grated nutmeg
½ cup chopped scallions
1½ cups heavy cream

- Preheat oven to 375 degrees. Butter a 4½ to 5 cup ring mold.
- Cut fish into cubes; place in processor. Add eggs and seasoning and blend coarsely. Gradually add cream pouring through funnel, and continue to blend until mixture is thick, about 45 seconds. Spoon into ring mold. Cover with ring of waxed paper cut to fit. Place mold in water, bring to a boil on top of stove; place in oven for 35 to 40 minutes until set. Let stand 10 minutes before unmolding.

Sauce

1 tablespoon butter
3 tablespoons finely chopped onion
1 tablespoon finely chopped shallots
⅓ cup dry white wine
2 cups cubed peeled tomato
Salt and pepper to taste
1½ cups heavy cream

- Melt butter, add onion and shallots. Cook until wilted. Add wine, tomatoes and seasoning. Cook for 10 minutes. Add cream; continue cooking for 10 minutes longer.
- Serve with fish mousse.

Fran Weisman
Scarsdale, New York

BREADED MUSHROOMS WITH ANCHOVY MAYONNAISE

A party pleaser!

Yield: Depending on number of mushrooms.

1 pound mushrooms (the larger the better)
½ cup flour
2 eggs, beaten
1 tablespoon olive oil
¼ cup water
Salt and freshly ground pepper to taste
2 cups fresh bread crumbs
½ teaspoon crushed oregano
¼ teaspoon red pepper flakes
¼ teaspoon dried thyme
Oil for frying, either peanut, vegetable or corn oil
*** Anchovy mayonnaise recipe follows**
Lemon wedges

- Rinse mushrooms and dry well. Dredge in flour.
- Blend eggs, oil, water, salt and pepper, beating well.
- Mix crumbs, oregano, pepper flakes and thyme. Dip mushrooms in egg mixture, then in crumbs. Repeat.
- Heat oil until hot, add mushrooms and sauté, stirring and turning with a slotted spoon, for 4 to 6 minutes or until nicely browned all over. Drain well. Serve with anchovy mayonnaise and lemon wedges.

Note: Can be done in advance and then heated.

* ***Anchovy Mayonnaise***

Yield: 1 cup

1 egg yolk
1 teaspoon Dijon style mustard
1 teaspoon lemon juice
Salt and freshly ground pepper, to taste
¾ to 1 cup peanut, vegetable or corn oil
1 to 2 tablespoons anchovy paste

- Place yolk in mixing bowl. Add mustard, juice, salt and pepper to taste. It is imperative that the yolk be combined with the acid provided by the mustard and juice before the oil is added. The acid will help prevent curdling.
- Gradually add oil to the yolk mixture while beating vigorously with wire whisk or electric beater. When approximately half the oil has been added, the remainder can be added more rapidly. It is best to use the full cup of oil. Add anchovy paste.
- If mayonnaise seems too thick, it may be thinned with a small amount of cold water.

Joan Safir
Stamford, Connecticut

BRIE EN CROUTE

Serves: 10 to 12

Prepare ahead

1½ cups all-purpose flour
Pinch salt
1 (8-ounce) package cream cheese, room temperature
½ cup sweet butter, room temperature
8 ounces (4-inch individual size) Brie cheese
Caraway seeds

- Preheat oven to 400 degrees. Use a pie plate or cookie sheet.
- Combine flour, salt, cream cheese and butter; roll into a ball. Refrigerate 20 minutes or longer.
- Cut in half. Roll half on floured surface into 11-inch circle. Sprinkle caraway seeds within 2-inches of border. Place brie in center, fold up and twist at top so that entire brie is covered. Refrigerate 1 hour or longer. Place on a pie plate or cookie sheet. Bake for 10 minutes in oven, reduce heat to 350 degrees and bake 20 minutes longer.
- Cool ½ hour before serving. Freeze dough (other half) for another time or make 2 and freeze before baking. If freezing, defrost fully before baking.

Serita Butwin
Woodmere, New York

CAPONATA

A great appetizer!

Yield: 3 cups

This recipe must be made at least 3 days before serving (4 to 5 days even better).

2 pounds Japanese eggplant or 1 large regular eggplant (preferably Japanese for this recipe)
1 tablespoon olive oil, more if necessary
1 clove garlic, whole
¾ cup onions, coarsely chopped
2 cups celery, coarsely chopped
⅓ cup wine vinegar
4 teaspoons sugar
3 cups plum tomatoes with basil
2 tablespoons tomato paste
*** 2 tablespoons capers, soaked in water, then drained**
*** 4 to 6 anchovies, soaked in water, then drained and cut into small pieces**
*** ½ cup green or black pitted olives, soaked and drained**
¼ cup Burgundy wine or dry sherry
Freshly ground pepper to taste; don't be shy in using pepper
½ cup pine nuts (optional)

- Cut Japanese eggplant into 1 inch slices or if using regular eggplant cut into 1 inch cubes. Do not peel.
- In a large skillet, heat olive oil and add garlic. When brown, discard. Add eggplant to oil. An additional amount of oil may be needed, but keep it to a minimum although original recipe calls for ½ cup. Sauté eggplant for a few moments, then transfer to a bowl and set aside. In the same skillet, sauté onions until lightly brown, about 5 minutes. Another small amount of oil may be needed. Add celery, sautéing 3 minutes longer. Tranfer eggplant, onions and celery to a saucepan. Add all other ingredients including "lots" of freshly ground pepper. Simmer for 20 minutes or until eggplant is soft but has not lost its shape. When cool, add ½ cup of pine nuts and stir through.

Note: * Soaking capers, anchovies and olives will remove a great deal of salt. Store in refrigerator.

Dorothy Kagon
Malibu, California

CAVIAR PIE

This is sensational!

Serves: 10 to 12

Prepare 1 day ahead

6 hard-boiled eggs, chopped
¼ pound butter, room temperature
2 large onions, chopped
1 (8-ounce) package cream cheese, room temperature
3 tablespoons sour cream
2 small jars caviar

- Use an 8-inch cake pan.
- Mix eggs with butter. Press mixture into the cake pan, preferably with removable sides, and refrigerate for one hour.
- Press the onions down on top of the eggs. Return to refrigerator for another hour.
- Soften the cream cheese and combine with sour cream. Spread over the onions and again return to the refrigerator for one hour.
- When ready to serve, spread caviar over the cream cheese mixture.
- Serve with your favorite crackers, toasted bread cut into triangles with crusts removed.

Audrey Mann
Boca Raton, Florida

CHEESE BALL

Attractive and easy to prepare.

Serves: 10 to 12

½ pound cream cheese, room temperature
½ pound extra sharp Cheddar cheese, grated
2 cloves garlic, pressed
½ cup chopped pecans or pistachio nuts
Chili powder, as needed

- Combine cheeses, garlic and nuts. Blend by hand or in a food processor. Cover with plastic wrap and form into a ball. Remove plastic wrap and roll in chili powder.
- Store in refrigerator until ready to use. One hour before serving, remove from refrigerator and return to room temperature.

Note: Mixture can be shaped into log using same method to form. Chili powder can be eliminated and the ball or log can be rolled in chopped nuts or California fruit mixture.

Sugs Pulitzer
New Orleans, Louisiana

CHEESY ALMONDS

Unusual!

Yield: Approximately 5 cups

2 egg whites
1½ tablespoons Dijon-style mustard
Pinch of cayenne, more if you like
4 cups raw almonds, unsalted
⅔ cup grated Parmesan cheese

- Preheat oven to 300 degrees. Use a parchment-covered or Teflon baking sheet.
- Whisk egg whites until frothy. Whisk in mustard and cayenne. Add almonds and mix to coat evenly.
- Spread cheese on waxed paper. Remove almonds from egg white mixture with slotted spoon and toss in cheese until all are coated. Spread coated almonds on baking sheet.
- Bake for 25 minutes, until nicely browned. Stir occasionally during baking. Turn off heat and leave nuts in oven for 30 additional minutes.

Note: These freeze well or can be refrigerated.

Len Feiman
White Plains, New York

CHEDDAR CHEESE PUFFS

Yield: 3 dozen

4 tablespoons butter
¾ cup hot water
¾ cup flour
2 eggs
½ cup Cheddar cheese, grated
1 teaspoon salt
Dash cayenne pepper

- Preheat oven to 350 degrees. Butter a cookie sheet.
- In a saucepan, combine butter and hot water and bring to a boil. Add flour to water and stir quickly until the dough becomes a solid ball. Remove from heat and beat in 1 egg. Add second egg and beat until dough is glossy. Beat in grated cheese, salt and pepper.
- Drop by teaspoonfuls onto cookie sheet and bake 10 minutes or until well-browned and crisp.

Susan Katz
Teaneck, New Jersey

CHUTNEY DIP

Yield: 1 cup

8 ounces cream cheese, room temperature
¼ cup chutney
¼ teaspoon dry mustard
1 teaspoon curry powder
Toasted almonds, chopped

- Combine all ingredients, except almonds, and blend by hand. Top with almonds. Serve with crackers or vegetables.

Margo Ruddy
Short Hills, New Jersey

CUCUMBER AND SMOKED SALMON CANAPES

Elegant!

Yield: 24 Canapes

1 (8-ounce) package cream cheese, softened to room temperature
1 small onion, sliced
2 tablespoons fresh dill
¼ pound Nova Scotia salmon for mixture, plus ¼ pound for rosettes (topping)
2 large cucumbers, peeled and sliced ¼ inch thick
Capers or sprigs of dill for garnish

- Purée first four ingredients in an electric blender until light pink. Transfer to a small bowl and refrigerate until chilled and stiff.
- Score cucumbers with a fork before slicing. Cut small slices of salmon and roll up into a rosette. Spread some of the cheese mixture on each slice of cucumber and garnish with a rosette and sprig of dill or caper in the center. Chill before serving.

Sherry Lieb
Livingston, New Jersey

FANCY NUTS

Not for nibblers only!

Serves: 4 to 6

1 egg white, room temperature
1 (8-ounce) can walnuts, unsalted, or equivalent mix
½ cup sugar
1 to 2 tablespoons butter

- Preheat oven to 325 degrees. Use a 9-inch cake pan.
- Beat egg white until foamy. Stir the nuts into the egg white, making sure they are all coated. Toss wet nuts into sugar, again be sure they are all coated.
- Place butter in pan and put in oven. When butter is melted, add the nuts to the pan.
- Bake for 10 minutes. After baking 10 minutes, stir the nuts and bake for 20 minutes more. You may (if you are busy) turn off the oven after 15 minutes and leave nuts in oven, removing them when they look dry and brown.

Variations:

1. Add ¼ cup cornstarch to ½ cup sugar: mix well. This will give a candied appearance.
2. Add ½ teaspoon vanilla to the egg white.
3. Heat oven to 250 degrees and bake for 1 to 1½ hours.

Marilyn and Al Fields
Delray Beach, Florida

GOUGERE

A French specialty.

Serves: 8 to 10

Páte Á Chou

¼ pound butter
1 cup water
1 cup flour
4 eggs

- Heat butter and water. When boiling, add flour all at once and stir until mixture forms a ball and leaves sides of pan.
- Place in processor and add eggs. Process until incorporated, or stir briskly (by hand) one egg at a time until thoroughly mixed.

Add the following:

½ cup grated Swiss cheese
½ cup finely diced Swiss cheese (or 1½ cups coarsley grated total) this part is quite flexible.
1 teaspoon Dijon-style mustard
½ teaspoon dry mustard

- Preheat oven to 375 degrees. Butter and flour cookie sheet.
- Using a pastry bag with a #6 or #8 tip or large rosette, fill and pipe large ring shape onto baking sheet. Bake for about 40 minutes.
- Mixture may also be spooned onto sheet to form a ring, and baked in the same manner. If desired, a wash of egg yolk and 1 tablespoon of heavy cream, may be brushed over top before baking. Serve warm.

Note: Mixture can be prepared early in day. Cover with plastic wrap until ready to pipe onto baking sheet.

- Ingredients for pâte á chou remain constant. To reduce proportions to serve 4 to 5 use ¼ cup butter, ½ cup water, ½ cup flour and 2 eggs.

Len Feiman
White Plains, New York

HERB BREAD STICKS

Yield: Approximately 5 dozen

½ pound butter, melted
1 teaspoon dill, dried
½ teaspoon oregano
½ teaspoon savory
½ teaspoon thyme
½ teaspoon parsley
1 large loaf very thinly sliced white bread, crusts removed

- Preheat oven to 250 degrees. Use cookie sheets.
- Melt butter and add seasonings.
- Cut bread slices into thirds. Place on a cookie sheet. Spread the butter mixture with a pastry brush on bread slices. Bake for 1 and ½ hours.

Margot Sider
Boca Raton, Florida

MARINATED MEATBALLS

Tastes as good as it looks!

Yield: 40 meatballs

2 pounds lean ground beef
2 eggs, lightly beaten
2 medium onions, chopped fine
1½ cups corn flakes (crush before measuring)
½ cup cold water
1 teaspoon garlic powder
Salt and pepper to taste

- Mix all ingredients together and shape into balls.

Sauce For The Above

1 (26-ounce) bottle ketchup
1¼ cups cold water
4 tablespoons Worcestershire sauce
1½ cups brown sugar
2 bay leaves
½ cup raisins
½ teaspoon rosemary

- Mix all ingredients together in a saucepan and cook until bubbling. Add the meatballs gently and simmer for 1 hour covered over low heat.
- Serve in a chafing dish or *pumpernickel basket.

**Directions for making a bread basket*

2 pound loaf of pumpernickel bread

- With a sharp knife, make two vertical cuts, one inch apart, down the center and halfway through the bread. This will be the handle.
- Starting at one end of the loaf, make a horizontal cut, ending at the vertical cut. Do the same thing to the other side. Lift off the two end pieces.
- Cut the bread away from the crust and under the handle. Scoop out the remaining bread to form a hollow shell, but leave enough bread to cushion the meatballs and sauce.

Dorothy Kramer
Hallandale, Florida

MERINGUE COATED PECANS

Lovely for parties and to serve with drinks.

Serves: 8 to 10

2 egg whites
2 tablespoons water
2 cups whole pecans
1 cup sugar
1 teaspoon cinnamon
1 teaspoon nutmeg
¼ teaspoon cloves
½ teaspoon salt

- Preheat oven to 300 degrees. Use a buttered cookie sheet with sides.
- Beat egg whites with the water until fluffy. Pour over nuts and stir. Combine sugar, cinnamon, nutmeg, cloves, salt and pecans.
- Spread on cookie sheet. (Mixture will run.) Bake for 25 minutes. Stir several times during baking.

Ethel Halpern
Pittsburgh, Pennsylvania

Editors Note: Keep in a tightly sealed container in refrigerator or freezer.

MUSHROOM HORS D'OEUVRE TURNOVERS

Prepare ahead

Yield: 6 to 8 dozen

Dough

8 ounces cream cheese, room temperature
8 ounces butter, softened
2¼ cups flour
1 teaspoon salt
1 egg, lightly beaten

- Preheat oven to 325 degrees.
- Knead cheese, butter, flour and salt into a dough. Shape into a ball. Wrap in waxed paper and chill at least four hours.
- Prepare mushroom filling.
- Roll out dough on a floured board to ⅛th-inch thickness. Cut into rounds with a 2½-inch cutter.
- Place 1 small teaspoonful of filling on each half, fold over to make a half circle. Seal edges with water, pressing together with a fork. Cut a small hole on top of each turnover. Place on a cookie sheet and freeze. After freezing transfer to a plastic bag.
- Before serving, remove the turnovers from freezer, place on greased cookie sheet, brush lightly with egg and bake for 30 minutes or until brown.

Mushroom Filling

3 tablespoons butter
1 large onion, finely chopped
½ pound fresh mushrooms, chopped
¼ teaspoon thyme
½ teaspoon salt
2 tablespoons flour
Freshly ground pepper
¼ cup sweet or sour cream

- In a skillet, heat the butter and brown the onion. Add mushrooms and cook for 3 minutes. Add seasonings. Sprinkle with flour. Stir in cream until thickened.

Sandy Butwin
Upper Saddle River, New Jersey

MUSHROOM TURNOVERS

Melts in your mouth.

Yield: 20 to 25 turnovers

Rich Pie Crust Pastry

2 cups flour
⅔ cup vegetable shortening
4 tablespoons ice water
1 egg yolk, beaten

- Preheat oven to 350 degrees. Grease a cookie sheet.
- Using a pastry blender, mix the flour and shortening, gradually add ice water. Blend well.
- Roll out dough, cut into 2½ or 3-inch rounds with a cookie cutter or glass.
- Put a teaspoonful of filling on each round, fold over. Use tines of fork to seal edges. Brush with beaten egg yolk. Place on cookie sheet and bake about 30 minutes.

Filling

½ cup minced onion
1½ tablespoons margarine or butter
2 (4-ounce) cans mushrooms, stems and pieces, drained (or ½-pound chopped fresh mushrooms)
½ teaspoon salt
⅛ teaspoon white pepper
1 teaspoon lemon juice
2 teaspoons flour
1 tablespoon sherry or dry Vermouth

- In a small saucepan, sauté onion in butter until golden in color for 5 minutes. Add mushrooms. Add salt, pepper and lemon juice and mix. Sprinkle in the flour and stir until thickened and smooth. Add the sherry. Set aside to cool.

Eve Ebenhart
Delray Beach, Florida

MY MOTHER'S CHOPPED LIVER

Yield:2 pounds

6 medium onions, thinly sliced
⅓ cup chicken fat, more if necessary
2 pounds fresh chicken livers
4 to 5 hard boiled eggs, chopped
Salt and pepper, to taste
Dash of garlic powder

- In a skillet, sauté onions in fat until golden brown. Remove onions and place in a wooden bowl. Chop with a hand chopper.
- Sauté chicken livers in the same skillet (use more fat if necessary) until done.
- Remove and chop with the onions. Add the chopped eggs and seasonings and mix again.
- Add a little more chicken fat, if too dry.
- Chill until one hour before serving.

Note: Do not use a food processor.

Hope Hirschhorn
Harrison, New York

ORIENTAL TUNA STEAK KEBABS

Picture perfect!

Serves: 12

Prepare ahead

1 pound tuna steaks, cut into 1-inch cubes
24 snow pea pods, cut in half
1 (11-ounce) can mandarin oranges, drained
1 to 2 (8-ounce) cans water chestnuts, drained

Marinade

1 (6-ounce) can frozen concentrated orange juice, thawed
2 to 3 tablespoons soy sauce
2 cloves garlic, crushed
3 to 4 slices ginger, or ½ teaspoon powdered ginger

• Soak kebab ingredients in marinade about 3 hours. Place on 6-inch skewers, or a long toothpick in the following order:

½ pea pod
1 water chestnut
1 cube fish
1 mandarin orange
½ pea pod

• Broil 3 to 5 minutes and serve.

Susan Berenson
Armonk, New York

PATÉ OF CHICKEN LIVER

Serves: 6

½ pound chicken livers
¼ teaspoon salt
Pinch cayenne pepper
½ cup unsalted margarine, room temperature
¼ teaspoon nutmeg
1 teaspoon dry mustard
⅛ teaspoon ground cloves
1 tablespoon sherry or port wine
2 tablespoons minced onion

- In a covered saucepan, bring chicken livers to boil in just enough water to cover and simmer 15 to 20 minutes. Drain. Purée livers inblender or food processor.
- Mix in remaining ingredients, blending well. Pack the mixture in a crock and chill in refrigerator. When ready to serve, unmold, slice and serve with crustless toasted bread triangles.

Note: A few truffles may be added.

Doe Koppana
Cincinnati, Ohio

PATÉ STRUDEL SLICES

Yield: 8 to 10 servings

1 onion, chopped
6 tablespoons margarine
1 pound chicken livers
¼ pound mushrooms, sliced
2 tablespoons cognac
¼ cup soft bread crumbs
Salt and pepper to taste
1 egg, lightly beaten
Pinch allspice
2 tablespoons chopped parsley
¼ pound phyllo pastry (approximately)
Melted margarine

- Preheat oven to 375 degrees. Large baking sheet with low sides.
- In skillet, sauté onion in two tablespoons margarine until tender. Add remaining margarine and livers. Cook quickly until browned on all sides. Add mushrooms and cook three minutes longer.
- Turn liver mixture onto chopping board and chop until fine, or process in food processor. Scrape mixture into bowl and add cognac, bread crumbs, salt, pepper, egg, allspice and parsley. Mix. Allow to cool.
- Place 2 sheets of phyllo pastry on a damp cloth. Brush with melted margarine, top with two more sheets, brushing with margarine until each step has been repeated totaling 10 sheets phyllo pastry.
- Mold liver mixture into a cylindrical shape along the longest side of pastry and roll up like a jelly roll. Lift carefully and place seam side down on baking sheet, preferably one with low sides in case fat oozes out while baking. Bake until pastry is crisp and golden, 30 to 40 minutes. Slice and serve.

Note: If making ahead of time, cool. Chill and wrap in aluminum foil and cover to freeze. Remove from freezer ½ hour before serving. Preheat oven to 375 degrees. After 10 to 15 minutes thawing, the roll can be cut in slices and set upright or on sides on a baking sheet. Bake about 15 minutes or until heated through.

Sherry Lieb
Livingston, New Jersey

PIZZA MUFFETS

Serves: 16 pieces per whole muffin

1 cup mayonnaise
½ cup green onions with tops, chopped
½ to ¾ cup Parmesan cheese, grated
1 tablespoon Worcestershire sauce
3 to 4 drops Tabasco sauce
6 to 9 English muffins, split
Paprika

- Mix ingredients and marinate overnight in refrigerator. Spread thinly on buttered English muffins that have been sliced in two. Broil until mixture bubbles. Sprinkle with paprika.
- Cut into 8 pie-style wedges for hors d'oeuvres.

Note: Mixture will keep in refrigerator for weeks in a closed container. I always keep this on hand for unexpected company.

Marianne Beyl
Greenwich, Connecticut

PUFFED MUSHROOMS

Light and wonderful!

Serves: 6 to 8

Sauce

¾ cup mayonnaise
3 tablespoons chopped dill
2 teaspoons chopped parsley
2 teaspoons chopped capers
1 teaspoon anchovy paste
1 teaspoon Dijon-style mustard
1 tablespoon chopped onions
Salt
1½ pounds small mushrooms (6 per person with stems cut)

Batter

1 cup flour
1 teaspoon salt
½ teaspoon pepper
Pinch of ginger
1 egg (extra large)
1 cup bread crumbs
Oil for frying

- Mix all ingredients for sauce, except the mushrooms. Set aside.
- Wipe the mushrooms. Dredge in flour which has been mixed with the salt, pepper and ginger.
- Dip in beaten egg. Roll in bread crumbs quickly. Fry in deep hot oil until golden.
- Serve with sauce.

Maureen Berkman
Scarsdale, New York

ROQUEFORT STUFFED HORS D'OEUVRE

(This recipe is for stuffing endive, mushrooms, cherry tomatoes, celery or any vegetable of your choice).

Yield: 1 cup

3 ounces cream cheese, room temperature
1 ounce Roquefort, Danish Bleu or Gorgonzola cheese
1 tablespoon Cognac
1 teaspoon prepared Dijon-style mustard
2 scallions, finely minced
½ cup fresh parsley, finely minced, for garnish

- Put all ingredients, except parsley, into a blender or food processor and purée until mixture is smooth and pale green in color. Transfer to a small bowl. Cover and chill until firm. Sprinkle top with parsley.

Note: Can be used for various vegetables and may be made a day ahead.

Joanne Bross
Mamaroneck, New York

SALMON PARTY BALL OR MOLD

Your guests will love this!

Serves: 8 to 10

Prepare ahead

1 (16-ounce) can red salmon
1 (8-ounce) package cream cheese, room temperature
1 tablespoon lemon juice
2 teaspoons grated onion
1 teaspoon horseradish
¼ teaspoon salt
¼ teaspoon liquid smoke
½ cup chopped pecans or walnuts
3 tablespoons snipped parsley

- Drain and flake salmon, removing skin and bones. Combine all ingredients, except nuts and parsley, in a food processor using the plastic blade. Mix thoroughly and chill for several hours.
- Combine nuts and parsley. Shape salmon into a ball and roll in nut mixture. Another method is to place the nuts and parsley mixture in a mold first and then fill with the salmon mixture.
- Serve with crackers.

Sandy Butwin
Upper Saddle River, New Jersey

SALMON ROLLS

Yield: 16 to 32 pieces

2 (8-ounce) packages cream cheese, room temperature
2 tablespoons white horseradish (well-drained) or to taste
16 slices smoked salmon
Black pepper to taste
Sprigs of dill or parsley for garnish

- Mix the softened cream cheese with horseradish. Put a tablespoonful on each slice of salmon. Sprinkle with black pepper. Roll each piece. Pierce with a toothpick to secure each roll. Insert sprig of dill or parsley just before serving.

Note: This serves 16 or can be cut in half to yield 32. They freeze well (on aluminum pie pan) and defrost in ½ hour. Do not use colored toothpicks.

Len Feiman
White Plains, New York

SPANAKOPETES

Yield: 8 to 9 dozen

4 tablespoons butter
1 onion, finely chopped
2 to 3 scallions, chopped
¼ cup chopped fresh dill
1 (10-ounce) package frozen spinach, chopped (defrosted, drained and squeezed dry)
Salt, pepper, dash nutmeg to taste
½ pound feta cheese, cut into chunks
½ pound dry cottage cheese (preferably farmer's or pot cheese)
¼ cup finely grated bread crumbs
3 eggs, lightly beaten
1 (1-pound) package Phyllo dough, defrosted
1 pound butter, melted

- Preheat oven to 400 degrees.
- Melt butter in skillet and gently sauté onion, scallions, dill, and spinach until onions are golden brown. Add salt, pepper, nutmeg and cheeses. Let cook until some of the liquid cooks down and evaporates. Add the bread crumbs and stir to mix. Remove from heat and stir in eggs. Mix to form a stuffing consistency. Let cool to room temperature.
- Open phyllo leaves and lay them out on a board. Cover with a damp towel to prevent them from drying out. Melt butter until hot and bubbly. Lay out one leaf on a board, the wide way, and with a pastry brush cover entire surface with butter. Lay another leaf on top and brush with butter. Do the same with the third leaf. Cut the rectangle into eight 1-inch strips. Lay a teaspoon of filling at bottom of each strip and roll up into small triangles. Starting at the bottom left corner, fold the left corner up to the right side, enclosing filling. Continue from left to right until a traingle is formed. Seal each triangle with melted butter. Continue until all ingredients are used, using three leaves of phyllo each time.
- Bake about 20 minutes until puffy and golden brown.

Note: The triangles can be frozen, unbaked until needed.

Sherry Lieb
Livingston, New Jersey

SPICED PECANS

Yield: 2 cups

1/4 cup butter
1/2 teaspoon Tabasco sauce
1 teaspoon Worcestershire sauce
1 tablespoon garlic salt
2 cups large pecan halves

- Preheat oven to 375 degrees. Use a jelly roll pan.
- Melt butter in a medium size saucepan; add spices. Mix well. Add nuts and stir to coat them.
- Place nuts on a jelly roll pan and toast them in oven for 20 minutes. Stir occasionally as they toast.
- Drain on paper toweling.

Penny Weill
Scarsdale, New York

STUFFED MUSHROOMS ALLA VALDOSTANA

Yield: Two pounds mushrooms

2 pounds mushrooms
1 small onion, chopped
1 clove garlic, chopped
4 tablespoons butter
4 tablespoons olive oil
1 tablespoon chopped parsley
1/2 cup white wine
1/2 teaspoon salt
1/4 teaspoon pepper
1/2 cup Fontina cheese, grated

- Preheat oven to 400 degrees.
- Wash and dry mushrooms. Remove stems and chop. Sauté stems, onion and garlic in 2 tablespoons butter and 2 tablespoons oil for 5 minutes. Add parsley, wine, salt and pepper. Cook over low heat for 10 minutes longer. Remove from stove. Add cheese and stir.
- Fill mushroom caps with stuffing mixture. Pour remaining oil in baking dish and arrange mushrooms stuffed side up. Dot with butter and bake uncovered for 15 to 20 minutes.

Sherry Lieb
Livingston, New Jersey

TANGY MEAT BALLS

An especially tasty combination.

Yield: 25 meat balls

1 pound ground beef
½ small onion, diced
½ cup bread crumbs
1 egg, beaten
½ teaspoon oregano
Pinch nutmeg
¾ cup chili sauce
1 cup jellied cranberry sauce
¼ cup brown sugar
2 teaspoons lemon juice

- Combine first 6 ingredients and form into balls.
- In a saucepan combine chili sauce, cranberry sauce, brown sugar and lemon juice. Stir until smooth. Add meat balls and simmer for 1 hour.
- Serve hot.

Ethel Halpern
Pittsburgh, Pennsylvania

TORTILLA OLÉ!

Yield: 20 triangles

Oil enough for frying 20 triangles
1 (12½-ounce) package flour tortillas (found in the dairy section)
1 large tomato, peeled, seeded and chopped
1 (4-ounce) can green chili peppers, mild, drained and chopped
½ pound Monterey Jack cheese

- Preheat oven to 350 degrees.
- In an electric skillet, pour enough oil for frying, and set temperature at 400 degrees.
- Remove tortilla skins from package and cut the rounds in half.
- Boil water and poach the tomato for 20 seconds just enough for the skin to come off easily. Peel skin, cut tomato into 4 parts, and remove as many seeds as possible. Cut each quarter in half. Chop in a food processor or blender. Do not over do, as texture should be chunky. Pour the tomato into a strainer over a bowl and let drain.
- Drain the green chili peppers and chop in a food processor or blender. Texture should be chunky.
- Slice the Monterey Jack cheese into ⅛-inch thin slices about 2-inches in length and 1½-inches wide. You will need 2 pieces for each tortilla. On one end of the cut tortilla skin, place two thin slices of cheese, keeping it ½-inch from the edges. Down the center of the cheese, place a thin single row of chopped tomatoes (no wider than ½-inch). On top of the tomatoes, add the chili peppers, making a thin row. Fold the tortilla skin in half, covering the mixture and making a triangle. Repeat the process until all the tortillas are used; you will have twenty.
- Make sure the oil is hot and ready. Fry lightly and quickly on both sides one to two minutes at most. Drain on paper toweling. Place on a cookie sheet and heat in oven for about 10 to 15 minutes or until warm.

Note: Freezes well. To serve, remove from freezer, place on a pizza pie tin and bake for 10 minutes in a 350 degree oven. Makes a wonderful light lunch or serve as a first course appetizer topped with your favorite hot sauce (salsa) using one heaping tablespoon per triangle.

Corrine Katz
White Plains, New York

VEGETARIAN CHOPPED LIVER

Tastes like the real thing.

Yield: 3 cups

Prepare ahead

1 cup lentils
3 cups water
1 cup onions, minced
4 teaspoons oil
½ cup hazel nuts, finely chopped
½ cup unsalted peanuts, finely chopped
3 eggs, hard boiled
2 teaspoons salt
¼ teaspoon pepper

- Soak lentils for about 3 hours in 3 cups water. Boil for an hour or until all water is absorbed.
- Sauté onions in oil until light brown. Mince all ingredients in a food processor until smooth.

Reba Etra
New York, New York

VEGETARIAN CHOPPED LIVER

Not for vegetarians only.

Yield 1½ pints

1 cup onions, diced
1 cup celery, diced
¼ cup green pepper, diced
2 tablespoons margarine
1 (8-ounce) can mushrooms, drained or 8-ounces fresh mushrooms, sautéed
1 (8-ounce) can string beans, drained or 8-ounces fresh string beans, cooked
½ cup walnuts
4 hard boiled eggs
1 to 2 tablespoons mayonnaise
Salt and pepper to taste

- Sauté onions, celery and green pepper in margarine.
- Chop or grind mushrooms, string beans, walnuts and eggs. Add this to the cooked vegetables and add enough mayonnaise to make a spread. Add salt and pepper to taste.
- Serve with crackers or bread.

Sarah Jane Fuchs
New York, New York

Bay Basil Savory Coriander Sage Rosemary Parsley Mint Coriander Sage Rosemary
Sage Rosemary Parsley Mint Cinnamon Marjoram
BREADS
namon Marjoram Thyme Juniper Bay
Bay Basil Savory Coriander Sage Rosemary Parsley Mint Cinnamon Parsley
Sage Rosemary Parsley Mint Cinnamon Marjoram Thyme Juniper Coriander Sage Rosemary
namon Marjoram Thyme Juniper Bay Basil Savory Coriander Bay Basil

PERTINENT PARTICULARS

- Use bread flour for superior bread and rolls.

- Check the date on yeast packages to insure freshness, otherwise bread will not rise.

- Liquids used to dissolve active dry yeast should be between 105 degrees to 115 degrees. When yeast is added directly to flour, hotter liquids (120 degrees to 130 degrees) should be used. A thermometer should be used to determine accurate water temperature.

- A temperature of 80 degrees to 85 degrees is ideal for bread rising.

- When making yeast breads, knead dough until smooth and satiny; about 10 to 15 minutes. More flour may be needed if dough is sticky.

- Always cool bread at least 1 hour before slicing.

- To cut fresh bread easily, warm the knife.

- Bread is done when loaf shrinks slightly from pan and when tapping the top makes a hollow sound.

CHALLAH

(Egg Bread)

The aroma and taste are worth the effort!

Yield: 4 loaves

3 packages dry yeast
¾ cup very warm water (105 degrees to 115 degrees)
½ cup sugar plus 2 teaspoons
¼ pound margarine, room temperature
1 cup boiling water
¼ cup vegetable oil
¼ cup honey
3 tablespoons coarse salt
8 extra large eggs, room temperature
9 to 10 cups unbleached flour
*** Glaze (recipe follows)**
Poppy seeds for topping

- Use ungreased cookie sheets.
- In a bowl dissolve yeast in ¾ cup water. Add 2 teaspoons sugar and set aside.
- In large bowl of electric mixer with dough hook in place, soften margarine by pouring 1 cup boiling water over it. Add oil, honey, salt and the remaining sugar. Mix thoroughly. Beat in eggs one at a time. Stir in yeast mixture.
- Gradually add 8 cups flour. Continue mixing, adding 1 cup of flour at a time. Knead for 5 minutes more. Dough will be soft.
- Put about 1 cup of flour on a board or counter top. Turn dough out and knead with the heel of your hand until dough is smooth and elastic.
- Place dough into a very large bowl, sprinkled with flour (dough will more than double in size). Sprinkle flour on top and cover with a towel. Place in a warm, draft free area and allow to rise, about 2 hours.
- Punch down, cover and let rise again about 1 to 1½ hours.
- Divide dough into 4 parts and form into desired shapes (braided or round).
- Place on cookie sheets and let rise uncovered for about 1 to 1½ hours.
- Preheat oven to 350 degrees.

Glaze

1 egg yolk
1 tablespoon water

- Mix egg yolk with water. Brush mixture on the loaves and sprinkle with poppy seeds.
- Place in the middle of the oven and bake for 35 to 40 minutes until golden brown. Remove from oven and turn out onto wire rack to cool.

Note: If necessary, second rising can be eliminated.

Gail Goldey
Harrison, New York

CHEESE ONION BREAD

Serves: 12 to 16

1 whole French bread
¼ cup scallions, diced fine
½ pound butter, room temperature
1 tablespoon poppy seeds
1 teaspoon dry mustard
2 (8-ounce) packages Swiss cheese

- Preheat oven to 400 degrees.
- Slice bread in half lengthwise. Do not cut through to bottom. Cut off side crusts and ends. Cut diagonally and almost to the bottom at 1-inch intervals.
- Mix together scallions, butter, poppy seeds and mustard. Spread over top and down inside slices.
- Cut Swiss cheese slices diagonally. Insert 1 slice cheese, point end up, between each slice of bread. Wrap in foil and bake for 20 minutes. Open foil and continue to bake for 5 minutes.

Penny Weill
Scarsdale, New York

DATE AND NUT BREAD

Yield: 1 loaf

1 cup water
1 teaspoon baking soda
1 (8-ounce) package pitted dates, snipped
½ cup raisins
2 cups flour
1 teaspoon baking powder
¼ teaspoon salt
6 tablespoons butter, room temperature
1 cup light brown sugar (firmly packed)
2 eggs
1 cup walnuts, chopped

- Preheat oven to 350 degrees. Butter a loaf pan 9-inch x 5-inch x 2¾-inch; sprinkle with flour.
- Bring water and baking soda to boil. Pour over dates and raisins to soften.
- Sift flour, baking powder and salt together.
- Cream butter and sugar and beat until fluffy. Add eggs, one at a time, beating well to incorporate. Add water-date mixture, then dry ingredients, and blend thoroughly. Fold in nuts.
- Pour into loaf pan and bake for 50 minutes or until cake tester comes out clean.

Lois Gallant
Harrison, New York

DILL BREAD

Delicious, flavorful and easy to make.

Yield: 1 round bread

2¼ cups flour, unsifted
2 tablespoons sugar
1 teaspoon salt
1 tablespoon instant minced onion
2 teaspoons dill seed
¼ teaspoon baking soda
1 package or 1 scant tablespoon dry yeast
1 tablespoon margarine, room temperature
¼ cup very hot tap water (120 degrees to 130 degrees)
1 cup creamed cottage cheese
1 egg

- Grease a 1½-quart round casserole (2-quart is suitable too).
- In large bowl of electric mixer, thoroughly mix ¼ cup of flour and the rest of the dry ingredients.
- Add softened margarine and gradually add the hot water to dry ingredients and beat for 2 minutes at medium speed, scraping bowl occasionally. Add cottage cheese, egg, and ½ cup flour (make a thick batter). Beat at high speed 2 minutes, scraping bowl. Stir in remaining flour to make a stiff batter. Cover. Let rise in a warm place until doubled in bulk, about 1 hour and 15 minutes.
- Stir batter down with a large wooden spoon. Turn into casserole. Cover and let rise in a warm place until doubled in bulk, about 50 to 60 minutes.
- Bake in a preheated 350 degree oven about 30 minutes or until done. Remove from casserole and cool on a wire rack.

Ellie Schwartz

DUFFY'S HEALTHY BREAD

Yield: 3 loaves

Ingredients For First Rising

3 tablespoons active dry yeast
6 cups lukewarm water (105 degrees to 115 degrees)
¾ cup honey
7½ tablespoons salt
7½ cups gluten flour
5¾ cups whole wheat flour
½ cup cracked wheat
½ cup bran flakes
½ cup millet
½ cup wheat germ
1 to 2 tablespoons cardamon
1 tablespoon or less cinnamon
¼ teaspoon nutmeg
½ to 1 tablespoon mace

Ingredients For Second Rising

½ cup raisins
½ cup chopped walnuts
⅜ cup oil
Approximately 1 tablespoon yeast, optional
1½ cups gluten flour
3 cups whole wheat flour

- You will need three 9-inch x 5-inch x 3-inch bread pans.
- Dissolve the yeast in the lukewarm water that has been mixed with honey.
- Measure the other ingredients and pour into a large bowl. Stir together with the yeast mixture. Let rise about 45 minutes to one hour in a warm dry place.
- When doubled, add the raisins, walnuts, oil, yeast, 1 and ½ cups gluten flour and 3 cups whole wheat flour. Knead in more whole wheat flour until elastic. Knead for 10 minutes to develop gluten.
- Preheat oven to 350 degrees.
- After doubling in size, shape loaves as follows: Divide into 3 equal parts. Flatten each piece in a big circle. Fold in half. Stretch and roll until it is rectangular in shape. Roll the short ends to form a loaf. Pinch ends in, flatten and seal. Place in large bread pans and let rise about 15 minutes. Bake in oven for 1 hour. Test for doneness.
- Remove from pans and cool on a rack.

Note: Freezes well.

Duffy Lyon
Mill Valley, California

FIVE STAR HONEY GLAZED BRAN MUFFINS

Truly a five star muffin.

Yield: 12 muffins

1 cup bran cereal
1 cup buttermilk
1 cup all-purpose flour
1 teaspoon baking powder
½ teaspoon baking soda
1 teaspoon ground cinnamon
½ teaspoon salt
⅓ cup butter, room temperature
½ cup brown sugar
1 large egg
¼ cup molasses
⅓ cup raisins
⅓ cup chopped dates

- Preheat oven to 400 degrees. Grease a 12-cup muffin tin.
- In a medium mixing bowl, combine bran and buttermilk. Mix together flour, baking powder, baking soda, cinnamon and salt. Add this dry mixture all at once to the bran mixture. Stir only to mix.
- In another bowl, cream butter, sugar, egg and molasses together. Stir into bran mixture. Stir in raisins and dates. Spoon into muffin tin, fill ¾ full.
- Bake 20 to 25 minutes. With a pastry brush, spread glaze on muffins while still warm and before removing from muffin tin.

Glaze

½ cup honey
⅓ cup corn syrup
1 tablespoon butter, room temperature

- Mix together.

Debbie Simon
Scarsdale, New York

HAMBURGER ROLLS

Yields: 22 to 24 rolls

2 cups warm water (use thermometer to test water 125 degrees to 130 degrees)
2 packages dehydrated yeast
¼ cup sugar
¼ cup margarine or shortening, room temperature
1 egg, beaten
2 tablespoons dehydrated onion
1½ teaspoons coarse salt, optional
6½ to 7 cups flour, either unbleached or bread flour
1 beaten egg for tops of rolls
Sesame seeds for tops of rolls

- Grease cookie sheets.
- Put water in a large bowl and stir in yeast. Add sugar, shortening, beaten egg and onion. Add half the flour and stir well. Add rest of flour, cover with foil, and place in refrigerator for at least 2 hours. Dough will rise and you can press down.
- Pull off pieces of dough the size of half dollar or larger, depending on size of roll. Place on cookie sheet, cover and set aside to rise until doubled. Brush tops with beaten eggs. Sprinkle sesame seeds over tops.
- Preheat oven to 425 degrees.
- Bake for 10 minutes. Reduce heat to 400 degrees and bake another 10 minutes.

Note: Dough can be kept in refrigerator for 2 to 3 days.

Eve Ebenhart
Delray Beach, Florida

HARRIET'S DATE NUT BREAD

Yield:2 breads

1 (8-ounce) package dates, cut in small pieces
2 tablespoons butter, room temperature
2 cups boiling water
2 teaspoons baking soda
2 eggs
2 cups sugar
4 cups flour, sifted
Pinch salt
1 cup walnuts, coarsely chopped
1 teaspoon vanilla

- Preheat oven to 300 degrees. Generously grease two (46 to 48-ounce) tomato juice or (48-ounce) vegetable shortening cans.
- Combine the dates, butter, boiling water and baking soda; let stand.
- Cream eggs and sugar until light. Blend in cooled date mixture. Gradually beat in flour and salt. Fold in walnuts and vanilla.
- Fill cans half-way (bread will rise) and bake for 1½ hours. Cool on cake rack 10 minutes. When cool, slip out of cans. This bread keeps well, wrapped in foil.

Gloria Svirsky
Scarsdale, New York

LEMON BREAD

This is very special!

Yield: 1 loaf

2½ cups flour
2 teaspoons baking powder
½ teaspoon salt
1 cup sugar
5 tablespoons butter, room temperature
2 eggs, beaten
Grated zest of 1 lemon
1 cup milk
*** Topping (recipe follows)**

- Preheat oven to 325 degrees. Grease a 9-inch x 5-inch x 3-inch loaf pan. Line with waxed paper.
- In a small bowl, combine flour, baking powder and salt. Set aside.
- In a mixing bowl, cream sugar and butter until light and fluffy. Add eggs and grated lemon zest. Mix thoroughly. Add milk alternately with dry ingredients. Blend well. Pour into prepared pan and smooth top with knife.
- Bake 50 to 60 minutes or until cake tester comes out clean.
- Cool 5 minutes, then remove from pan onto cake rack.
- Spoon topping over bread while still warm

* ***Topping***

⅓ cup superfine sugar
Juice of ½ lemon
Zest from ½ lemon

- Mix sugar and lemon juice into a paste. Spoon half of topping onto bread, sprinkle with lemon zest. Put remainder of topping on bread and return to warm oven for 1 to 2 minutes, until sugar bubbles and caramelizes.

Penny Weill
Scarsdale, New York

MISSISSIPPI CORN BREAD

Serves: 8

1 cup plain corn meal
3 teaspoons baking powder
¼ cup sugar
½ teaspoon salt (optional)
2 eggs, beaten
⅓ cup vegetable oil
1 cup sour cream
1 (8½-ounce) can cream style corn

- Preheat oven to 375 degrees. Grease an 8-inch square pan.
- Mix corn meal, baking powder, sugar and salt together. Stir in eggs, oil, sour cream and corn.
- Pour into pan and bake for 35 minutes. Cool and cut into squares.

Zilota Walters
Teaneck, New Jersey

MIXER-MADE YEAST BREAD

Yield: 1 loaf

5 cups unbleached white flour
3 tablespoons sugar
1 tablespoon salt
2 envelopes active dry yeast
1 cup milk
1 cup water
2 tablespoons butter
¾ cup wheat germ

- Grease a 9-inch x 5-inch x 3-inch loaf pan.
- In a large bowl of electric mixer, with a dough hook attachment, mix 1½ cups flour, sugar, salt and yeast together, at medium speed.
- In a saucepan heat the milk, water and butter over low heat until warm. (120 to 130 degrees)
- Gradually add to flour; beat 2 minutes at medium speed, scraping occasionally.
- Beat 1½ cups of flour in at low speed; then beat for 2 minutes at high speed.
- Add rest of flour and wheat germ, beating at low speed and scraping inside of bowl until well blended.
- Cover with a clean cloth; let rise in a warm place until double in bulk (about 40 to 60 minutes).
- Heat oven to 375 degrees.
- Punch batter down. Turn into the loaf pan. Bake immediately for 40 to 50 minutes. Remove from pan; cool on wire rack.

Susan Abrams
Katonah, New York

PENNY'S ZUCCHINI BREAD

An exceptionally tasty bread.

Yield: 2 loaves

3 beaten eggs
1 cup oil
2 cups sugar
2 teaspoons vanilla
2 cups grated raw zucchini (do not peel)
2 cups flour
1 teaspoon salt
1 teaspoon baking soda
¼ teaspoon baking powder
3 teaspoons cinnamon

- Preheat oven to 350 degrees. Grease and flour two 9-inch x 5-inch x 3-inch loaf pans.
- In a large mixing bowl, mix eggs, oil, sugar, zucchini and vanilla by hand.
- Add flour, salt, baking soda, baking powder and cinnamon. Mix well.
- Pour into prepared pans and bake for 50–60 minutes.
- Cool on wire rack before removing from pan.

Penny Weill
Scarsdale, New York

Note: This recipe must be done by hand.
Editor's Note: We used two 8½-inch x 4½-inch x 2¾ inch pans.

PUMPKIN BREAD

This recipe was given to Greg in 3rd grade from his teacher. It has become our family tradition to serve pumpkin bread on Thanksgiving.

Serves: 10 to 12

3 cups flour, unsifted
1 teaspoon baking soda
1 teaspoon salt
1½ teaspoons ground cloves
3 teaspoons cinnamon
1 teaspoon nutmeg
2 cups sugar
2 cups canned pumpkin
4 eggs, beaten
1½ cups vegetable oil
½ cup chopped nuts (optional)

- Preheat oven to 350 degrees. Grease two 9-inch x 5-inch x 3-inch loaf pans.
- In a large bowl, mix together all dry ingredients. Add wet ingredients. Mix well.
- Pour into 2 loaf pans and bake for 1 hour.

Gregory Weill
Scarsdale, New York

RAISIN BROWN BREAD

This is very easy to prepare and has a most delicious taste.

Yield: 1 loaf

3 cups whole wheat flour
½ teaspoon baking soda
1 cup nonfat dry milk powder
2 cups water
1 tablespoon vinegar
3 tablespoons molasses
1 cup dark raisins

- Preheat oven to 350 degrees. Generously grease and flour a 9-inch x 5-inch x 3-inch loaf pan.
- In a large mixing bowl, sift together flour, baking soda and powdered milk.
- Add water, vinegar and molasses. Mix thoroughly with a wooden spoon. Add raisins and mix again.
- Pour into the loaf pan and bake for 1 hour or until a cake tester inserted in the center comes out clean. Remove from oven and cool on rack for 5 to 10 minutes. Use a wide spatula to remove bread from pan and continue to cool on rack.

Lisa Katz
White Plains, New York

RYE BREAD

Yield: 3 loaves

1 cup medium rye flour
5 cups all-purpose flour
1½ tablespoons dry yeast
1½ tablespoons kosher salt
2 tablespoons caraway seeds (optional)
2½ cups warm water (120 degree to 130 degree)
Egg white
Cornmeal

- In a large mixing bowl, mix together all dry ingredients except cornmeal. Add water and mix to form a dough. (If you have a large mixer with a dough hook, knead in the mixer for about 2 minutes, or just until dough becomes elastic. Do not overwork.) Turn out onto a floured board and knead just until dough is smooth and elastic.
- Turn dough into a large bowl, cover with clean dish towel, and allow to rise until 2½ times its original bulk. (You can sprinkle top of dough with a small amount of flour to prevent its sticking to the cloth).
- Punch dough down, turn onto floured board, cover with the towel and allow to rest for 20 minutes.
- Form into 3 loaves, approximately 3 to 4 inches wide and 5 to 6 inches long, kneading dough lightly and making the loaves fairly tight as you don't want much spread as they rise.
- Sprinkle a baking sheet with cornmeal and set the loaves on the sheet. Make 3 horizontal slashes on top of each loaf, cover and allow to rise to about 1½ times original size.
- Meanwhile, preheat oven to 450 degrees. When loaves are ready, brush tops with lightly beaten egg white. Spray some water into oven with a spray bottle, or scatter drops with your hand, to create some steam. Place sheet in oven. Bake for approximately 35 minutes, spraying the oven again twice during the first 10 minutes. Remove from oven and allow to cool on rack.

Note: If you have unglazed quarry or pizza tiles, cover the oven rack (leaving space around the sides) and bake bread directly on the tiles.

Gail Goldey
Harrison, New York

RYE BREAD STICKS WITH CARAWAY SEEDS

Yield: 2 dozen

1 package active dry yeast
1¼ cups warm water (105 degrees to 115 degrees)
¼ cup margarine, room temperature, minus 1 tablespoonful
1 level tablespoon sugar
½ teaspoon salt (optional)
1 scant cup whole rye flour
1 scant cup whole wheat flour
Caraway seeds to taste (or sesame seeds)
1 heaping teaspoon dehydrated minced onion
2 cups all-purpose flour
1 egg yolk

- Grease a cookie sheet.
- Dissolve yeast in the water in a large mixing bowl. Add margarine, sugar, salt, whole rye flour, whole wheat flour, caraway seeds and minced onion. Beat until smooth.
- Cover and let rise in a warm place for 45 minutes.
- Stir in all-purpose flour, ½ cup at a time. Turn onto lightly floured board. Knead until smooth and elastic (add a little more flour if too sticky). Divide in half. Shape into sticks, about 4-inches long, or make into rolls, if desired.
- Place on cookie sheet, cover, and let rise for 40 minutes. Preheat oven to 375 degrees. Brush tops with egg yolk and sprinkle with caraway or sesame seeds. Bake for 15 to 20 minutes.

Eve Ebenhart
Delray Beach, Florida

STRAWBERRY BREAD

Yield: 2 loaves

3 cups flour
2 cups sugar
1 teaspoon baking soda
1 teaspoon salt
1 teaspoon cinnamon
2 cups crushed strawberries, fresh or frozen
1¼ cups oil
4 eggs, beaten
1¼ cups chopped pecans

- Preheat oven to 350 degrees. Grease and flour two 9-inch x 5-inch x 2½-inch loaf pans, or a Bundt pan.
- Sift dry ingredients together. Add remaining ingredients and mix well. Bake for 1½ hours. I check the bread after an hour, because it doesn't seem to take the full 1½ hours to bake.

Note: You can make a thin icing of confectioners sugar and strawberry juice and pour over the bread.

Kim and Spencer Joyce
Denver, Colorado

ZUCCHINI BREAD

An exceptionally tasty bread.

Yield: 1 loaf

1½ cups shredded zucchini, unpeeled
2 cups flour
¾ teaspoon salt
¾ teaspoon baking soda
½ teaspoon baking powder
1½ teaspoons cinnamon
1 cup sugar
2 beaten eggs
½ cup oil
1½ teaspoons vanilla
½ cup walnuts

- Preheat oven to 325 degrees. Grease a 9-inch x 5-inch x 3-inch loaf pan.
- Wash zucchini. In a food processor with shredding disc in place, run zucchini through tube. Transfer to a mixing bowl.
- Reassemble processor with steel blade. Put in the flour, salt, soda, baking powder, cinnamon and sugar. Process just until blended. Remove cover and add eggs, oil, vanilla and walnuts. Process only until blended. Add to zucchini in bowl, stirring very well to blend.
- Spoon into pan and bake for 1 hour and 15 minutes or until bread pulls away from sides. Cool on wire rack before removing from pan.

Rita Glanzer
Washington, D.C.

BRUNCH

Bay Basil Savory Coriander Sage Rosemary Parsley Mint Coriander Sage Rosemary
Sage Rosemary Parsley Mint Cinnamon Marjoram
Marjoram Thyme Juniper Bay
Bay Basil Savory Coriander Sage Rosemary Parsley Mint Cinnamon Parsley
Sage Rosemary Parsley Mint Cinnamon Marjoram Thyme Juniper Coriander Sage
Marjoram Thyme Juniper Bay Basil Savory Coriander Bay Basil

BLINTZ SOUFFLÉ

An unusal treat and so easy to make.

Serves: 8 to 10

¾ cup butter
18 cheese blintzes, frozen
6 eggs, beaten
1½ pints sour cream
1½ teaspoons vanilla extract
6 tablespoons orange juice
6 tablespoons sugar
Dash cinnamon
1 (10-ounce) package frozen strawberries, thawed and sliced

- Preheat oven to 350 degrees.
- Melt butter and cover bottom of 3-quart oblong baking pan.
- Layer the frozen blintzes over the butter.
- Beat eggs, add sour cream and remaining ingredients, except strawberries. Mix thoroughly and pour over blintzes. Bake 1 hour.
- Serve with strawberries.

Elinore Skalet
White Plains, New York

CAVIAR MOLD

Serves: 10

1 tablespoon unflavored gelatin
2 tablespoons sherry
2 tablespoons lemon juice
6 hard-cooked eggs
1 teaspoon anchovy paste
1 teaspoon Worcestershire sauce
1 cup mayonnaise
Pinch onion powder
1 (2½-ounce) jar caviar

- Oil a 3-cup mold.
- Dissolve gelatin in sherry and lemon juice in a bowl large enough to hold all ingredients.
- Put eggs through a sieve and add rest of ingredients, except caviar, and combine with gelatin. Add caviar last and mix in gently.
- Place mixture in mold and chill in refrigerator until ready to serve. Unmold onto a platter.

Note: Potato masher may be used to sieve eggs.

Audré Lemler
New Rochelle, New York

CHILES RELLENOS

A spicy tidbit.

Serves: 6

½ pound each Monterey Jack and Cheddar cheese, cut into strips
2 (4-ounce) cans green chilies drained, pat dry
3 eggs, separated
3 tablespoons flour
Salad oil

- Insert a strip of each cheese in each chili.
- In a medium bowl, beat egg whites until they form peaks.
- In a small bowl, beat yolks until thick and lemon colored. Blend in 3 tablespoons of flour. Fold this mixture into whites, until just blended.
- In a heavy saucepan, slowly heat 1½ to 2 inches oil to 400 degrees. Roll cheese stuffed chilies in flour.
- With a large slotted spoon, dip chilies in batter, coating very generously. Gently place stuffed chilies in hot oil, 2 at a time. Fry for about 3 to 4 minutes until golden on both sides. Drain on paper towel.

Note: Can be kept in oven at 350 degrees for ½ hour before serving.

Vicki Capin
Tucson, Arizona

COLD SALMON MOUSSE

Serves: 4 to 6

Mousse

3 tablespoons lemon juice
2 tablespoons cold water
2 envelopes gelatin
⅔ cup boiling water
2 stalks celery, each cut into 3 pieces
1 small onion, halved
¼ cucumber, peeled, seeded and quartered
½ carrot, cut into 2 pieces
2 sprigs parsley
* ½ cup mayonnaise (homemade is best!)
1 teaspoon salt
¼ teaspoon white pepper
3 sprigs dill
1 cup heavy cream
2 (7¾-ounce) cans salmon, drained or 1 pound fresh salmon, poached

- Put lemon juice, 2 tablespoons cold water and gelatin into a food processor and let stand for 1 minute.
- Add the boiling water and process 10 seconds. Add all other ingredients and process until fine. Pour into 5 cup mold and chill.
- ** Serve with Dill Sauce.

**** Mayonnaise-In Food Processor***

3 egg yolks
1 tablespoon wine vinegar
Juice of 1 lemon
½ teaspoon salt
½ teaspoon white pepper
1 envelope rich brown seasoning mix
½ teaspoon mustard
2 to 2½ cups oil
Dash Tabasco sauce

- In bowl, with metal chopping blade in place, beat 3 egg yolks until creamy. Add remaining ingredients except oil. Slowly add oil (through top tube) and blend until thick. Add a dash of Tabasco sauce.

***** Dill Sauce***

1 egg
½ teaspoon salt
Pinch white pepper
Pinch sugar
1 tablespoon lemon juice
1 cup sour cream
2 tablespoons finely chopped dill

- Beat egg until light and fluffy. Add salt, pepper and sugar. Beat in lemon juice and sour cream. Blend in dill.

Len Feiman
White Plains, New York

CROISSANT FILLINGS

Yield: To fill 6 croissants

Chicken and Almond Filling

2 tablespoons slivered almonds
¼ of a cooked chicken, finely chopped
1 tablespoon chopped chives
½ cup mayonnaise
Salt and pepper to taste

- Preheat oven to 325 degrees.
- Toast almonds for 8 minutes.
- Combine chopped chicken, chives, almonds and mayonnaise. Season to taste.
- Fill the croissants and heat for 10 minutes.

Cream Cheese and Chive Filling

½ pound cream cheese, room temperature
1 tablespoon butter, room temperature
1 teaspoon mustard
6 croissants, heated in a 325 degree oven
1 teaspoon lemon rind
1 teaspoon lemon juice
¼ cup chopped chives

- Beat cheese, butter, mustard, lemon rind and juice until soft and creamy. Stir in chives and spread onto hot croissant.

Maureen Berkman
Scarsdale, New York

EASY CHEESE SOUFFLÉ

Serves: 5 for luncheon

8 slices thinly sliced white bread, crusts removed
¾ pound sharp Cheddar cheese, grated
8 eggs, beaten
¼ teaspoon salt
⅛ pound melted butter (½ in batter, ½ to grease dish)
2 cups whole milk

- Preheat oven to 325 degrees. Butter an 8-inch soufflé dish.
- Place 3 slices of bread in soufflé dish.
- Mix the remaining ingredients (except bread) together.
- Pour one-third of mixture over the bread.
- Alternate bread and liquid in layers until all ingredients are used.
- Bake for 1 hour and 15 minutes.

Elaine Satuloff
Harrison, New York

EGGS IN ROLLS

Can be prepared and wrapped in foil several hours before cooking.

Serves: 8

8 round crisp bread rolls
10 to 12 spinach leaves, chopped
4 tablespoons butter
2 medium onions, chopped
2½ tablespoons barbeque sauce, jar or homemade
8 eggs
¾ cup Cheddar cheese, grated
Salt and pepper to taste

- Preheat oven to 350 degrees. Use a cookie sheet.
- Cut a slice from the top of the rolls and reserve lids. Scoop out the inside of the rolls, leaving a thin shell.
- Blanch spinach in a pot of boiling water and drain. Sauté in 2 tablespoons of melted butter for 1 minute. Divide the spinach between the 8 rolls.
- Sauté onions in 2 tablespoons butter until tender but not brown. Stir in the barbeque sauce and spoon over the rolls.
- Break an egg into each roll. Sprinkle with salt and pepper and top with cheese. Replace lids. Wrap each roll in foil.
- Place on a cookie sheet and bake for 15 minutes. Remove from oven and let stand for 5 minutes before removing foil.

Maureen Berkman
Scarsdale, New York

EGG SOUFFLÉ

Serves: 8

¼ cup butter, room temperature
2 cups grated cheese (any hard cheese of your choice)
2 teaspoons prepared mustard
1 cup light cream
12 eggs
Salt and pepper to taste

- Preheat oven to 350 degrees.
- Grease a soufflé dish with butter and sprinkle the grated cheese over the butter.
- Mix mustard and cream together. Pour half the mixture over cheese.
- Beat eggs with salt and pepper and add to dish. Pour rest of cream and mustard mixture over eggs.
- Bake for 45 minutes to 1 hour. Serve immediately.

Mildred Goldberger
Scotch Plains, New Jersey

EXCELLENT OVEN FRENCH TOAST

Serves: 10

¼ cup butter or margarine
⅓ cup sugar
1 teaspoon cinnamon
1 teaspoon grated orange rind
5 eggs
1 cup orange juice
20 slices French or Italian bread; plain or seeded
Hot orange syrup (recipe follows)

- Preheat oven to 400 degrees. Use an 11-inch x 16-inch baking pan.
- Melt butter in the baking pan. Sprinkle sugar, cinnamon and orange rind on top of the melted butter.
- Beat eggs. Mix with orange juice.
- Dip each slice of bread into the egg-orange mixture. Place in the pan on top of the sugar mixture.
- Bake for 25 minutes. Remove from oven and let stand for 2 minutes. Tops of bread should be nicely toasted.
- Serve sugar side up on a warm platter. Top with hot orange syrup and coconut.

Orange Syrup

1 cup frozen orange juice, defrosted
½ cup butter
2 cups sugar

- Heat all ingredients together and boil a few minutes.

Topping

1 cup grated coconut

Note: Oven can be turned off after 20 minutes of baking and toast allowed to stand in oven, if serving is delayed.

Gen Vergari
Yonkers, New York

HONEY ORANGE BUTTER

Yield: 1 Cup

½ pound butter, room temperature
1 teaspoon grated orange rind
2 tablespoons orange juice
½ cup honey
¼ teaspoon cinnamon

• Beat butter until creamy. Beat in remainder of ingredients.

Maureen Berkman
Scarsdale, New York

LAYERED MUSHROOM AND TOMATO PANCAKE

Serves: 6

The fillings may be prepared the day before serving. The pancakes may be filled as directed in the recipe up to 3 hours before baking.

Mushroom Filling

¾ pound fresh mushrooms, sliced
6 shallots, chopped
3 tablespoons butter
1 teaspoon cornstarch
1 tablespoon sour cream
Salt and pepper to taste

• Sauté mushrooms and shallots in butter for 3 minutes. Add cornstarch and sour cream and stir until thickened. Season with salt and pepper.

Tomato Filling

1 onion, chopped
3 tablespoons butter
1 (16-ounce) can peeled chopped tomatoes, drained
1 teaspoon cornstarch
1 teaspoon water
1 teaspoon sugar

• Sauté onion in butter. Add tomatoes and cook for 2 minutes. Add cornstarch and water. Stir for 2 minutes. Add sugar and blend.

Pancakes

1 cup flour
3 eggs
1 cup milk
1 tablespoon oil

- Use a 8-inch Crêpe pan.
- Beat eggs and milk gradually into flour. Keep beating until smooth. Stir in oil and let mixture stand for 30 to 45 minutes.
- Heat crêpe pan and grease lightly with butter. Pour about 2½ to 3 tablespoons batter into the pan and cook until lightly browned underneath. Turn and cook the other side. Continue until all the batter has been used.
- Place one pancake in an ovenproof dish and spread a small amount of mushroom filling over the pancake. Top with another pancake. Spread a small amount of tomato filling over the pancake. Top with another pancake. Repeat until all pancakes are layered.
- Cover with aluminum foil and bake in a preheated 350 degree oven for 15 minutes.
- Cut into wedges and serve.

Maureen Berkman
Scarsdale, New York

MY GRANDMOTHER'S PETITE CHEESE BLINTZES

Passed down from one generation to another.

Yield: 40 blintzes

Batter

8 eggs
3½ cups water
4 cups flour
½ teaspoon salt

- Beat eggs and water together in an electric mixer. Add flour and salt and beat until the ingredients are blended together. Set aside.

Filling

3 (7½-ounce each) packages farmer cheese, room temperature
1 (8-ounce) package cream cheese, room temperature
1 (3-ounce) package cream cheese, room temperature
4 tablespoons sugar
1 egg plus 1 egg yolk, beaten
1 teaspoon vanilla
Butter for frying

- Use a 6-inch skillet or crepe pan.
- Mix the cheeses together with the sugar.
- Add the beaten eggs and vanilla, combining thoroughly.
- In a 6-inch skillet or crepe pan heat butter until it sizzles. Pour about 2 tablespoons of batter into pan. Immediately roll pan around so the batter spreads evenly. When underside is brown and top is dry, turn out bottom side up on a dish towel. Repeat in this manner until all the batter has been used.
- Place 1 tablespoon of filling on cooked side of the crepe, at the end closest to you. Fold over the sides, and roll the blintzes as you would a jelly roll.
- Sauté in butter on a low flame until golden brown.

Linda Berk
Greensburg, Pennsylvania

ONION AND CHEESE PIE

Serves: 8

1 pound Swiss cheese, grated
2 tablespoons flour
2 large onions, sliced
4 eggs, lightly beaten
1 cup heavy cream
1 cup milk
½ teaspoon curry powder
¼ teaspoon nutmeg, ground
2 drops Tabasco sauce
1 teaspoon salt
Freshly ground black pepper, to taste
One 10-inch unbaked pie shell

- Preheat oven to 350 degrees.
- Combine grated cheese with flour and spread evenly in pie shell. Separate onion slices into rings and arrange on cheese mixture.
- Beat eggs lightly. Beat in cream, milk, curry powder, nutmeg, Tabasco, salt and pepper. Pour egg mixture over cheese and onion rings.
- Bake in moderate oven for 45 minutes.

Note: 1 pint half and half may be substituted for milk and cream.

Nataly Ritter
Mamaroneck, New York

QUICK QUICHE

(Crustless)

Serves: 4 to 6

1 cup milk
6 to 8 ounces Cheddar or Swiss cheese, grated
3 to 4 beaten eggs
¾ cup whole wheat flour
½ to 1 cup vegetables (any kind or mixture)
½ teaspoon dill
½ teaspoon basil
⅛ teaspoon pepper
¾ teaspoon oregano

- Preheat oven to 350 degrees. Grease a 9-inch pie pan or 9-inch quiche pan.
- Mix all ingredients together. Pour into pan and bake for 30 minutes or until top is puffy and golden brown.

Judi Paseltiner
South Huntington, New York

Editors Note: To make a larger quiche use a 10-inch pie plate or quiche pan and increase ingredients as follows:

8 ounces grated cheese
4 large eggs
2 to 2½ cups vegetables, such as 5 large mushrooms sliced, ½ head (small) broccoli flowerets, ½ red pepper diced, 2 onions sliced

SALMON MOUSSE

Serves: 8 to 10

1 envelope plain gelatin
⅔ cup boiling water
2½ tablespoons lemon juice
1 medium onion, cut into 4 quarters
⅔ cup mayonnaise
¼ teaspoon paprika
1½ teaspoons dry dill
1 (1 pound) can salmon, drained
1 cup heavy cream
2 teaspoons horseradish
A few drops of liquid smoke seasoning

- Use a greased fish-shaped or other 1½ pint mold.
- Dissolve gelatin in boiling water. When dissolved pour into food processor. Add all remaining ingredients and process until smooth. Pour into mold and refrigerate. When ready to serve, unmold on platter.

Sharon Strongin
Scarsdale, New York

SCONES

What a lovely way to start the day.

Yield: 15 Scones

1 tablespoon sugar
2 cups flour
4 teaspoons baking powder
Pinch salt
6 tablespoons butter, room temperature and cut into 1-inch cubes

1 beaten egg
1 cup sour cream
1 egg yolk
1 tablespoon water

- Preheat oven to 400 degrees. Lightly grease a cookie sheet.
- Mix dry ingredients together. Add cut up butter. Add beaten egg and cream. Blend all ingredients together very quickly.
- Pat out on a lightly floured surface. Cut into 2-inch circles with a cookie cutter or juice glass. Place on cookie sheet and brush tops with egg wash.
- Bake for 10 to 15 minutes.

***Egg Wash**

- ***Mix 1 egg yolk with a tablespoon water.***

Maureen Berkman
Scarsdale, New York

SPECIAL EGGS BENEDICT

Serves: 10

2 red peppers, sliced
2 green peppers, sliced
2 medium onions, sliced
¼ pound butter
10 poached eggs
5 English muffins, split and toasted

- Sauté peppers and onions in ¼ pound butter until tender.

Hollandaise Sauce

¼ pound butter
3 egg yolks
1 teaspoon Dijon-style mustard
2 teaspoons lemon juice
Freshly ground black pepper

- Melt butter over low heat.
- Beat egg yolks, mustard, lemon juice and pepper in a blender or food processor. Gradually blend in the hot melted butter.

To Assemble:

- Preheat oven to 350 degrees.
- On a cookie sheet, place 10 toasted English muffin halves.
- Spoon pepper and onion mixture onto muffin halves. Top with poached eggs and sauce.
- Heat in oven for 3 minutes before serving.

Maureen Berkman
Scarsdale, New York

SPINACH AND SALMON ROULADE

This will become a brunch classic.

Serves: 8

Roulade

1 (10-ounce) package frozen chopped spinach
⅛ pound butter
⅓ cup flour
1 cup milk
4 eggs, separated

Filling

1 (15½-ounce) can salmon, drained and flaked
3 shallots, finely chopped
½ cup mayonnaise
1 tablespoon chives, finely chopped

- Combine all ingredients and mix well. Set aside.

- Grease a jelly roll pan with oil, line with waxed paper, and grease the waxed paper.
- Preheat oven to 400 degrees.
- Cook frozen spinach over medium heat until all the liquid has evaporated.
- Melt butter in a separate pan, add the flour gradually and whisk for one minute. Add milk gradually and whisk until mixture thickens. Quickly stir in egg yolks and spinach. Transfer the mixture to a large bowl.
- Beat egg whites until soft peaks form and fold into the spinach mixture.
- Pour mixture into the prepared pan and bake for 12 to 15 minutes.
- Remove from the oven and turn onto a wooden board covered with a tea towel or 2 large pieces of waxed paper. Carefully remove the lining paper.
- Spread evenly with the filling (recipe follows).
- Holding the tea towel or waxed paper with both hands, gently roll the Roulade the long way.
- Serve immediately.

Maureen Berkman
Scarsdale, New York

STUFFED WHITE FISH

Serves: 10 to 12

1 large smoked white fish, boned (leave head and tail)
2 tablespoons mayonnaise, more or less, as desired
4 stalks celery, chopped or diced
Salt and pepper to taste
Onion powder to taste
Juice of half a lemon to taste

- Remove fish from skin and place in a large bowl. Flake or chop. Add remaining ingredients and mix to desired consistency.
- Spoon fish back into skin. Decorate platter with Romaine or Radicchio lettuce. Place fish in the center and garnish with sliced lemon, onions, radishes, olives and cucumber.

Ellie Stengel
Greenwich, Connecticut

TOMATO QUICHE

A delicious way to use your garden tomatoes.

Serves: 8 to 10

1 (10-inch) pie shell, unbaked
3 tablespoons butter or margarine
3 to 4 ripe tomatoes, peeled and chopped
3 large scallions, chopped
1 tablespoon fresh basil, chopped or 1 teaspoon dried basil
1 teaspoon salt
Fresh ground white pepper, to taste
3 large eggs
1 cup half and half
½ pound natural Swiss cheese, diced

- Preheat oven to 400 degrees.
- Bake pie crust shell for 10 minutes and remove from oven. Raise oven temperature to 425 degrees.
- Melt butter in saucepan. Add tomatoes, scallions, salt, pepper and basil. Cook until mixture is reduced to ½ (about 10 minutes). Drain off excess liquid. Set saucepan in bowl of ice cubes for 10 minutes or so to cool down.
- Sprinkle cheese into pie crust and spread tomato mixture over cheese. Beat eggs with half and half and pour over all. Bake 10 minutes then reduce temperature to 375 degrees and bake another 30 to 35 minutes.
- Serve hot or at room temperature, as a first course or luncheon dish. Also good for a picnic.

Marilyn Wilkes
Armonk, New York

VEGETABLE SOUFFLÉ

A delicious buffet dish.

Serves: 10

Prepare ahead

1 medium onion, coarsely chopped
1 medium green pepper, chopped
½ pound mushrooms, chopped
5 scallions, chopped
1 tablespoon butter

- Vegetables should total 1½ cups.
- Sauté vegetables in butter until wilted. Set aside.

14 large eggs
1 quart half and half
1 large challah (egg bread), sliced thin, crust removed
1 pound Cheddar cheese, grated (any hard cheese of your choice)
Salt to taste, if desired

- Preheat oven to 350 degrees. Butter a 3-quart soufflé dish or a 9-inch x 13-inch pan.
- In a large bowl, beat eggs with half and half. Layer the soufflé dish with bread-cheese-vegetable, bread-cheese-vegetable until all ingredients are used.
- Pour egg mixture over layers. Let sit 4 or more hours in refrigerator or overnight.
- Bake for 45 minutes.

Debbie Simon
Scarsdale, New York

CAKES
Bay
Basil
Savory
Coriander
Sage
Rosemary
Parsley
Mint
Coriander
Sage
Sage
Rosemary
Parsley
Juniper
Mint
Cinnamon
Marjoram
Thyme
Coriander
Juniper
Bay
Bay
Basil
Savory
Coriander
Sage
Rosemary
Parsley
Mint
Cinnamon
Parsley
Sage
Rosemary
Parsley
Mint
Cinnamon
Marjoram
Thyme
Juniper
Coriander
Sage
Marjoram
Thyme
Juniper
Bay
Basil
Savory
Coriander
Bay
Basil

PERTINENT PARTICULARS

- All ingredients should be at room temperature.
- All measurements must be exact.
- Use glass measuring cups for liquid measure.
- Use aluminum cups for dry ingredients. Pile the ingredients lightly into the cup with a spoon and level off with a metal spatula or knife.
- When measuring syrup rub the spoon or cup with oil and syrup will slip off easily.
- When sour milk is indicated, add one tablespoon of vinegar to one cup of milk.
- Add 1 teaspoon of vinegar to baking soda when baking a chocolate cake; it will be moist and fluffy.
- Four tablespoons of cocoa and ½ teaspoon of butter equals one square of chocolate.
- Substitute orange juice for water in making a sponge cake.
- When "flouring" a cake pan before baking a chocolate cake, use cocoa instead of white flour.
- All purpose flour may be substituted for cake flour, but use 2 tablespoons less per cup.
- Always dust raisins with flour when adding to cake recipes. This prevents raisins from sinking to the bottom.
- Eggs are easier to separate when cold; then bring to room temperature before beating egg whites.
- When making recipes using egg whites; substitute superfine sugar for granulated sugar to increase volume. Cream of tartar may also be used to increase volume.
- When creaming butter, margarine or cream cheese, always have at room temperature.
- To keep cake fresh longer, put a slice of apple in the cake tin or plate.
- Always cool cake on a metal cake rack.

APPLE SQUARES

Serves: 12

Prepare ahead

Dough

4 cups flour
2 teaspoons salt
1 teaspoon baking powder
6 tablespoons sugar
1½ cups butter, room temperature
2 eggs, beaten
Confectioners sugar for top

- Preheat oven to 375 degrees. Grease a 9-inch x 13-inch pan.
- Sift dry ingredients together; cut in butter and add eggs.
- With a pastry blender and then fingertips combine to form soft dough.
- Refrigerate for 5 hours or overnight.

Filling

8 Granny Smith apples
3 tablespoons lemon juice
1 teaspoon cinnamon
1 cup sugar

- Peel, core, and slice apples in eighths. Sprinkle with lemon juice. Add sugar and cinnamon and toss together to coat the apples.
- Cut dough in half. Pat half the dough into prepared pan. Place the apples on the dough. Roll out remainder of the dough and cover the apples. Seal dough on all sides.
- With a very sharp knife, cut into squares. Bake for 1 hour.
- Sprinkle with confectioners sugar while still warm.

Hope Hirschhorn
Harrison, New York

BAKLAVA

One of the best Baklava's you'll ever taste.

Yield: 3 dozen

Must be prepared a day ahead

2 pounds almonds, blanched and coarsely chopped
2 cups sugar
1 cup bread crumbs
1¼ pounds sweet butter, melted
1½ pound phyllo dough (preferably fresh)

- Preheat oven to 275 degrees. Grease an 18-inch x 12½-inch x 2¾-inch pan.
- Mix almonds with sugar and bread crumbs. Set aside.
- Melt butter. Brush butter over bottom and sides of pan.
- Place one sheet of phyllo in pan. Brush generously with butter. Repeat with 4 additional phyllo sheets.
- Sprinkle ⅔ cup nut mixture over buttered sheets. Cover with single sheet of phyllo, brushing generously with butter. Repeat until all nut mixture is used.
- Cover with 5 sheets of phyllo, brushing each with butter.
- With a sharp knife, cut three horizontal lines into baklava. Do not cut through to bottom.
- Bake for 2½ hours. Increase oven temperature to 375 degrees and bake 10 to 15 minutes more or until top is nicely browned. Do not refrigerate.
- On the following day pour syrup (recipe follows) over baklava.

Syrup

3 cups water
6 cups sugar
3 tablespoons lemon juice
1 strip lemon peel

- Boil water and sugar 4 minutes. Add lemon juice and peel and continue cooking 4 more minutes.
- Slowly pour hot syrup over cold baklava.

Maria Kokinakis
Queens, New York

Editor's Note: Don't panic! This is not too much syrup; it will be absorbed by the baklava and is delicious.

BANANA CAKE Á LA AMERICANA

Serves: 10 to 12

2½ cups sifted cake flour
1 teaspoon baking powder
¾ teaspoon baking soda
½ teaspoon salt
½ cup milk
1⅓ cups mashed, ripe bananas
⅔ cup butter, room temperature
1½ cups sugar
3 eggs
½ cup chopped pecans
*** 1 cup vanilla patisserie cream, recipe follows**
2 tablespoons diced maraschino cherries
2 bananas, thinly sliced
*** ⅓ cup apricot glaze, recipe follows**

- Preheat oven to 350 degrees. Butter and flour two 9-inch round baking pans.
- Sift together twice: flour, baking powder, baking soda and salt (be sure to read cake flour ingredients. If salt and baking powder are already in cake flour, do not add).
- Blend together milk and mashed bananas.
- In a large mixing bowl, cream butter and sugar. Add eggs, one at a time, beating well after each addition. Add banana mixture, then sifted ingredients to egg mixture. Beat rapidly to obtain smooth batter. Stir in the chopped nuts. Divide evenly into 2 prepared pans.
- Bake for 35 minutes or until a cake tester inserted through the center comes out dry. Cool on cake racks about 15 minutes, then remove from pans.

Vanilla Patisserie Cream

¼ cup sugar
Dash of salt
3 tablespoons flour
1 cup milk
1 egg yolk, lightly beaten
½ teaspoon vanilla

- Mix sugar, salt, and flour in heavy saucepan and stir in milk. Cook over low heat, stirring constantly with whisk to prevent scorching. Allow the mixture to come to a boil and cook until thick and smooth. Remove from heat and stir a small amount of hot mixture into beaten egg yolk. Return egg yolk to mixture and stir in vanilla until well combined. Chill.
- Place 4 strips of waxed paper on serving plate. Place a layer of cake upside down on top of waxed paper. Combine vanilla cream with cherries and spread on layer. Place top layer right side up on top of filling.

Apricot Glaze

½ cup apricot preserves
⅛ cup water

- Combine preserves and water in saucepan. Heat until ingredients just come to boil. Strain and cool to lukewarm.
- Cover top layer of cake with sliced bananas arranged in circles, one overlapping the other. Coat with apricot glaze. Remove waxed paper strips. Refrigerate until ready to serve.

Sherry Lieb
Livingston, New Jersey

BEST CHOCOLATE CHIP FUDGE CAKE

Rich, delicious and festive.

Serves: 8 to 10

Cake Layers

⅔ cup unsalted butter, room temperature
2 cups granulated sugar
3 eggs
2 cups sifted all-purpose flour
¾ cup unsweetened cocoa powder
1¼ teaspoons baking soda
¼ teaspoon baking powder
½ teaspoon salt
1½ cups milk
1 teaspoon vanilla
¼ cup chocolate-mint liqueur

- Preheat oven to 350 degrees. Line two 9-inch cake pans with waxed paper; butter and flour the pans; tap out excess.
- In a large mixing bowl, beat butter until light and fluffy. Gradually add the sugar; continue beating until smooth. Beat in eggs one at a time, until well blended.
- Sift together flour, cocoa, baking soda, baking powder and salt. Add to egg mixture in thirds, alternating with the milk, mixing only until blended. Blend in vanilla and liqueur.
- Divide the batter evenly between the two pans. Bake until the tops of cakes are springy to the touch, 40 to 45 minutes. Remove from oven. Cool on racks for 30 minutes. Loosen edges with a knife and unmold. Peel off waxed paper. Set cakes on rack and cool completely.

Chocolate Fudge Filling

2/3 cup sugar
1/2 cup heavy cream
2 1/2 ounces unsweetened baking chocolate
1 tablespoon light corn syrup
2 tablespoons unsalted butter

- Combine sugar, cream, chocolate and corn syrup in a small heavy saucepan. Bring to a simmer over moderate heat, stirring frequently. Reduce heat to low and cook for 5 to 10 minutes or until thickened.
- Remove from heat, dot top with butter and let cool at room temperature (about 15 minutes). When cool, stir in butter until fudge filling is smooth and creamy.

Chocolate Cream

2 1/2 cups heavy cream
3 1/2 tablespoons unsweetened cocoa powder
7 tablespoons confectioners sugar

- Beat cream and cocoa until soft peaks form. Gradually add confectioners sugar and continue beating until stiff.

Chocolate Syrup

2 tablespoons unsweetened cocoa powder
2 tablespoons light corn syrup
1 tablespoon granulated sugar
2 tablespoons water

- To prepare syrup combine cocoa, corn syrup, sugar and water in a small heavy saucepan. Bring to simmer over low heat and cook, stirring constantly, for two minutes. Transfer syrup to a small bowl and cool to room temperature, stirring once or twice to prevent a skin from forming.

To Assemble Cake

3 tablespoons semi-sweet chocolate chips

- Cover one cake layer with all the fudge filling. Sprinkle evenly with chocolate chips. Spread 1/2 cup chocolate cream on top of chips.
- Cover with second cake layer and cover top and sides of cake with remaining chocolate cream. Use the remainder in a pastry bag to decorate the cake as desired.
- Refrigerate for up to three hours before serving.
- Just before serving, drizzle the syrup over the top of the cake in a lacy design.

Arnold Gross
Ryebrook, New York

Editors Note: Any liqueur of your choice may be substituted.

BLUEBERRY SQUARES

Yield: Nine 3-inch squares

1½ cups sifted flour
1½ teaspoons baking powder
1½ cups dark brown sugar, firmly packed
Scant ½ cup vegetable shortening
3 eggs, well beaten
½ teaspoon lemon rind, grated
1½ cups blueberries, either fresh or fresh frozen, unsweetened
¾ cup chopped walnuts

- Preheat oven to 325 degrees. Grease a 9-inch x 9-inch pan lightly, line with waxed paper, grease paper.
- Sift flour with baking powder and brown sugar.
- In a large bowl, beat vegetable shortening; add beaten eggs. Stir in flour mixture, beating well. Fold in lemon rind, blueberries and nuts. Pour into pan. Bake 50 minutes or until cake tester comes out clean. Cool. Remove from pan, peel off paper and cut cake into squares.

Eve Ebenhart
Delray Beach, Florida

CARROT CAKE

Serves: 8 to 10

4 eggs
1½ cups sugar
1½ cups vegetable oil
2 cups flour
2 teaspoons cinnamon
2 teaspoons baking powder
2 teaspoons baking soda
1 teaspoon salt (optional)
3 cups grated carrots
½ cup raisins
½ cup chopped pecans

- Heat oven to 350 degrees. Butter and flour a 10-inch Bundt pan.
- Beat eggs until frothy. Beat in sugar a little at a time until light and lemon-colored. Gradually beat in oil.
- Sift dry ingredients together and fold into egg mixture. Fold in carrots, raisins and pecans.
- Bake for 30 minutes (until "tester-dry"). Remove from pan when cooled.

Icing (optional)

8 ounces cream cheese, room temperature
¼ pound unsalted butter, room temperature
1 pound confectioners sugar
1 cup crushed pineapple, very well drained
1 teaspoon vanilla

- Cream the cheese and butter with confectioners sugar until light. Blend in pineapple and vanilla.

Len Feiman
White Plains, New York

LEMON CREAM CHEESE ICING

½ cup butter, room temperature
1 (3-ounce) package cream cheese, room temperature
1½ teaspoons vanilla
2½ cups sifted confectioners sugar
Grated rind and juice of ½ lemon

- Mix butter, cream cheese, vanilla and blend. Add sugar gradually and mix well. Add lemon rind, juice and blend.

Gen Vergari
Yonkers, New York

CHEESE CAKE

Serves: 10 to 12

Make one day ahead

Crust

¼ pound butter, melted
2 cups graham cracker crumbs
¼ cup brown sugar

- Preheat oven to 350 degrees. Use an ungreased 9-inch springform pan.
- Mix all ingredients together and pat into the bottom and ¼ inch up the sides of the pan.
- Bake for 8 minutes. Cool completely on wire rack.

Filling

1 pound cream cheese, room temperature
1 cup sugar
5 eggs, separated
1 pint sour cream
3 tablespoons lemon juice
1 teaspoon vanilla

- Preheat oven to 310 degrees.
- In a large mixing bowl cream the cheese and sugar together, creaming until smooth. Beat the egg yolks until light and lemon colored. Add to the creamed mixture and blend. Fold in sour cream, lemon juice and vanilla. Beat egg whites until stiff and fold into the mixture.
- Pour into prepared crust and bake for 1 hour. Turn heat off and leave cake in oven for another hour. Open oven door and leave cake in for ½ hour.
- Remove to wire rack to cool completely. Refrigerate.

Topping

1 (12-ounce) jar raspberry preserves
1 pint whole strawberries
1 teaspoon Cointreau

- In a saucepan, heat the preserves until melted. Strain to remove the seeds; add the Cointreau and stir. Dip whole strawberries into preserves and cover top of cooled cake. Refrigerate until 10 minutes before ready to serve.

Note: For a heavier cake do not separate eggs. Add the beaten eggs to the cream cheese and sugar mixture and blend.

Hope Hirschhorn
Harrison, New York

CHOCOLATE ROLL

Elegant to serve, delicious to taste.

Serves: 12

8 squares semisweet chocolate
5 tablespoons strong coffee
8 eggs, separated
1 cup sugar
¾ cup heavy cream
2 teaspoons vanilla
3 tablespoons confectioners sugar
Semi-sweet cocoa

- Preheat oven to 350 degrees. Oil a jelly roll pan. Place waxed paper on pan so it extends over sides. Oil waxed paper.
- In a double boiler, melt chocolate and add coffee. Stir until velvety and smooth. Remove from stove and cool completely.
- Separate eggs and beat yolks with sugar until light and lemon colored. Add chocolate to egg yolks slowly while mixing well. Whip egg whites until peaks form. Fold into cake mixture slowly.
- Pour into pan and bake for 15 minutes. Turn heat off and leave cake in oven for 5 minutes longer. Meanwhile, wet 4 pieces of paper toweling; wring dry. Remove cake from oven; place towels over top and cool completely. Remove towels, sprinkle semi-sweet cocoa over cake. On a large wooden board, place 2 large pieces of waxed paper and turn cake out on paper. Peel paper off top.
- Whip the cream, add confectioners sugar and vanilla. Spread over cake and roll lengthwise.
- Sprinkle on additional cocoa to cover cracks, if necessary. Remove to serving platter.

Hope Hirschhorn
Harrison, New York

CRANBERRY CRUNCH

Serves: 9

1 cup quick-cooking oatmeal
½ cup flour
1 cup dark brown sugar, firmly packed
¼ pound sweet butter, room temperature
1 (16-ounce) can whole berry cranberry sauce
Vanilla ice cream or whipped cream

- Preheat oven to 350 degrees. Grease an 8-inch x 8-inch pan.
- In a large bowl combine oatmeal, flour, sugar. Cut in butter and mix until crumbly.
- Spread ½ mixture into pan. Cover with cranberry sauce. Spread rest of mixture on top of cranberries.
- Bake in oven for 45 minutes.
- When ready to serve, cut into squares. Top with vanilla ice cream or whipped cream.

Pearl Smith
Scarsdale, New York

FROZEN CHOCOLATE NUT CAKE

Absolutely decadent!

Serves: 10 to 12

Prepare ahead

1½ cups chopped nuts
1 (8½-ounce) package chocolate wafers, crushed
1 (12-ounce) package chocolate chips
½ teaspoon salt
1 cup sugar
2 heaping tablespoons powdered instant coffee
1 cup milk
6 eggs, separated
1½ envelopes unflavored gelatin
½ cup hot water
½ pint heavy cream
1 teaspoon vanilla

- Rinse a 10-inch springform pan in cold water. Leave damp. Line sides with waxed paper extending 2 inches above rim to form a collar.
- Mix nuts with chocolate wafer crumbs. Cover bottom of springform with half the mixture.
- Melt chocolate chips, salt, ½ cup sugar, instant coffee and milk in double boiler. Remove once melted. Beat egg yolks with a wire whisk and add to mixture.
- Dissolve gelatin in hot water and add. Chill until mixture begins to thicken.
- Beat egg whites with vanilla until frothy. Slowly add remaining ½ cup sugar and continue beating until stiff. Whip cream and fold both into chocolate mixture. Pour into springform. Top with remaining cookie crumb mixture and freeze, preferably overnight, or at least 6 hours.
- When ready to serve, remove springform. If desired, keep some of the extra crumb mixture to sprinkle on sides for a finished look.

Fran Weisman
Scarsdale, New York

Nataly Ritter
Mamaroneck, New York

GREEK NUT CAKE

(Karithopita)

Serves: 32 to 36

4 cups flour
2 tablespoons baking powder
1 pound walnuts, ground
3 cups sugar
¼ pound butter, melted
1 cup water
12 eggs
1 teaspoon vanilla

- Syrup, recipe follows.
- Preheat oven to 350 degrees. Grease 12-inch x 18-inch baking pan with butter.
- In a large mixing bowl, combine flour, baking powder and walnuts. In bowl of mixer place sugar, butter, water, eggs and vanilla. Beat well. Add dry ingredients and mix thoroughly until smooth.
- Pour mixture into pan. Bake for 40 minutes until golden brown. Cut into serving sized portions.

Syrup

6 cups sugar
3 cups water
1 teaspoon lemon juice
4 whole cloves
1 tablespoon cinnamon

- In a large saucepan combine all ingredients except cinnamon. Bring to boil, lower heat,and simmer for 5 minutes. Cool.
- Remove cloves.
- Slowly pour syrup over cake and sprinkle cinnamon on top.

Eve Lefes
Hartsdale, New York

HONEY CAKE

As good as Grandma made.

Serves: 12

4 cups sifted flour
2 teaspoons baking powder
1 teaspoon baking soda
¼ teaspoon salt
1 teaspoon cinnamon
1¼ cups dark raisins (dust with flour)
4 extra large whole eggs, room temperature
1½ cups sugar
1 pound honey
1 cup cold, dark coffee
½ cup vegetable oil
1 large apple, peeled, cored, and grated
Grated rind (zest) of 1 medium orange
½ cup orange juice
Grated rind (zest) of 1 large lemon
2 tablespoons brandy
1 heaping cup chopped walnuts, plus ¼ cup for topping

- Preheat oven to 325 degrees. Place rack in center of oven. Line the bottom of a 9-inch x 13-inch pan using a brown paper bag or parchment paper as a liner. Do not grease.
- In a bowl,sift all dry ingredients together. Dust the raisins with flour (this keeps them from sinking to the bottom in the batter mixture).
- In large bowl of electric mixer, beat the eggs until foamy. Gradually add sugar and beat until lemon colored. Add honey and blend until smooth. Add cold coffee and oil. Add the grated apple, juice, lemon and orange zests. Mix thoroughly. Add dry ingredients, ½ cup at a time. Blend by hand until well incorporated. Beat just enough so that all the flour has disappeared. Add brandy. Fold in the nuts and raisins by hand. Pour batter into baking pan. Sprinkle with remaining nuts.
- Bake for 1 hour plus 10 to 15 minutes more. Test cake after 1 hour. Cake should be done when a cake tester inserted in center comes out clean. Cool on cake rack in pan. After 15 minutes run a knife around the edge. When completely cool, use a cookie sheet to turn cake out. Peel off paper. Invert back, by using another cookie sheet.

Corrine Katz
White Plains, New York

INDIVIDUAL CHEESE CAKES

Yield: 40 cakes

2 (8-ounce) packages cream cheese, room temperature
¾ cup sugar
2 eggs
1 teaspoon vanilla
8 ounces sour cream
2 cups crushed vanilla wafers or graham cracker crumbs
1 (21-ounce) can pie filling, either blueberry or cherry

- Preheat oven to 350 degrees. Line miniature muffin tins with paper cupcake liners.
- In a bowl, cream the cream cheese, add sugar and beat in eggs, one at a time. Blend in vanilla and sour cream.
- Place 1 tablespoon crumbs in cupcake liner, pour mixture filling a little more than half full. Bake for 10 to 15 minutes. Cool, then top with 1 tablespoon pie filling.

Helen Peck
Scarsdale, New York

Editor's Note: See Strawberry Glaze on Page 101.

LADY FINGER MOCHA

Serves: 8

1½ tablespoons powdered coffee
1½ tablespoons cocoa
5 tablespoons confectioners sugar
1½ teaspoons vanilla extract
1 pint heavy sweet cream
24 (2 packages) lady fingers
½ pound almond Rocca*, finely chopped

- Add coffee, cocoa, sugar and vanilla to the cream and whip until stiff.
- Open lady fingers and place half the amount in a glass bowl or other serving dish that is about 4-inches deep. Arrange in any manner you desire.
- Spread whipped cream mixture on the lady fingers and sprinkle with half of the chopped Rocca on top.
- Place remaining lady fingers over Rocca bits and spread with remaining cream. Top with Rocca bits and chill until ready to serve.

*Tin of candy.

Wendy Shemer
New Rochelle, New York

LEMON CUSTARD SPONGE CUPS

Serves: 6

3 tablespoons butter or margarine, room temperature
1 cup sugar
3 eggs, separated
5 tablespoons flour
Grated rind of 1 lemon
5 tablespoons lemon juice
1½ cups milk
Whipped cream, or berries, optional

- Preheat oven to 325 degrees. Use 6 large custard cups.
- Cream butter and sugar and add egg yolk to mixture. Beat thoroughly. Add flour, lemon juice and rind and mix well. Stir in milk and blend. Fold in stiffly beaten egg whites.
- Pour into custard cups or a large pudding dish. Set in a pan of cold water and bake in slow oven for 45 minutes. When done each cup will have custard on bottom with sponge-like texture on top.
- Serve plain or with whipped cream; may be topped with berries or with other fruit.

Gail Hoffman
Larchmont, New York

LIGHT AND EASY COFFEE CAKE

Delicious too!

Serves: 12

½ pound butter, room temperature
2 eggs
1 cup sour cream
1 teaspoon vanilla
1 cup sugar
2 cups flour
1 teaspoon baking soda
1 teaspoon baking powder
½ cup raisins or chocolate chips

- Preheat oven to 375 degrees. Grease a 10-inch tube pan.
- Cream butter, eggs, sour cream, and vanilla in a bowl. In another bowl mix sugar, flour, baking soda and baking powder.
- Combine ingredients in large bowl of electric mixer; beat for about 2 minutes.
- Stir in raisins or chocolate chips.

Topping Mixture

Combine:

⅔ cup sugar
3 teaspoons cinnamon
1 cup chopped walnuts

To Assemble

- Line pan with ⅓ of topping mixture, spoon in ½ of the batter and spread smoothly. Add another third topping, spoon remainder of batter, spread evenly and add rest of topping.
- Bake for 40 minutes. Cool on cake rack and remove from pan.

Elaine Satuloff
Harrison, New York

NAN'S CHEESE CAKE

From Grandmother with love.

Serves: 8 to 10

Prepare a day ahead

Graham cracker crumbs
½ teaspoon cinnamon (¼ teaspoon for crumbs and ¼ teaspoon for topping)
3 (8-ounce) packages cream cheese, room temperature
4 eggs, room temperature
16 ounces sour cream
8 ounces heavy cream
2 cups sugar
*** 1 teaspoon lemon juice**
*** 1 teaspoon vanilla extract**
*** Zest of one lemon**
or
*** 2 ounces Amaretto may be substituted for the starred *items.**

- Preheat oven to 350 degrees. Butter a 9-inch or 10-inch springform pan. Spread graham cracker crumbs on bottom and sides of springform pan. Crumb layer on bottom of pan should be ¼ inch deep and a dusting on the sides. Sprinkle with ¼ teaspoon of cinnamon.
- Beat cream cheese and eggs until thoroughly mixed. Add remaining ingredients and beat well. Pour into prepared pan and rap sharply on counter top to eliminate air bubbles. Let settle for a few minutes. Sprinkle teaspoon cinnamon over top.
- Bake for 40 minutes if using a 10-inch springform pan or 50 minutes if using a 9-inch pan. Cheese cake will be done when batter has risen to the top of pan. Watch carefully.
- When cake is finished baking, place under broiler for 40 to 60 seconds. Turn off oven and leave cake inside for several hours. Remove and refrigerate for a day before serving.

Phillip Martino
Chicago, Illinois

NUT ROLL

Serves: 8

7 eggs, separated
6 tablespoons sugar
¾ cup ground nuts-any kind or mixture will do, unsalted only
1 teaspoon ground ginger
½ teaspoon cinnamon
Confectioners sugar
1½ cups heavy cream
4 tablespoons praline liqueur

- Preheat oven to 350 degrees. Grease a 10-inch x 15-inch jelly roll pan. Line with waxed paper and grease paper.
- Beat egg yolks and sugar until *very* thick and creamy. Beat egg whites until very stiff.
- Fold whites, nuts and spices into yolk mixture.
- Pour cake mixture into pan and spread evenly.
- Bake 25 minutes or until cake springs back when lightly touched. Let cool. Remove from pan and peel off paper.
- Beat cream with liqueur and sugar to taste. Spread on cooled cake and roll up. Sprinkle with confectioners sugar.

Susan Berenson
Armonk, New York

COOKIE ICE CREAM CAKE

Prepare ahead

Serves: 12 to 16

36 chocolate sandwich cookies, crushed
⅓ cup melted butter
2 quarts vanilla or coffee ice cream
1 (13-ounce) can evaporated milk
⅓ cup butter
4 squares unsweetened chocolate
1 cup sugar
1 cup heavy cream
½ cup coconut

- Preheat oven to 350 degrees. Use a 10-inch springform pan.
- Crush 36 cookies and add melted butter. Mix thoroughly and press into pan, coating bottom and sides. Bake for 10 minutes. Remove from oven and cool.
- Add 2 quarts of softened vanilla or coffee ice cream. Freeze at least 1 hour.
- In a saucepan, over low heat, cook evaporated milk, butter, chocolate and sugar, stirring constantly until thickened. Cool slightly and pour on top of ice cream. Freeze again.
- When ready to serve, whip the cream and fold in coconut. Spread on top of chocolate. Serve immediately or refreeze.

Stephanie Green
New York, New York

PAULETTE'S FUDGE CAKE

Serves: 8 to 10

12 ounces semisweet chocolate
5 tablespoons strong coffee
1 cup butter
2 cups sugar
6 eggs, separated
1 cup flour

- Preheat oven to 350 degrees. Use a 9-inch greased and floured springform or removable bottom pan.
- In top of double boiler, melt chocolate in coffee. Let cool.
- Cream butter and sugar together. Add egg yolks, one at a time to the creamed mixture, beating well after each addition. Blend in flour.
- Beat egg whites until stiff. Gently fold chocolate into egg whites. Fold into batter.
- Pour into prepared pan. Bake for 60 to 70 minutes. When done, the top will be crusty and cracked and the middle will be slightly moist.

Paulette Howard
New Rochelle, New York

PLUM CAKE

Serves: 6 to 8

¼ pound butter, room temperature
3 tablespoons sugar
1 egg
1¼ cups flour
12 purple plums, halved and pitted
Juice of ½ lemon

Topping

3 tablespoons butter
½ cup sugar (scant)
1½ tablespoons flour
Cinnamon

- Preheat oven to 350 degrees. Grease a 9-inch pie plate.
- Cream butter, sugar and egg together in a bowl. Add flour and mix again. Press into pie plate. Layer plum halves skin side up over mixture. Sprinkle with lemon juice and topping.
- Bake in oven for 45 minutes.

Grace Oshin
White Plains, New York

POUND CAKE

Serves: 24

1 pound cake flour (sifted, 4½ to 5 cups)
1 pound butter, room temperature
1 pound sugar (2¼ to 2½ cups)
1 pound eggs weighed in shell (9 or 10)
2 tablespoons vanilla or brandy

- Preheat oven to 300 degrees. Line three 9-inch x 5-inch x 3-inch loaf pans (or 10-inch tube pan) with waxed paper.
- Sift flour, weigh or measure and sift again.
- Cream butter well; add sugar gradually and beat until light and fluffy.
- Add eggs (without shell) 2 at a time; beat well after each addition. Add flavoring. Add flour gradually and beat until smooth.
- Pour mixture into pans and bake 1 hour and 15 minutes, a little longer for tube pan.

Penny Weill
Scarsdale, New York

RUTH KRANZ'S ORANGE NUT CAKE

Friends have requested this recipe more than any other.

Serves: 8 to 10

¾ cup butter, room temperature
1½ cups sugar
3 eggs, separated
2 cups flour
1 teaspoon baking powder
1 teaspoon baking soda
¾ cup sour cream
¾ cup chopped walnuts
1 lemon, grated rind and juice
1 orange, grated rind and juice

- Preheat oven to 350 degrees. Butter a 9-inch springform pan.
- In a large bowl, cream butter and 1 cup sugar. Add egg yolks. Sift together flour, baking powder and soda; add alternately with sour cream. Add chopped nuts, grated rind of lemon and orange.
- Beat egg whites until stiff and fold into batter.
- Bake for 45 minutes. Mix orange and lemon juice with remaining ½ cup sugar. When cake is done, baste with juice until all is absorbed.

Estelle Silverstone
Harrison, New York

SACHER TORTE

Serves: 12

3 (1-ounce) squares unsweetened chocolate
⅔ cup sugar
½ cup milk
1 egg, lightly beaten
½ cup butter
1 cup sugar
1 teaspoon vanilla
2 eggs
2 cups sifted flour
1 teaspoon baking powder
¼ teaspoon salt
⅔ cup milk
1 (12-ounce) jar apricot preserves, strained
1 recipe Chocolate Icing, recipe follows
Whipped cream

- Preheat oven to 350 degrees.
- Prepare two 9-inch cake pans by buttering the bottom lightly and sprinkling with flour. Shake off excess flour.
- Combine chocolate, ⅔ cup sugar, ½ cup milk and beaten egg in a saucepan. Cook and stir over low heat until chocolate melts and mixture thickens. Do not boil. As soon as chocolate is melted and the mixture smooth, remove from heat and cool.
- With an electric mixer, cream butter adding 1 cup sugar gradually, beating until light and fluffy. Add vanilla and the eggs, one at a time, beating well after each addition.
- Sift flour, soda and salt together. Add to the butter/sugar mixture alternately with ⅔ cup milk, beginning and ending with flour. Beat after each addition. Blend in the cooled chocolate mixture. Pour into prepared pans and bake in the center of oven for 25 to 30 minutes or until cake shrinks slightly from sides of pan and springs back lightly to the touch. Remove cakes from oven, turn onto racks and cool thoroughly.
- When cakes cool, split each layer in half with a serrated knife. You should now have 4 layers. Spread each layer with the apricot preserves and with 2 tablespoons of the icing. Continue layering and spreading leaving enough icing to frost the sides and top of cake. Serve Viennese style with whipped cream.

Chocolate Icing

6-ounces unsweetened baking chocolate
½ cup butter
2 cups confectioners sugar
Pinch of salt
2 teaspoons vanilla extract
3 to 4 tablespoons boiling water

- Place chocolate and butter in top of a double boiler. Melt over simmering water until smooth. Remove from heat and transfer mixture to electric mixer bowl. Beat in sugar, salt, vanilla and enough water to make a smooth and shiny glaze consistency.

Sherry Lieb
Livingston, New Jersey

STRAWBERRY GLAZED CHEESE CAKE

Serves: 10 to 12

Must be made 1 to 2 days ahead

Crust

¾ cup ground walnuts
¾ cup crushed graham crackers
3 tablespoons sweet butter, melted

- Preheat oven to 350 degrees. Lightly butter a 9-inch or 10-inch springform pan.
- Combine above ingredients and press into bottom of pan.

Filling

4 (8-ounce) packages cream cheese, room temperature
4 eggs
1¼ cups sugar
1 tablespoon fresh lemon juice
2 teaspoons vanilla

- In a large bowl of electric mixer beat cream cheese until smooth. Add eggs, sugar, lemon juice and vanilla beating until thoroughly mixed. Pour over crust. Position rack in center of oven.
- Bake in 10-inch pan 40 to 45 minutes; 9-inch pan 50 to 55 minutes. (Cake may rise slightly and crack; it will settle and topping will cover it.) Remove from oven and let cool 15 minutes. Retain oven at 350 degrees.

Topping

2 cups sour cream
¼ cup sugar
1 teaspoon vanilla

- Combine cream, sugar and vanilla and blend. When cake has cooled, spoon topping over top to ½ inch of edge. Return to oven and bake 5 minutes. Let cool and refrigerate for at least 24 to 48 hours.

Glaze

1 quart strawberries
1 (12-ounce) jar raspberry jelly
1 tablespoon cornstarch
¼ cup Cointreau
¼ cup water

- Wash, hull and dry berries. Combine a small amount of jelly with cornstarch and mix. Add remaining jelly, Cointreau and water. Cook over medium heat, stirring until thickened and clear, about 5 minutes. Cool
- Loosen cake from pan with knife. Remove springform. Arrange berries pointed ends up on top of cake. Spoon glaze over berries allowing some to drip down the sides. Return to refrigerator until glaze is set.

Aileen Karp
Mamaroneck, New York

VIV'S APPLE OR PEACH CRISP

Delicious and effortless.

Serves: 12

4 to 5 apples, peeled, cored and sliced
Juice of 1 lemon
1 to 2 tablespoons cinnamon
1 cup sugar
1 cup flour
1 teaspoon baking powder
1 egg, beaten
¼ cup sweet butter, melted

- Preheat oven to 350 degrees. Grease an oblong 9-inch x 13-inch pan.
- Place sliced apples in the pan. Sprinkle with lemon juice and cinnamon.
- In a mediun bowl, add sugar, flour, baking powder and egg. With two forks, mix until crumbly. Sprinkle the crumb topping evenly over the apples.
- Pour melted butter over the top. Sprinkle with additional cinnamon and sugar. Bake for 40 minutes. Remove from oven. Serve either warm or cold.

Note: In summer use 6 to 7 medium peaches, peeled and sliced.

Amy Satuloff Lemle
Scarsdale, New York

YEAST CAKE

Serves: 12 to 14

Allow 2 days to prepare

½ pound unsalted butter, room temperature
4 tablespoons sugar
3 eggs, separated (put whites in refrigerator overnight)
½ cup warm milk
1 package granulated yeast
¼ cup warm water
3 cups flour
1 cup sugar
½ cup chopped nuts
½ cup raisins
1 teaspoon cinnamon

- Preheat oven to 350 degrees. Use a greased 10-inch springform pan.
- Combine nuts, raisins and cinnamon.
- In a large bowl, mix butter and 4 tablespoons sugar until smooth. Add egg yolks to milk. Dissolve yeast in warm water. Add egg and yeast mixtures to butter-sugar mixture. Blend well. Stir in flour, a little at a time, mixing well. Place in refrigerator overnight. Next day divide dough in half.
- Roll out on a lightly floured board about 12-inch x 8-inch and about ¼-inch thick.
- Beat egg whites with 1 cup sugar. Spread ⅓ mixture over the dough, add half the nuts, raisins and cinnamon. Roll up jelly roll fashion and place into springform. Repeat procedure with remaining dough. Place over first portion. Spread remaining beaten whites over top. Let rise, covered, until double in size.
- Bake for 50 to 55 minutes.

Note: You can also shape and place into 2 greased 9-inch x 5-inch x 3-inch loaf pans. Bake for 45 minutes.

Eve Ebenhart
Delray Beach, Florida

COOKIES
Bay
Basil
Savory
Coriander
Sage
Rosemary
Parsley
Mint
Coriander
Sage
Rosemary
Sage
Rosemary
Parsley
Mint
Cinnamon
Marjoram
Marjoram
Thyme
Juniper
Bay
Bay
Basil
Savory
Coriander
Sage
Rosemary
Parsley
Mint
Cinnamon
Parsley
Sage
Rosemary
Parsley
Mint
Cinnamon
Marjoram
Thyme
Juniper
Coriander
Sage
Marjoram
Thyme
Juniper
Bay
Basil
Savory
Coriander
Bay
Basil

PERTINENT PARTICULARS

- Use a cool cookie sheet to bake each batch of cookies to prevent spreading.
- Bake cookies on the middle rack of the oven unless otherwise specified.
- Remove soft or sticky cookies from cookie sheet by greasing the spatula.
- Cool cookies on a metal rack or they will become soggy.
- Cookies stored in an air-tight metal container will last longer.

ALMOND TARTLETS

Love at first bite.

Yield: 12 to 14 tartlets
or one 10-inch tart

Pastry

8 tablespoons butter, room temperature
2 tablespoons sugar
1 egg
½ teaspoon baking powder
1 cup flour

- Preheat oven to 400 degrees. Use lightly greased individual small fruit tart pans or one 10-inch tart pan. Cookie sheet.
- Cream butter and sugar thoroughly. Add egg and mix. Add baking powder and flour and mix thoroughly.
- Press small amounts of pastry into tart pans (approximately ¼ inch thick).
- Cool in refrigerator on a baking sheet.

Filling

6 tablespoons butter
4 tablespoons sugar
1 teaspoon vanilla
1 tablespoon milk
½ cup sliced almonds

- Melt butter, sugar, vanilla, and milk
- Add sliced almonds and stir into the mixture. Bring to a simmer and remove from heat.
- Spoon mixture into the shells. Place on cookie sheet and bake for 20 minutes.
- Remove from oven and cool on cake rack for 10 minutes. Remove from tart pans and cool completely on cake rack.

Maureen Berkman
Scarsdale, New York

BEST LACE COOKIES

These really are the best!

Yield: 48 cookies

½ cup margarine
½ cup brown sugar, tightly packed
½ cup Karo light corn syrup
1 cup flour
1 cup shredded coconut
1 cup chopped nuts (pecans, almonds or combination of each)
1 teaspoon vanilla

- Preheat oven to 350 degrees. Foil covered cookie sheets.
- Melt margarine, sugar and syrup in 2½-quart saucepan. Bring to boil over medium heat, stirring constantly. Remove from heat and add flour, coconut, nuts and vanilla.
- Stir thoroughly to incorporate all flour.
- Drop on foil covered cookie sheet by scant teaspoon 3 inches apart (they spread).
- Bake for 8 to 10 minutes. Cool 4 to 5 minutes before removing from foil. Finish cooling on rack with double thickness of paper towels on it to absorb margarine.

Icing for Lace Cookies

1 (6-ounce) package semi-sweet chocolate chips
6 tablespoons butter
1 teaspoon vanilla

- Melt chocolate chips and butter. Lay waxed paper on a flat surface and arrange cookies in a single layer. Working quickly, dip a fork in chocolate and drizzle across cookies to obtain a lacy effect.

Roxene Feinberg
Scarsdale, New York

BUTTER COOKIES

You can't eat just one!

Yield: 96 to 120 cookies

Prepare one day ahead

1 pound butter, room temperature
1 cup sugar
5 tablespoons vanilla
2 eggs
Dash salt
5 cups flour
1 teaspoon of Amaretto liqueur
Sugar and cinnamon for sprinkling

- Preheat oven to 350 degrees. Use a large cookie sheet.
- Cream butter and sugar in a large bowl. Add vanilla, eggs and salt. Beat in flour until smooth. Add the liqueur. Shape into roll 2½ inches wide, wrap in waxed paper, and refrigerate overnight.
- Remove paper and cut crosswise into thin slices. Sprinkle sugar and cinnamon over cookie tops. Bake for 8 to 10 minutes or until golden brown.

Fritzi Bertuch
Bal Harbour, Florida

BUTTER NUT SQUARES

Yield: 24 squares

½ pound butter, room temperature
⅔ cup sugar
1 egg yolk (save white)
½ teaspoon cinnamon
1 cup chopped walnuts, divided
1⅔ cups unsifted flour

- Preheat oven to 275 degrees. Use an ungreased 11-inch x 16-inch jelly roll pan.
- In a large bowl, cream together butter and sugar. Add egg yolk, cinnamon, ½ cup chopped walnuts and flour.
- Spread mixture on pan. Brush with egg white. Sprinkle additional ½ cup chopped nuts on top of egg white. Bake for 1 hour. Cut into squares immediately.

Elaine Weiser
Great Neck, New York

CHEESE HORNS

Unusually Good!

Yield: 32 horns

¼ pound margarine or butter, room temperature
1 (3-ounce) package cream cheese, room temperature
3 teaspoons sugar
1 egg yolk
2 cups sifted flour
Raspberry preserves, chopped nuts, sugar and cinnamon for filling
Additional sugar

- Preheat oven to 350 degrees. Cover a cookie sheet with aluminum foil and grease foil.
- In a bowl, cream margarine, cream cheese, sugar and egg yolk. Add flour and mix well. Chill overnight or several hours in refrigerator. (Can be made a day ahead and kept refrigerated).
- Divide dough into 4 equal parts. Roll each part (one at a time) into a thin circle. Spread jam (not too much) an inch in from the circle edge. Sprinkle with nuts, sugar and cinnamon. Cut circle into 8 pie-shaped wedges. Roll each wedge, widest part first, into a horn shape; then roll in sugar. Place on cookie sheet and bake for 20 to 25 minutes.

Note: This dough can also be made in a food processor. Margarine and cream cheese must be ice cold. Cut cream cheese into 4 parts and margarine into 6 to 8 sections. Put all ingredients including flour into processor at one time. Turn on and off about 3 to 4 times, then let machine run until dough is in one mass and to one side of work bowl. Remove dough and wrap in waxed paper. Refrigerate until cold. Can also be made a day ahead.

Eve Ebenhart
Delray Beach, Florida

CHOCOLATE CHUNK COOKIES

Spectacular!

Yield: 15 to 18 cookies

Prepare ahead

¼ pound unsalted butter, room temperature
½ cup packed brown sugar
¼ cup granulated sugar
1 teaspoon vanilla
½ teaspoon salt
1 egg
½ teaspoon baking soda
1 cup all purpose flour
¾ cup walnuts, coarsely chopped
12-ounces semi-sweet chocolate morsels or four (3-ounce) bars imported chocolate, coarsely chopped

- In a large mixing bowl, combine the butter, brown sugar, sugar, vanilla and salt. Beat until fluffy. Beat in the egg and baking soda. Stir in the flour, walnuts and chocolate. Transfer to a bowl just large enough to hold the dough. Cover and refrigerate until firm, about 4 hours or overnight.
- Preheat oven to 350 degrees. Lightly coat 1 or 2 baking sheets with vegetable shortening. Using 2 to 3 tablespoons of dough for each cookie, shape the dough into balls. Place one in the center of the cookie sheet and evenly space four others a few inches in from each corner. Bake for 10 to 12 minutes until the cookies spring back when lightly touched.
- Cool on the sheets for 2 minutes. Transfer to paper towels to cool for 2 minutes, and then transfer to racks to cool.

Audrey Wiley
Briarcliff, New York

DATE CRESCENTS

Yield: 60 crescents

3 cups flour
½ pound butter or margarine, room temperature
½ cup water

- Mix the flour, butter and water; knead well. Set aside for a few minutes.

Date Filling

1 pound dates, pitted
1 cup water
2 tablespoons butter or margarine
1 teaspoon grated orange rind
½ cup walnuts, chopped
¼ teaspoon cinnamon
Confectioners sugar

- Cook dates in water over very low heat for 15 minutes. Stir and mix well. Add butter or margarine and heat through until dates are well cooked. Add rind, walnuts and cinnamon. Let cool.
- Preheat oven to 350 degrees. Use an ungreased cookie sheet. Roll dough into balls the size of a walnut; roll out to make a 3-inch circle. Place 1 teaspoonful dates toward the bottom of the circle; roll into a log. Bend to form crescent shape.
- Bake for 15 minutes or until bottoms are light brown. Sprinkle with confectioners sugar.

Betty Laboz
Brooklyn, New York

Editors Note: This dough blends easily in a food processor.

FRUIT ROCKS

Yield: 8 to 10 dozen

1 scant cup butter
1½ cups brown sugar, firmly packed
3 eggs
2 level teaspoons baking soda dissolved in 2 tablespoons hot water
1 teaspoon cinnamon
¼ teaspoon cloves
2¾ cups flour
1 pound dates, cut into small pieces
1 pound currants
1 pound raisins
½ pound walnuts, coarsely chopped

- Preheat oven to 325 degrees. Grease cookie sheet.
- Flour fruit with ¾ cup flour.
- In a large mixing bowl, cream butter and sugar until smooth. Add eggs mixing well. Stir in baking soda, spices and 2 cups flour. Fold in fruits and walnuts.
- Using about 1 teaspoonful for each, form into balls and place on cookie sheets.
- Bake for 10 to 12 minutes.

Audré Lemler
New Rochelle, New York

HAMANTASCHEN

A traditional Purim favorite.

Yield: 30

Filling

8 ounces lekvar (prune butter)
½ cup apricot jam
½ cup walnuts, chopped
¼ cup sugar
¼ cup raisins
Grated rind and juice of ½ lemon

- Combine all ingredients and set aside.

Cookie Dough

½ cup margarine, room temperature
⅔ cup sugar
1 egg
2½ cups flour
2 teaspoons baking powder
½ teaspoon vanilla
¼ cup orange juice
Rind of 1 lemon
1 beaten egg, for brushing tops

- Preheat oven to 350 degrees. Use a greased cookie sheet.
- Cream margarine and sugar in a bowl. Add egg and blend. Add remaining ingredients to form dough. Add a little more flour if dough is too wet.
- Divide dough in half for easy rolling, and roll ⅛-inch thick. Cut circles with 3-inch cutter or larger, if desired.
- Place about 2 teaspoons of filling in center of each circle of dough. Pull circle together over filling to form a triangle. Pinch corners. Brush with beaten egg.
- Bake for 20 minutes or until golden brown.

Note: Dough can be rolled out to fit a 9-inch x 13-inch glass dish, filled with apples or blueberries and sprinkled with ½ cup sugar. Roll out rest of dough and cover top. Brush with beaten egg. Bake in a 375 degree oven for 45 minutes. Cut into squares.

Eve Ebenhart
Delray Beach, Florida

HELLO DOLLIES

Easy and fun to make!

Yield: 16 squares

- Preheat oven to 350 degrees. Use a 9-inch square baking pan.

Crust

1 cup graham cracker crumbs mixed with
4 tablespoons butter, melted

- Press mixture into baking pan.
- Layer these ingredients in the following order on top of crust:

1 cup coconut, shredded or flaked
1 cup semi-sweet chocolate chips
1 cup walnuts, chopped
1 (15-ounce) can condensed milk

- Bake for 30 minutes. Cut into small squares while warm.

Audré Lemler
New Rochelle, New York

JANICE'S BROWNIES

Chewy and moist!

Yield: 1 dozen

14 tablespoons butter
4 ounces unsweetened chocolate
3 eggs
2 cups sugar
½ cup flour
1 teaspoon vanilla
1 cup chopped walnuts

- Preheat oven to 350 degrees. Grease a 9-inch x 13-inch glass baking dish.
- In a double boiler, melt the butter and chocolate over low heat. Let cool.
- Beat the eggs until foamy and gradually beat in sugar. Add butter-chocolate mixture to eggs; mix. Add flour and mix thoroughly. Add vanilla and nuts. Spread evenly in pan.
- Bake 20 to 25 minutes. Cool and cut into squares. DO NOT OVERBAKE!

Roxene Feinberg
Scarsdale, New York

LACE COOKIES

Crisp and light.

Yield: 36 cookies

2 tablespoons light corn syrup
½ cup quick-cooking oats
½ cup flour
½ cup sugar
Pinch salt
⅓ cup butter, melted
¼ teaspoon baking powder
2 tablespoons heavy cream
1 teaspoon vanilla

- Preheat oven to 375 degrees. Grease a cookie sheet.
- Mix all ingredients together in a large bowl. It will seem to be a small amount of batter, but the cookies spread on cookie sheet. Use ½ teaspoon for each cookie; place well apart. Bake for 6 to 8 minutes.

Note: ¼ cup ground almonds may be added.

Joy Klebanoff
Scarsdale, New York

LEMON SQUARES

Yield: 12 to 15 squares

¾ cup butter, room temperature
½ cup confectioners sugar
1½ cups flour
3 eggs
¾ to 1 cup sugar
2 tablespoons flour
Juice and grated rind of 1 lemon
Confectioners sugar for topping

- Preheat oven to 350 degrees. Use a 9-inch by 13-inch pan.
- Blend the butter, confectioners sugar and flour in a food processor or by hand. Pat into the baking pan. Bake 10 to 20 minutes or until light brown. Remove from oven. Maintain oven at 350 degrees.
- Combine the eggs, sugar, 2 tablespoons flour, lemon juice and rind in a processor or blender. Pour over hot crust. Bake again 15 to 20 minutes (until set). Cool 5 minutes. Sprinkle with confectioners sugar. Cut into squares while warm.

Harriet Meyers
White Plains, New York

MANDELBRODT
(Almond Bread)

Yield: 60 slices

3 eggs
1 scant cup sugar
7 tablespoons oil
½ to 1 teaspoon vanilla or almond extract
⅓ cup blanched almonds or walnuts, coarsely chopped
2 rounded teaspoons baking powder
3 scant cups flour

- Preheat oven to 350 degrees. Grease a cookie sheet.
- Beat eggs and sugar together until light. Mix in oil, vanilla or almond extract. Add nuts.
- Add flour which has been sifted with baking powder. Spoon mixture 3 inches wide and ¾ inch high onto cookie sheet, two to a sheet. Bake for about 20 to 25 minutes. *Do not overbake.*
- Slice while still warm into ⅜-inch slices. Brown quickly in oven or under broiler on both sides.

Variations: ½ to 1 cup slivered almonds, chopped almonds, coarsely chopped walnuts or coarsely chopped filberts may be used. One to two teaspoons whiskey, the grated rind of an orange or lemon, or any combination of both may also be used for flavoring.

Mary Barnhard
Lilly Block
Fae Boczko, New Rochelle, New York
Eve Ebenhart, Delray Beach, Florida
Marcia Singer, Harrison, New York
Lotty Stein, Short Hills, New Jersey

MERI BARS

Yield: 12 squares

Prepare ahead

Bottom Layer

23 chocolate wafer cookies
22 vanilla wafer cookies
½ cup butter, melted

Top Layer

1 (12-ounce) package semi-sweet chocolate morsels
1 (6-ounce) package either peanut butter morsels or butterscotch morsels, or a combination of both
½ cup chopped nuts, optional
1 (4-ounce) package coconut flakes
1 (14-ounce) can condensed milk

- Preheat oven to 350 degrees. Use an 8-inch x 12-inch x 1½-inch glass dish.
- Crush chocolate and vanilla cookies in a food processor. Mix cookie crumbs with melted butter and pat into dish.
- Mix the remaining ingredients and place on top of cookie crumb mixture.
- Bake for ½ hour or until top is lightly toasted.
- Cool and cut into squares.
- Put into freezer overnight. Flavor seems to improve if frozen and brought to room temperature.

Note: Other flavors of cookies may be substituted. We tried graham crackers instead of vanilla wafers and they were delicious. If one does not want these too sweet, use less butterscotch morsels, coconut and vanilla wafers; add more chocolate and chopped nuts.

Meri Ritter
Mamaroneck, New York

NANA'S SUGAR COOKIES

Light and not too sweet!

Yield: 60 to 64 cookies

4½ cups sifted flour
1 teaspoon baking soda
1 teaspoon cream of tartar
1 cup sugar
1 cup confectioners sugar
1 cup margarine, room temperature
1 cup vegetable oil
2 eggs
1 teaspoon vanilla

- Preheat oven to 350 degrees. Grease 4 cookie sheets.
- Sift together flour, baking soda and cream of tartar. Set aside.
- In bowl of electric mixer beat together sugar, confectioners sugar, margarine and oil.
- Add eggs one at a time, beating well after each.
- Slowly add flour mixture and beat well. Add vanilla. Dough will be soft.
- Roll dough into large, walnut size balls.
- Place 16 on each cookie sheet.
- Flatten each cookie with a small glass (2-inch x 2½-inch diameter) dipped in sugar.
- Bake for 10 to 12 minutes. Do not allow to brown.
- Cool for 3 to 5 minutes and remove to cookie rack to finish cooling.

Note: Store in air-tight containers. Cookies will remain soft.

Cynthia Hogan
Chevy Chase, Maryland

PEANUT MERINGUES

Yield: 24 cookies

2 egg whites, room temperature
¾ cup sugar
2 cups minced peanuts, unsalted

- Preheat oven to 350 degrees. Grease a cookie sheet.
- In a bowl, beat egg whites until frothy. Slowly add sugar and continue to beat until egg whites are stiff and glossy in color. Fold in the peanuts, blending thoroughly.
- Drop mixture by teaspoonful onto cookie sheet and bake 15 minutes or until golden brown.

Beryl Levitt
Larchmont, New York

PECAN DREAM COOKIES

A recipe handed down to me by my mother.

Yield: 45 cookies

2 cups flour
½ teaspoon salt
1 cup butter, room temperature
½ cup sugar
2 teaspoons vanilla
1 egg white
2 cups coarsley chopped pecans
½ cup sifted confectioners sugar

- Sift together flour and salt. Set aside.
- In a large bowl, cream the butter; add sugar and vanilla beating with a wooden spoon until fluffy. Add egg white and blend. Gradually add flour and salt. Add chopped pecans and blend. Chill for about 30 minutes or longer.
- Preheat oven to 325 degrees. Use ungreased cookie sheets.
- Roll about a teaspoon of dough quickly between the palms of your hands to form finger-like cookies. Place closely together on cookie sheet.
- Bake on shelf in the middle of the oven for 20 minutes. Do not put two trays of cookies in the oven at once. Place carefully onto paper toweling or brown paper bags and allow to cool completely at room temperature.
- Sift confectioners sugar over cookies, then turn carefully and sift more sugar on the other side.

Gen Vergari
Yonkers, New York

PEPPERMINT CREAM CHOCOLATE BARS

Delicious and impressive.

Yield: 100 bars

1 cup sweet butter
4 ounces unsweetened chocolate
4 eggs
2 cups sugar
1 cup unsifted flour
1 cup sliced, unblanched almonds

- Preheat oven to 350 degrees. Grease a 17-inch x 11½-inch jelly roll pan.
- In a saucepan, melt together butter and chocolate. In a bowl, beat the eggs and sugar together. Add flour, almonds and butter-chocolate mixture. Stir until smooth. Spread into jelly roll pan and bake about 25 minutes. Cool completely; cover with filling.

Filling

2¼ cups confectioners sugar
4½ tablespoons sweet butter, room temperature
4 tablespoons heavy cream
1 teaspoon peppermint flavoring
Few drops green food coloring, to make a pale green filling

- Beat together all ingredients until smooth. Spread filling over cake. Cover with plastic wrap and chill 1 hour or until firm. Cover with glaze.

Glaze

8 ounces semisweet chocolate
8 tablespoons butter
1 teaspoon vanilla

- Melt ingredients together over hot water in double boiler. Pour glaze over cake and chill again until firm. Cut into small bars.

Note: Cut into very small bars, 1½-inch x 1½-inch or 2-inch squares.

Phyllis Fass
Scarsdale, New York

REMARKABLE BROWNIES

Chewy and moist-everyone's favorite!

Yield: 18 squares

4 eggs
2 cups sugar
½ pound butter or margarine
4 ounces unsweetened chocolate
2 teaspoons vanilla
1 cup flour, unsifted
1 cup chopped walnuts
1 cup raisins

- Preheat oven to 250 degrees. Grease and flour a 9-inch x 13-inch glass baking dish.
- Beat eggs until foamy. Add sugar and beat well.
- Melt together in double boiler the butter and chocolate. Cool slightly. Add to egg mixture blending well. Add vanilla and fold in flour, nuts and raisins.
- Pour into baking pan and bake for 1 hour. Test for doneness with a cake tester. Long slow baking is the secret of success. When cool, cut into desired sizes.

B. Terri Trieger
Larchmont, New York

SIS CHAUTIN'S YEAST CRESCENTS

Yield: 5 dozen crescents

1 cake yeast (or 1 package)
½ cup lukewarm milk
4 tablespoons sugar plus 1 heaping teaspoon
1 cup butter, room temperature
2 egg yolks
3¼ cups flour (or more)
¼ pound butter, melted
Cinnamon, to taste
Sugar, to taste
1 cup ground nuts
1 cup raisins
Confectioners sugar

- Dissolve yeast in milk. Add 1 heaping teaspoon sugar. Let stand 25 minutes.
- Cream butter and remaining 4 tablespoons of sugar; add yolks. Add yeast and milk and work in flour. Divide dough into 8 parts. Roll each part into an 8-inch circle. Brush with melted butter. Sprinkle with cinnamon, sugar, ground nuts and raisins. Cut in triangles (8 pieces) and roll from outside to center. Shape in form of a crescent. Let stand for 2 hours.
- Preheat oven to 375 degrees. Use a cookie sheet.
- Bake for 15 to 20 minutes until slightly browned. Before serving, sprinkle with confectioners sugar.

Estelle Silverstone
Harrison, New York

SNOW BALL COOKIES

Yield: 36 cookies

½ pound sweet butter, room temperature
½ cup confectioners sugar
1 teaspoon vanilla
2¼ cups flour
1 cup walnut halves
Confectioners sugar for coating

- Preheat oven to 400 degrees. Grease a cookie sheet.
- Beat butter and sugar until light and fluffy. Blend in vanilla. Gradually add the flour, mixing until smooth.
- Form mixture into 1-inch balls, forming each around one nut half. Bake for 12 to 15 minutes.
- Pour confectioners sugar into two small bowls. When cookies are done and still warm, place one at a time in one bowl, rolling to coat the surface. Remove and place in second bowl, repeating the procedure, until heavily coated.

Beverly Picker
Scarsdale, New York

SUPER BLONDIES

Yield: 24 squares

⅔ cup butter, room temperature
2 cups brown sugar, firmly packed
3 eggs
1 teaspoon vanilla
1¾ cups flour
1½ teaspoons baking powder
¼ teaspoon salt
½ cup chopped nuts
2 cups semi-sweet chocolate bits

- Preheat oven to 350 degrees. Grease and flour a 9-inch x 13-inch pan.
- In a large bowl, cream butter with sugar until smooth. Add eggs one at a time, beating well after each addition. Add vanilla.
- Sift flour, baking powder and salt. Add to egg mixture and blend well. Fold in nuts and chocolate bits.
- Bake for 30 minutes. Cool in pan on a cake rack. When completely cooled, cut into squares.

Blanche Orlofsky
White Plains, New York

TASSIES

Yield: 24

Dough

½ pound butter or margarine, room temperature
6 ounces cream cheese, room temperature
2 cups flour
Confectioners sugar

- Blend butter and cream cheese. Stir in flour and mix well. Chill for 1 hour.

Filling

8 ounces cream cheese, room temperature
1 egg
½ cup sugar
1 teaspoon vanilla

- Mix all ingredients together and set aside.
- Preheat oven to 350 degrees. You will need two 12-cup ungreased muffin tins and 24 fluted paper cups.
- Shape dough into 1-inch balls. Press dough against sides and bottom of muffin tins. Top with filling.
- Bake for 25 to 30 minutes. When cool, place in fluted paper cups and sprinkle with confectioners sugar.

Marilyn Fields
Delray Beach, Florida

TEENY PECAN CUPCAKES

Yield: 24

Prepare ahead

Dough

¼ pound butter, room temperature
¼ pound cream cheese, room temperature
1 cup flour

- Mix all ingredients until a ball forms, and refrigerate for 2 hours.

Filling

1 tablespoon butter or margarine, room temperature
1 egg
1 teaspoon vanilla
1 cup brown sugar
1 cup pecans, chopped

- Preheat oven to 350 degrees. Use two miniature muffin tins.
- Mix all ingredients together except pecans.
- Divide dough into quarters. Make 6 balls from each quarter. Place each ball in muffin tins, patting around to make a shell.
- Spoon filling into each shell about ½ full, not more than ¾. Sprinkle pecans over all.
- Bake for 15 minutes. Lower oven to 250 degrees and bake 20 minutes longer. Cool in pan.
- Remove from pan and place in small fluted paper cups. Sprinkle with confectioners sugar.

Elaine Strauss
Harrison, New York

DESSERTS
Bay
Basil
Savory
Coriander
Sage
Rosemary
Parsley
Mint
Cinnamon
Marjoram
Thyme
Juniper

PERTINENT PARTICULARS

- To bake a pie shell; cover pie shell with aluminum foil and weigh down with beans or rice.
- When baking a fruit pie, brush bottom crust with egg white. This prevents the crust from becoming soggy.
- For a two crust pie, cut slits in the top crust to allow the steam to escape.
- For extra light pastry, try using whipped unsalted margarine.
- Slightly chilled pie dough rolls out more easily.
- Sprinkle lemon juice over apples or any other fruit to prevent them from discoloring.
- Before whipping heavy cream, place the bowl and beaters in the refrigerator for 1 hour.

APPLE PIE

An all American favorite.

Yield: One 2-crust pie

Crust

2 cups flour
½ teaspoon salt
⅔ cup solid shortening (part butter may be mixed with it)
3 to 4 tablespoons ice water

- Use a 9-inch pie pan.
- Sift together the flour and salt. Cut in the shortening with pastry blender, or use two table knives, cutting in opposite directions, until pieces are the size of small peas. Sprinkle 1 tablespoon of water over part of the mixture. Gently toss with fork; push to one side of bowl. Sprinkle next tablespoon of water over dry part; mix lightly and push to moistened part at side. Repeat until all is moistened. Gather the dough; wrap it in waxed paper and refrigerate it for at least ½ hour before rolling.

Filling

7 to 8 tart-sweet, unblemished cooking apples, such as Granny Smith's, Greenings, Winesaps, or Rome Beauties (about 2½ pounds)
⅓ cup, plus 2 tablespoons sugar
⅓ cup brown sugar
⅛ teaspoon salt
2 tablespoons flour
½ teaspoon cinnamon
⅛ teaspoon nutmeg, if desired
2 tablespoons butter, room temperature
1 tablespoon lemon juice

- Preheat oven to 450 degrees.
- Cut the pastry in half. Roll out half of it on a lightly floured surface and line a 9-inch pan with the dough. Let the dough overlap the edges of the pan about ½-inch thick. Set aside the rest of the dough that is left over.
- Pare the apples and cut them into quarters. Cut away the cores. Cut the quarters lengthwise into pieces about ½-inch thick. Put the slices into a mixing bowl. Mix all the ingredients together, except the butter and lemon juice; sprinkle over apples, coating them well. Spread just 1 tablespoon butter on top of the pastry in the pie pan. There should be a "goodly mountain" of apple slices. Dot the top with the remaining butter and sprinkle lemon juice over all.

Note: If you want to pare apples ahead of time, possibly the night before using, pour the lemon juice over the slices and place in a plastic bag, thus preventing them from turning brown; then refrigerate.

- Roll out the second half of the dough, quite thin, so that it measures about 1½ inches wider all around than the pie pan. Moisten the rim of the bottom pie crust with a little water. Cover the apple slices with the second crust. Press the two edges together, rolling them together, away from you. Flute edges or press with fork all around. Cut small slits in the top of the pie to allow steam to escape. Place a piece of aluminum foil on the oven shelf to catch any drippings. Place pie directly on foil in the center of the shelf in the middle of the oven. Bake for 10 minutes at 450 degrees, then reduce oven to 375 degrees for about 45 minutes or until pie is pretty brown, and not a "pale-faced" pie.

Gen Vergari
Yonkers, New York

APPLE TART

Beautiful as well as delicious.

Serves: 8 to 10

1¾ cups flour
10 tablespoons butter, well-chilled and cut into ½-inch pieces
Scant ¼ cup sugar
2 egg yolks
¼ teaspoon water
½ teaspoon vanilla
1 (12-ounce) jar apricot jam, heated and strained
10 Granny Smith apples, peeled, cut in half and sliced
Lemon juice to cover sliced apples

- Use an ungreased 12-inch tart or flan pan with removable bottom.
- In a food processor combine flour, butter and sugar. Mix, turning on and off until mixture resembles coarse meal, for about 45 seconds. Add yolks, water and vanilla and continue mixing until dough is crumbly. Gather into a ball; flatten into a disc and wrap tightly in plastic wrap. Refrigerate for two hours.
- Preheat oven to 375 degrees.
- Roll out dough and place in pan. Paint with half of the apricot jam. Refrigerate for 15 minutes. Place sliced apples, which have been sitting in lemon juice, over apricot jam, in a concentric circle. Sprinkle 2 to 4 tablespoons sugar over apples. Bake for 40 minutes.
- Remove from oven and paint apples with remaining apricot jam while hot. Cool completely before removing bottom.

Susan Berenson
Armonk, New York

BAKED PEARS

Serves: 6

½ cup water
Juice and zest of one lemon
¼ cup port wine
1 cup sugar
6 slices lemon
2 to 3 tablespoons orange marmalade (optional)
6 Bosc pears, whole, unpeeled

- Preheat oven to 350 degrees.
- Put all ingredients, except pears, in a saucepan and cook down until strongly flavored and syrupy.
- Pour the mixture over the pears which have been placed upright in a Pyrex dish, just large enough to hold them.
- Bake until tender, basting often.

Note: This may be prepared a day ahead and served warm or cold. If desired, 2 to 3 tablespoons of orange marmalade may be added to the sauce. Serve on a glass plate, with a slice of lemon, lemon leaf, mint leaves, or top with vanilla ice cream.

Dorothy Kagon
Malibu, California

Editor's Note: Use ¾ cup wine; omit water. Pears may be peeled if preferred.

BRANDY TART

Yield: Two 9-inch tarts

Prepare two days in advance.

2 ounces butter, room temperature
1 cup sugar, superfine
1 egg, beaten
1 cup boiling water
1 teaspoon baking soda
1½ cup dates, chopped
1 cup walnuts, coarsely chopped
1½ cups flour
¼ teaspoon baking powder
Pinch salt

- Preheat oven to 350 degrees. Grease two 9-inch Pyrex dishes.
- Cream butter and sugar well; add egg.
- Pour boiling water and baking soda over dates and nuts.
- Add butter, sugar and egg mixture.
- Add the flour, baking powder and salt which have been mixed together.
- Pour half of the mixture into each baking pan and bake for 30 minutes. Allow to cool.

Brandy Sauce

1½ cups sugar
¼ cup brandy
1 teaspoon vanilla
1 cup cold water
2 teaspoons butter

- Boil all ingredients for 5 minutes.
- Prick the tart all over with the tip of a knife (do not slit completely down - just halfway). Pour the syrup over the tarts.
- Serve with whipped cream or crème fraîche. Can be served warm.
- Allow tarts to stand at room temperature or in the refrigerator for 2 days before serving.
- They freeze well.

Maureen Berkman
Scarsdale, New York

CARAMEL BAKED APPLES

Apples done to perfection.

Serves: 4 to 6

4 to 6 baking apples, (such as Rome Beauties)
½ cup chopped apricots
½ cup light seedless raisins
½ cup dark seedless raisins
3 tablespoons flour
⅓ cup light brown sugar
½ teaspoon cinnamon
3 tablespoons butter, room temperature
¼ cup chopped walnuts
½ cup water
½ cup orange juice

- Preheat oven to 325 degrees.
- Core the apples and peel off the skin around the top of each apple.
- Place in a baking dish and fill the centers with chopped apricots and raisins.
- Combine flour, sugar and cinnamon in a small mixing bowl. Cut butter in with a pastry blender. Add nuts. Sprinkle mixture over apples. Combine water and juice and pour over all.
- Bake uncovered for 1½ hours or until apples are tender, basting occasionally with syrup. More liquid may be needed if all is absorbed.

Pat Wagner
Short Hills, New Jersey

CHOCOLATE MOUSSE TORTE

Serves: 8

8 ounces semisweet chocolate
1 tablespoon instant powdered coffee
¼ cup boiling water
8 eggs, separated
⅔ cup sugar
1 teaspoon vanilla
⅛ teaspoon salt
1 cup heavy whipping cream
1 tablespoon sugar

- Preheat oven to 350 degrees. Butter a 9-inch pie plate.
- Place chocolate in top of double boiler. Dissolve coffee in boiling water and pour over chocolate. Cover and let stand over low heat, stirring occasionally until chocolate has melted. Remove from heat to cool.
- In electric mixer, beat egg yolks at high speed until pale lemon-colored and thickened. Gradually add sugar and beat until very thick. Add vanilla and chocolate and mix until well blended.
- In a separate bowl, beat egg whites with salt until stiff but not dry. In 2 or 3 small additions fold half the whites into chocolate. Then fold chocolate into remaining whites gently but thoroughly.
- Set aside 4 cups mousse, cover and refrigerate. Turn balance into pie plate. Bake for 25 minutes; turn heat off and leave in oven for 5 minutes longer. Remove and cool on rack. When completely cool, take reserved mousse from refrigerator and place in center of shell. Refrigerate for at least 2 to 3 hours. Whip cream with 1 tablespoon sugar and cover torte or pipe a lattice pattern from a pastry tube.

Sherry Lieb
Livingston, New York

CHOCOLATE SOUFFLÉ PIE

Serves: 8

Prepare ahead

Meringue Pecan Shell

2 egg whites
1/8 teaspoon cream of tartar
1/2 cup sugar
1 cup chopped pecans

- Preheat oven to 275 degrees. Generously grease a 9-inch pie plate.
- Beat egg whites until foamy. Add cream of tartar and beat until meringue is stiff, but not dry. Gradually beat in sugar. Fold in chopped pecans.
- Spread mixture over bottom and sides of pie plate.
- When spreading meringue, make a nest-like shell, building sides up 1/2-inch above edge of pan.
- Bake in oven about 1 hour or until browned and crisp. Cool.

Filling

1 envelope unflavored gelatin
1/4 cup water
1/4 pound sweet chocolate
1/2 cup milk
3/4 teaspoon vanilla
1 pint vanilla ice cream
3/4 cups chopped pecans

- Soften gelatin in 1/4 cup water. Combine chocolate with milk and melt over hot (not boiling) water. Remove from hot water. Add gelatin and vanilla to chocolate mixture and stir until gelatin dissolves.
- Soften ice cream in mixing bowl. Add chocolate mixture and blend with wire whisk or electric mixer for 2 minutes.
- Pour into baked meringue shell and sprinkle with chopped pecans.
- Place in freezer until firm. Remove from freezer 10 minutes before serving.

Note: May be used for Passover omitting cream of tartar.

Hope Hirschhorn
Harrision, New York

CLAFOUTIS

Serves: 8 to 10

4 eggs, plus 2 egg yolks
Pinch salt
½ cup sugar
1 cup, minus 2 tablespoons, flour
2 tablespoons butter, room temperature
2½ cups milk
1 teaspoon vanilla
1 (17-ounce) can Bing cherries, pitted and well-drained
Confectioners sugar

- Preheat oven to 350 degrees. Butter a fairly shallow glass baking pan about 10-inch diameter, or a 12-inch glass pie plate.
- In a large bowl, beat the eggs, egg yolks and salt. Add sugar and beat until very light and creamy. Add flour gradually, beating until smooth.
- Melt 1 tablespoon butter and beat into the mixture. Add milk and vanilla beating until batter is smooth and well blended. (This can be done in a blender, mixer or food processor.)
- Scatter the drained cherries over the bottom of the baking dish. Pour batter over all.
- Dot with remaining tablespoons of butter and sprinkle a little bit of sugar over top.
- Bake for 45 minutes or until top is golden and puffy and a silver knife inserted in center comes up clean.
- Serve lukewarm with confectioners sugar sprinkled over the top of cake.

Sherry Lieb
Livingston, New Jersey

CZECHOSLOVAKIAN TORTE

Suprisingly easy and an all-time favorite.

Yield: 20 squares

½ pound butter or margarine, room temperature
1 cup sugar
2 egg yolks
2 cups flour
1 heaping cup finely chopped nuts
1 teaspoon vanilla
1 (18-ounce) jar jam or preserves, flavor optional

- Preheat oven to 350 degrees. Grease and flour a 9-inch x 13-inch pan.
- Cream butter and sugar in a large bowl. Blend in egg yolks. Fold in flour, nuts and vanilla.
- Gather dough into a ball and divide in half.
- Press half of the batter into the baking pan, spread with your favorite jam, and crumble rest of dough over jam.
- Bake for 45 to 50 minutes. Cut immediately into squares.

Mildred Goldberger
Scotch Plains, New Jersey

Editor's Note: You can use a thin narrow spatula to evenly spread dough on bottom of pan. We found apricot preserves to be an outstanding flavor. Freezes well.

DIVINE CHOCOLATE MOUSSE

The title says it all!

Serves: 8 to 10 or 4 Chocoholics!

1 pound imported semisweet chocolate
1 dozen eggs, separated
2 tablespoons liqueur (Grand Marnier, Kahlua, Frambois, or Cointreau)

- Place egg whites in large bowl of electric mixer and let come to room temperature.
- Melt chocolate in top of double boiler. Add liqueur to melted chocolate. Remove from heat, stir well and allow to cool completely.
- Beat egg whites until dry but not stiff. A pinch of cream of tartar helps.
- Add slightly beaten egg yolks to cooled chocolate and incorporate thoroughly.
- Fold ⅓ of chocolate mixture into beaten egg whites. Pour into remaining chocolate and fold carefully and completely.
- Pour into a soufflé dish, decorative bowl, or individual serving dishes and refrigerate until ready to serve.
- May be decorated with whipped cream and/or shaved chocolate.

Note: Any fine imported semisweet chocolate may be used. Mousse may be frozen; defrost 1 hour before serving.

Len Feiman
White Plans, New York

EASY PECAN PIE

This couldn't be easier!

Serves: 8

¼ cup butter, room temperature
3 eggs, well beaten
¾ cup sugar
1 cup white corn syrup
1 teaspoon vanilla
¼ teaspoon salt
One 9-inch pie shell, unbaked
2 cups pecans

- Preheat oven to 350 degrees.
- Mix first 6 ingredients together and pour into pie shell. Top with pecans.
- Bake for 1 hour. Can be served warm.

Marcia Hendler
Harrison, New York

FROSTED GRAPES

Do not prepare on a humid day as the frost will not dry.

Serves:6

1 pound black grapes or seedless red grapes
1 pound seedless green grapes
2 egg whites, room temperature
1 pound superfine sugar

- Wash and thoroughly dry grapes. Cut into bunches, leaving them on the stems.
- In a medium-size bowl, beat the egg whites lightly and set aside.
- Pour the sugar into a large bowl and set aside.
- Dip each small bunch of grapes into the egg whites and coat thoroughly. Hold each bunch over the bowl until all the dripping stops. Toss the grapes in the sugar and coat all over.
- Place the grapes on a wire rack and dry at room temperature for at least 1 hour. Do not refrigerate or the "frosted" effect will be ruined.

Note: This can be placed in a beautiful bowl to be used as a centerpiece, and then eaten at dessert time.

Eve Ebenhart
Delray Beach, Florida

FROZEN HALVA DESSERT

You will receive a standing ovation on this dessert.

Prepare ahead

Serves: 10

6 extra large eggs, separated
⅔ cup sugar
1 pint heavy cream
½ pound halva, preferably with nuts

- Slightly oil a 12 cup mold.
- Beat egg yolks with sugar until light and fluffy.
- Whip the cream until stiff and fold into egg yolks.
- Beat egg whites stiffly and fold into cream and yolks.
- Flake the halva; fold into above mixture. Spoon into mold and set in freezer overnight.
- When ready to serve, unmold onto a serving platter. Decorate with chocolate sauce drizzled over and flakes of halva.

Maureen Berkman
Scarsdale, New York

FROZEN LEMON SOUFFLÉ

Prepare ahead

Serves: 8 to 10

2 envelopes unflavored gelatin
1½ cups cold water
12 egg yolks
2 cups sugar
1⅓ cups lemon juice
2 tablespoons lemon rind, grated
8 egg whites, stiffly beaten
3 cups heavy cream, whipped

- Butter two three-inch bands of waxed paper and fasten around top of two 1-quart buttered soufflé dishes, or use a 2-quart soufflé dish and butter one three-inch band.
- Soften gelatin in water.
- Beat egg yolks and sugar until thick and light colored. Stir in lemon juice. Pour into saucepan and cook egg yolk mixture over low heat beating steadily until mixture is thickened and coats the spoon. Mix in dissolved gelatin, then lemon rind. Remove from heat and cool, mixing occasionally.
- Fold in beaten egg whites and then the whipped cream into the lemon mixture. Slowly pour into soufflé dish. Mixture will rise above the top of dish. Freeze, then remove paper collar.
- Wrap in aluminum foil or plastic wrap and return to freezer.
- To serve: let stand in refrigerator for 3 hours.
- Decorate the top with whipped cream and lemon slices dipped in sugar or surround with raspberries or strawberries.

Rose Rabbino

FRUIT PIZZA

A lovely summer dessert.

Serves: 12

1(17-ounce) roll sugar cookies, cut into 1/8-inch slices

- Preheat oven to 375 degrees.
- Line sides and bottom of a 14-inch pizza pan with cookies, overlapping them slightly.
- Bake for approximately 12 to 14 minutes, until golden brown. Cool completely.

Cheese Filling

1(3-ounce) package cream cheese, room temperature
1/3 cup sugar
1 pint heavy cream, whipped
Assorted summer fruit, sliced (bananas, kiwis, strawberries, raspberries, blueberries, peaches)
Melted apricot jam

- Beat together the cream cheese and sugar. Add the whipped cream.
- Spread on the cooled crust. Arrange your favorite fruits on top of filling.
- Brush fruit with a small amount of melted apricot jam to keep it looking fresh. Refrigerate until ready to serve.
- May be served with whipped cream or ice cream on the side.

Amy Townsend
San Francisco, California

ICE CREAM PIE

Prepare ahead

Serves: 8 to 10

1 egg
¾ cup sugar
3 tablespoons flour
⅛ teaspoon salt
1½ teaspoons baking powder
1 teaspoon vanilla
½ cup chopped walnuts
½ cup pared apples, diced
1 quart coffee (or other flavor) ice cream

- Heat oven to 350 degrees. Use an 8-inch springform or a deep dish pie pan. In a large bowl, beat egg; add sugar and beat thoroughly. Sift flour, baking powder and salt. Blend with egg mixture. Add vanilla. Add walnuts and diced apples.
- Pour into pie plate and bake for 20 to 25 minutes. Cool. Break crust into small pieces.
- Mix ice cream with "crust". Freeze, cover with plastic wrap until ready to serve.

Stolen by Marilyn Fields
Delray Beach, Florida

ICE CREAM PIE

For ice cream lovers!

Serves: 6 to 8

Make A Day Ahead

1 (16-ounce) box peanut brittle
2 (½ pound) chocolate bars, with almonds
2 teaspoons powdered coffee
⅔ cup water
1 pint each of 3 different flavors of ice cream

- Lightly grease a 9-inch pie plate.
- Grind the peanut brittle in a food processor. Spread it in the pie plate.
- In a double boiler, melt the chocolate bars with the coffee and water . Let cool and pour into crust. Freeze overnight.
- Soften 1 pint of ice cream and spread it over the frozen crust. Return to freezer. Repeat with second pint and refreeze. Add third pint and refreeze again.
- Remove from freezer 15 minutes before serving. May be served with whipped cream if desired.

Marsha Pollack
Short Hills, New Jersey

INDIVIDUAL BAKED ALASKA

Serves: 8

Allow 2 days to prepare

Genoise Cake

6 eggs
1 cup sugar
1 cup sifted flour
¼ pound butter, clarified and cooled
1 teaspoon vanilla
8 maraschino cherries, drained

- Preheat oven to 350 degrees. Two greased 9-inch cake pans.
- Combine eggs and sugar in mixing bowl and beat with electric mixer for 10 to 15 minutes, until ingredients have tripled in bulk.
- At low speed add flour, butter and vanilla.
- Pour into pans. Bake for 25 to 30 minutes. Cool on cake rack.

Ice Cream

Fill 8 paper cupcake liners with 2 different ice cream flavors of your choice, layering the ice cream by filling the liners half way with each flavor. Place liners in cupcake pan, cover with plastic wrap, and freeze until solid.

Meringue

5 to 6 egg whites (⅔ cup)
¼ teaspoon cream of tartar
¼ teaspoon salt
⅔ cup sugar
½ teaspoon vanilla

- Beat egg whites until foamy; add cream of tartar and salt. Continue beating until soft and peaks form.
- Add the sugar, one tablespoon at a time, and continue beating until the peaks are stiff and shiny. Add the vanilla toward the end of beating.

To Assemble Baked Alaska

- Cut cake into 3-inch rounds using a glass as a guide. Peel liners from ice cream and set each ice cream mold in center of cake. Cover cake and ice cream with meringue, swirling meringue into peaks. Place onto cookie sheet and set in freezer.
- Preheat oven to 500 degrees. Take the Alaska directly from freezer to oven and bake for 1 minute or until meringue is lightly browned. Insert cherry in center of each and return to freezer until ready to serve.

Sherry Lieb
Livingston, New Jersey

INVERTED LEMON MERINGUE PIE

The meringue is the crust.

Serves: 8

Crust

4 egg whites
Pinch salt
¼ teaspoon cream of tartar
1 cup sugar

- Preheat oven to 275 degrees. Butter a 9-inch pie plate.
- Beat egg whites with salt and cream of tartar until stiff. Add sugar, a little at a time, and continue beating until mixture is glossy and sugar is dissolved.
- Spread into a well buttered pie plate, carrying it well out over the rim. Bake for 25 minutes. Raise temperature to 300 degrees and bake for another 25 minutes, or until a faint brown tinge has appeared. Remove from oven and allow to cool.

Filling

4 egg yolks
½ cup sugar
¼ cup lemon juice
Grated rind of 1 lemon
1 pint heavy cream

- Beat the egg yolks until thick; add sugar, lemon juice and rind of lemon. Stir and cook in top of double boiler until mixture thickens. (Use a whisk or spoon for this.) Remove from heat and cool.
- Whip the cream; fold half into cooled filling, then turn into the crust. Cover pie with plastic wrap and refrigerate until ready to serve.
- Save remaining whipped cream and use to decorate top of pie when serving.

Judy Rosenberg,
New York, New York

LIME CHIFFON PIE

Serves: 8

1 envelope unflavored gelatin
1¼ cups sugar, divided
6 eggs, separated
⅓ cup water
⅔ cup lime juice
2 teaspoons grated lime rind, plus 2 teaspoons for topping
½ teaspoon cream of tartar
1 (9-inch) baked pastry shell or crumb crust
½ pint heavy cream, whipped

- In a saucepan mix together gelatin and ½ cup sugar.
- Beat egg yolks with water and lime juice; stir into gelatin mixture. Cook, stirring constantly until gelatin dissolves and mixture thickens slightly, about 6 minutes. Add lime rind. Chill, stirring occasionally, until mixture mounds slightly when dropped from a spoon.
- Beat egg whites with cream of tartar until stiff but not dry. Gradually add remaining ¾ cup sugar and beat until very stiff. Fold into gelatin mixture. Chill until mixture holds its shape. Turn into pastry shell mounding high in center. Chill until set, several hours or overnight.
- Garnish with whipped cream and grated lime rind.

Corrine Katz
White Plains, New York

NANA'S FUDGE

Light and not too sweet.

Yield: 5 pounds

4½ cups sugar
1 (12-ounce) can evaporated milk
4 (5¾-ounce) packages milk chocolate morsels
½ pound butter or margarine
1 (7½-ounce) jar marshmallow fluff

- Line a jelly roll pan with aluminum foil.
- Combine sugar and milk; bring to a boil over low heat, stirring constantly for 11 minutes. Remove from heat, add all the chocolate, butter or margarine and marshmallow fluff. Stir until the chocolate is dissolved.
- Pour into pan. Allow to cool completely. Cut into small squares. Store in airtight containers in the refrigerator.

Cynthia Hogan
Chevy Case, Maryland

PARVE ICE CREAM

Prepare ahead

Serves: 6

2 cups Parve whipped topping
3 eggs, separated
¾ cup light corn syrup (white)
¼ cup sugar
1½ teaspoons vanilla

- Use 3 bowls.
- In first bowl, whip topping according to directions. In second bowl (largest) beat egg whites until frothy. Continue beating, adding corn syrup in a very thin stream. Beat about 10 minutes. In third bowl, beat yolks until light adding vanilla and sugar. Fold topping and yolks into whites together with any flavoring. (See note).
- Freeze at least overnight.

Note: Strawberry Flavor: Fold in 2 boxes drained, frozen strawberries plus 1 teaspoon strawberry syrup.
Coffee Flavor: Add ¼ cup powdered instant coffee or to taste.
Chocolate Flavor: Add ½ cup of any instant chocolate powder that does not contain milk.

Mildred Goldberger
Scotch Plains, New Jersey

PIE CRUST-NO FAIL

Yield: Two 9-inch crusts

2 cups all purpose flour
⅔ cup vegetable shortening
2 tablespoons butter, melted
1 tablespoon vinegar
5 tablespoons cold water

- Mix flour, shortening and melted butter with pastry blender.
- Add vinegar and cold water. Roll out immediately.
- Needs no refrigeration. Never falls apart.
  (My 4-year old rolls this out with ease!)

Wendy Friedrich
Short Hills, New Jersey

Variation: Eliminate: butter, vinegar and water.
Use 5 tablespoons of orange juice adding one at a time.
For a 10-inch pie, increase recipe 1½ times.

Eve F. Ebenhart
Delray Beach, Florida

STUFFED PEARS

Serves: 4

4 fresh pears, peeled, halved and cored
¼ cup white raisins
2 tablespoons chopped walnuts
2 tablespoons sugar
1 teaspoon lemon juice
2 tablespoons water
½ cup light corn syrup
3 tablespoons granulated sugar and 1 teaspoon cinnamon, combined

- Preheat oven to 350 degrees. Use a 9-inch x 13-inch baking pan.
- Fill opening of each pear half with a mixture of raisins, walnuts, sugar and lemon juice.
- Place in a baking pan, add water and corn syrup. Cover and bake 30 minutes. Remove cover, sprinkle with cinnamon and sugar mixture. Place under broiler to brown.
- Serve warm.

Ruth Abromowitz
Short Hills, New Jersey

FISH

Bay Basil Savory Coriander Sage Rosemary Parsley Mint Coriander Sage Rosemary
Rosemary Parsley Mint Cinnamon Marjoram
Marjoram Thyme Juniper Bay
Bay Basil Savory Coriander Sage Rosemary Parsley Mint Cinnamon Parsley
Sage Rosemary Parsley Mint Cinnamon Marjoram Thyme Juniper Coriander Sage Rosemary
Marjoram Thyme Juniper Bay Basil Savory Coriander Bay Basil

BRAISED SOY FISH

A piquant blending of flavors.

Serves: 2 to 3

1 sea bass (2 to 3 pounds) cleaned, boned, scaled and left whole (butterflied)
Flour, as needed
3 slices fresh ginger, minced
2 green onions, minced
1 cup water
4 tablespoons soy sauce
2 tablespoons sherry
½ teaspoon sugar
2 to 3 teaspoons black beans * (optional)
2 cloves garlic, minced
4 to 6 tablespoons vegetable oil

- Rinse the fish in cold water and score both sides with diagonal cuts. Sprinkle with flour coating fish lightly.
- Combine ginger, onions, water, soy sauce, sherry, sugar, black beans and garlic. Set aside.
- Heat the oil in a large heavy frying pan until almost smoking. Add the fish and fry over high heat, one minute on each side. Reduce heat to medium and fry 1½ minutes more on each side. Baste with hot oil.
  Remove all but one tablespoonful of oil. Pour the water containing seasonings and onions over the fish and bring to a boil. Cook covered over medium heat until done, 15 to 20 minutes. Turn the fish halfway through cooking.

* *Note:* Black beans may be purchased at Asian markets.

Michelle Lattman
New York, New York

CALIFORNIA STYLE FISH

They will definitely say "I must have that recipe!"

Serves: 4

½ to ¾ cups fresh salsa, recipe follows
1 ripe avocado, mashed
1 tablespoon lemon juice
1 teaspoon garlic powder
2 pounds any white fish fillets (scrod, perch, sea bass, butterfish or red snapper)
4 tablespoons sour cream

- Preheat oven to 325 degrees. Grease a 9-inch x 13-inch baking dish.
- Prepare avocado topping by mashing the avocado and adding lemon juice and garlic powder.
- Pour ½ of the salsa into prepared baking dish, and place fish on top of salsa. Spoon remaining salsa on top of fish. Bake for 20 minutes or until done.
- Serve fish with a dollop of sour cream on it, topped with the avocado mixture.

Rita Sloan
Van Nuys, California

GREEN CHILI SALSA

Yield: 2 cups

1 large tomato, diced
1 medium onion, diced
½ bell pepper, diced
1 (3½-ounce) can green chili, diced
1 to 2 tablespoons oil
1 teaspoon vinegar, or to taste
Salt and pepper to taste

- Mix together tomato, onion, pepper and chili. Add oil and vinegar (a little more of the vinegar, if desired). Season with salt and pepper.
- Great on salads, sandwiches and tacos.

Debbie Simon
Scarsdale, New York

COULIBIAC OF SALMON

Well worth the effort!

Serves: 10 to 12

Allow two days to prepare

Dough

½ pound cream cheese, room temperature
½ pound sweet butter, room temperature
Salt and pepper to taste
1 egg yolk, beaten
2½ cups flour

- In an electric mixer combine the cream cheese and butter. Add seasonings and the egg yolk. Gradually add flour until mixed.
- Roll dough into a ball. Coat with flour and cover with plastic wrap. Place in refrigerator overnight to chill.

Mushroom Sauce

2 tablespoons chopped shallots
1 cup chopped onion
¼ pound mushrooms, sliced
2 tablespoons butter
2 tablespoons flour
½ cup dry white wine
½ cup milk
Salt and pepper to taste
Drop of Tabasco sauce
1 egg yolk
4 tablespoons chopped dill

- Sauté shallots, onions, and mushrooms in butter. Add remaining ingredients except egg yolk and dill. Cook over low heat for 20 minutes. Remove from heat and add egg yolk and dill. Cool.
- Refrigerate until ready to serve.

Rice Mixture

1 tablespoon butter
2 tablespoons chopped onion
1¼ cups water
¾ cup raw rice
2 sprigs parsley

- Sauté the onion in butter, add water and bring to a boil. Add rice and reduce heat to low. Add parsley. Cover and cook for 20 minutes. Refrigerate.

Salmon

1½ to 2 pounds poached salmon

- In a large oblong baking pan flake the salmon so that it covers the whole surface. Spoon the mushroom sauce over the salmon. Place buttered waxed paper over the mixture. Refrigerate one day.

To Assemble

1 egg
½ cup water

- Preheat oven to 375 degrees.
- Divide dough in half. Roll out each piece to fit a 9-inch x 13-inch pan.
- Place one piece in the pan.
- Spread and alternate the following down the length of pastry to one inch from the end.
  ¼ cup rice mixture
  ½ cup salmon mixture
  ¼ cup rice mixture
  the remaining salmon mixture, and end with the remaining rice mixture.
- Cover with the other half of pastry and crimp the sides of the dough. Brush the entire piece with the egg and water combined. Cut a few slits on top of the pastry.
- Bake in a preheated 375 degree oven for 45 minutes or until lightly brown. Serve with heated mushroom sauce.

Note: Coulibiac can be made in individual portions. It is very elegant to serve for a small dinner party or luncheon. The top surface of the pastry can be decorated with flowers, leaves etc., cut from small pieces of leftover dough.

Blanche Gutstein
New York, New York

CHEDDAR FISH DISH

Serves: 2

1 pound fillet of lemon sole
Salt and pepper to taste
Juice of 1 lemon
¼ pound butter or margarine
¾ cup shredded sharp Cheddar cheese
¾ cup bread crumbs

- Preheat oven to 350 degrees.
- Rinse the fish and pat dry. Place in a baking dish. Add salt and pepper and squeeze lemon juice over fish.
- In a saucepan, melt butter or margarine; add cheese and bread crumbs. Pour over fish and bake for 25 minutes.

Linda Altman
Harrison, New York

FRESH TUNA STEAK ORIENTALE

Easy to prepare with a good blend of spices.

Serves: 8

1 (6-ounce) can frozen orange juice concentrate, thawed
2 to 3 tablespoons dark soy sauce
2 cloves garlic, crushed
3 to 4 slices ginger or ½ teaspoon powdered ginger
4 fresh tuna steaks, approximately 1 pound each

- In a large glass bowl mix all ingredients and pour over fish.
- Marinate for at least 1 hour.
- Broil about 5 to 6 minutes per side, depending on thickness of fish, or bake the fish for 15 minutes at 375 degrees.

Susan Berenson
Armonk, New York

ITALIAN JEWISH RED SNAPPER

Serves: 6

4 pounds small whole red snappers
Salt to taste
½ cup olive oil
1 teaspoon sugar
¼ cup red wine vinegar
½ cup pine nuts
1 cup dark seedless raisins

- Preheat oven to 400 degrees. Lightly oil a 9-inch x 13-inch baking dish.
- Wash fish thoroughly and pat dry with paper towels. Lightly sprinkle with salt. Arrange the fish in a single layer in the baking dish.
- Dissolve the sugar in the vinegar and pour over fish. Pour in remaining oil and sprinkle with pine nuts and raisins.
- Cover with aluminum foil and bake for about 20 minutes. Remove foil and bake another 30 minutes or until all liquid has evaporated and the snapper is golden.

PUFFED HALIBUT

Delicious and easy to prepare.

Serves: ¾ pound per person

Prepare ahead

Halibut, 1-inch thick
1 (12-ounce) bottle beer, or as needed
1 cup flour, or as needed
3 to 4 tablespoons dried rosemary, or as needed
2 to 4 cups oil, enough to cover fish

- Use a wok.
- Cut halibut into large cubes and marinate in beer for ½ to 1 hour.
- Mix flour and rosemary together. Place halibut in the flour mixture; shake off excess. Set aside and let stand 10 to 15 minutes.
- Heat oil in wok to 350 degrees. Slide fish pieces in one at a time and deep-fry until golden brown. Drain on paper toweling.
- Serve hot with tartar or cocktail sauce.

Jeffrey Katz
Beverley Shores, Indiana

RICE-STUFFED SEA BASS

Serves: 6

¼ cup chopped onion
4 tablespoons butter
¼ cup dry bread crumbs
2 cups cooked rice
1½ teaspoons salt
½ teaspoon pepper
½ teaspoon basil
1 teaspoon fresh dill, snipped
1 tablespoon fresh parsley, chopped
2 tablespoons lemon juice
1 fresh sea bass (about 4 pounds) cleaned and boned
Paprika

- Preheat oven to 400 degrees. Butter a 9-inch x 13-inch baking dish.
- In a skillet, sauté onion in 2 tablespoons butter until tender but not brown. Mix with bread crumbs, rice, ½ teaspoon salt, ¼ teaspoon pepper, basil, dill, parsley and 1 tablespoon lemon juice. Mix well.
- Fill cavity of fish with rice stuffing. Extra stuffing may be placed alongside fish in the baking dish. Season fish with remaining salt and pepper.
- Combine remaining butter and lemon juice and brush over fish. Sprinkle with paprika.
- Bake 10 minutes per pound or until fish flakes easily, basting frequently with the lemon butter.

Sherry Lieb
Livingston, New Jersey

ROLLED FISH FILLET

Serves: 4

1 cup mayonnaise
1 medium onion, diced
Grated Parmesan cheese to taste
2 pounds fillet of sole (or flounder)
1 (12-ounce) package frozen spinach soufflé
Paprika

- Preheat oven to 350 degrees. Grease an 8-inch square baking dish.
- Prepare a paste of mayonnaise, onion and cheese. Spread on slices of fish reserving some to cover outside of fish rolls. Slice frozen spinach soufflé into 1-inch "fingers" and place one on each fillet. Roll fish around the spinach. Spread remaining paste on outside of fish rolls. Sprinkle with paprika.
- Place in a prepared dish and bake for 20 minutes or until lightly browned.

Hilda Milton
Great Neck, New York

SALMON CROQUETTES

Yield: 5 to 6 croquettes

1 (7½-ounce) can salmon
1 large egg, beaten
2 heaping tablespoons cottage cheese
1 heaping tablespoon snipped chives (fresh or frozen)
¼ to ½ cup plain bread crumbs
Freshly ground pepper to taste
3 tablespoons margarine

- Drain juice from salmon. Mash salmon with a fork. Add egg, cottage cheese, chives, bread crumbs and pepper. Mix thoroughly.
- With wet hands, and using 2 tablespoons of the mixture, form round cakes.
- Melt margarine in a skillet and brown croquettes on both sides for 2 to 4 minutes. Be sure to use enough margarine or croquettes will stick.

Variation: Omit chives, add the following: 1 to 2 teaspoons dried dillweed or 1 tablespoon fresh, 1 teaspoon dried minced garlic or ½ teaspoon fresh, 1 teaspoon dried minced onion or 1 tablespoon fresh.

Corrine Katz
White Plains, New York

SALMON LOAF

Spectacular, served hot or cold!

Serves: 4

1 (16-ounce) can salmon, drained and flaked
½ cup bread crumbs
½ cup mayonnaise
½ cup chopped onion
¼ cup chopped celery
¼ cup chopped green pepper
1 egg, beaten
1 teaspoon salt

- Preheat oven to 350 degrees. Use a shallow baking dish.
- Combine all ingredients, mixing lightly. Shape into a loaf and place in baking dish. Bake 40 minutes. Serve with cucumber sauce.

Cucumber Sauce

½ cup mayonnaise
½ cup sour cream
½ cucumber, finely chopped
2 tablespoons chopped onion
½ teaspoon dillweed

- Combine ingredients and mix well.

Brenda Sichel
Short Hills, New Jersey

SALMON TROUT CASA DE ESPANA

This recipe is from La Paz, Bolivia.

Serves: 4

2 pounds salmon trout fillets
Salt and pepper to taste
4 potatoes, cut into wedges and boiled
4 tomatoes, cut into wedges
2 onions, diced and sautéed in 4 tablespoons margarine
Fresh parsley, chopped
Pimiento strips
Lemon wedges

- Preheat oven to 350 degrees. Grease a 9-inch x 13-inch baking dish.
- Place salmon trout in center of greased baking dish. Season to taste. Surround with potatoes and tomatoes. Place onions, parsley and pimiento strips over fish.
- Bake for 45 minutes. Garnish with lemon wedges.

Estelle Silverstone
Harrison, New York

SOUTH OF THE BORDER RED SNAPPER

For fish and non-fish lovers alike!

Serves: 4

1 large onion, chopped
¼ cup olive oil
1 (14½-ounce) can tomatoes, chopped into large pieces
2 pounds red snapper fillets
1 (2-ounce) can pimientos, coarsely chopped
2 tablespoons capers
¼ cup pimiento-stuffed green olives, sliced
Salt and pepper to taste

- In a large skillet, sauté onions in olive oil until wilted. Add tomatoes and cook about 5 minutes to blend flavors.
- Place fish in sauce, sprinkle pimientos, capers and olives over fish, and spoon sauce over all.
- Cook gently for 10 minutes or until fish flakes easily.
- This can be baked in a 350 degree oven for 25 minutes instead.

Note: Any other type of fillet may be substituted.

Rita Sloan
Van Nuys, California

STUFFED FILLET OF SOLE

Serves: 4

1 cup grated carrots
1 cup crushed saltines, or any crackers
2 ounces butter, melted
Salt and pepper to taste
2 pounds fillet of sole

- Preheat oven to 350 degrees. Grease a 9-inch x 13-inch baking dish.
- Mix all ingredients, except fish, together and set aside. Wash fillets and dry with paper towels. Sprinkle very lightly with salt and pepper.
- Arrange fillets in layers, covering each fillet with carrot mixture. These arranged fillets will be one on top of another, and when completed will have the appearance of one large fish.
- Cover with buttered waxed paper and bake 15 minutes.
- Pour off fish broth, strain and boil down to ¼ cup.

Mushroom Cheese Sauce

3 tablespoons butter
2 tablespoons flour
Salt and pepper to taste
¼ cup fish broth
1 cup milk
2 tablespoons Cheddar cheese, grated
2 tablespoons Parmesan cheese, grated
4 ounces canned mushrooms, drained or ¼ pound fresh mushrooms, sliced and sautéed
Additional grated Cheddar or Parmesan cheese for topping.

- Melt butter in saucepan. Remove from heat and stir in flour. Cook until flour is well blended. Add salt, pepper, fish broth and milk. Cook, stirring constantly until thickened. Add cheeses and mushrooms.
- Pour sauce over fish in baking dish. Sprinkle with additional grated cheese and dot with butter. Place under broiler until browned.

Variations:

1. Do not stuff fish. Add ½ cup dry Vermouth, 1 bay leaf, 2 peppercorns and ¼ teaspoon salt to baking dish. Bake fish as above. When done, cover with any sauce and bake 30 minutes, or until browned.
2. Do not cover fish with waxed paper. Dot with butter. Bake 30 minutes or until browned. Can be served without sauce.
3. Serve unstuffed fish with Mornay sauce.

Mornay Sauce

3 tablespoons butter
2 tablespoons flour
3 tablespoons cream
1 cup milk
¼ cup fish broth
2 tablespoons Parmesan cheese, grated
Salt and pepper to taste
Additional Parmesan cheese for topping

- Melt butter in saucepan. Remove from heat and stir in flour, cream, milk and fish broth.
- Cook, stirring constantly until thickened. Add grated cheese, salt and pepper. Simmer 5 minutes.
- Pour sauce over fish in baking dish. Dot with butter and sprinkle with additional cheese.

Estelle Silverstone
Harrison, New York

SWEET AND SOUR FISH

Serves: ½ pound per person

Prepare ahead

1 fresh whole red snapper
Salt and pepper to taste
1 tablespoon rice wine or dry sherry
1 tablespoon cornstarch, plus extra for dusting
3 egg yolks
2 tablespoons water
3 cups cooking oil

- Clean the fish and dry well. Make crosswise cuts on both sides about ½ inch deep. Rub inside and out with salt, pepper and wine. Soak in this mixture for about one hour.
- Mix the cornstarch with the egg yolks and water. Rub on fish. Dust extra cornstarch all over fish shaking off excess.
- Heat ¼ cup of oil in a wok or deep frying pan to 375 degrees. Gently slide fish into the pan and fry for 5 minutes on each side. Place on paper toweling and cool. Refry in 375 degree oil for 1 minute on each side.

Sweet and Sour Sauce

1 tablespoon ginger, sliced thinly
1 large onion, sliced in ½-inch wide strips
2 tablespoons oil
½ to ⅔ cup cider vinegar
1 teaspoon salt
⅔ cup sugar
2 cups fish stock
⅓ cup tomato ketchup
6 drops Tabasco sauce
1 green and 1 red pepper (sweet), cut in ½-inch wide strips
½ cup bamboo shoots, cut in strips
½ cup snow peas, sliced
2 tablespoons cornstarch dissolved in a little water

- Fry ginger and onion in oil until limp. Set aside. Boil together vinegar, salt, sugar and fish stock. Add tomato ketchup and Tabasco. Add all the prepared vegetables including the fried ginger and onions. Let boil only once, then thicken sauce with cornstarch which has been mixed with a small amount of water. Pour hot sauce over freshly fried fish. Serve hot.

Emily Landau
Rye, New York

TROUT STUFFED WITH FRESH DILL

Serves: 1

1 fresh stream trout per person, 1 pound each, boned but not filleted
Juice of ½ lemon for each fish
Enough flour to coat fish lightly
Minced garlic to taste
Ground thyme to taste
Freshly ground pepper to taste
Medium bunch fresh dillweed, 1 bunch per fish
Vegetable oil, mixed with a small amount of olive oil for sautéeing

- Wash fish and pat dry. Brush each fish with lemon juice; set aside.
- Wash and dry dillweed. Stuff each fish liberally with one bunch. Let the dill extend out over edges. Close fish with toothpicks, if necessary.
- Mix flour, garlic, thyme and pepper. Spread on a large plate. Coat fish with mixture and sauté approximately 5 minutes on each side in oil. (Time depends on size of fish).

Cynthia Hogan
Chevy Chase, Maryland

MEAT
Bay
Basil
Savory
Coriander
Sage
Rosemary
Parsley
Mint
Coriander
Sage
Sage
Rosemary
Parsley
Mint
Cinnamon
Marjoram
Thyme
Juniper
Bay
Bay
Basil
Savory
Coriander
Sage
Rosemary
Parsley
Mint
Cinnamon
Parsley
Sage
Rosemary
Parsley
Mint
Cinnamon
Marjoram
Thyme
Juniper
Coriander
Sage
Marjoram
Thyme
Juniper
Bay
Basil
Savory
Coriander
Bay
Basil

BEEF AND BOOZE

Serves: 4 to 6

Salt
2 pounds boneless chuck, cubed
2 large onions, chopped
1 green pepper, chopped
1 teaspoon paprika
2 teaspoons salt (optional)
1 bay leaf
¼ teaspoon allspice
¼ teaspoon white pepper
1 cup tomato juice
2 teaspoons Worcestershire sauce
½ cup Burgundy wine
¼ cup ketchup

- Salt bottom of a hot, heavy saucepan. Brown meat. Add onions and green pepper to brown. Add seasonings. Cover and simmer about 2 hours.
- After about 1 hour or when juices are reduced add tomato juice, Worcestershire sauce, Burgundy and ketchup. Uncover occasionally and add hot water if drying out.
- Cover and continue cooking for a total of 2½ to 3 hours or until tender.

Evelyn Colton
Scarsdale, New York

BEEF AND ONIONS

Serves: 3 to 4

½ pound onions, sliced into very thin rings
1 pound london broil slightly frozen so as to slice more easily
1 egg white
½ teaspoon salt
1 tablespoon cornstarch
4 tablespoons soy sauce
Oil for frying
1 tablespoon sugar
1 tablespoon sherry

- Slice the steak into little pieces and marinate in egg white, salt, cornstarch and 1 tablespoon soy sauce.
- Stir-fry onions in hot oil in a wok until very brown. Set aside.
- Add additional oil to deep fry and when hot, add meat and stir-fry for 30 seconds. Do in small batches so that oil stays hot. Wait for temperature to rise between batches. When finished, discard oil and wash wok to remove residue.
- Put onions, meat, 3 tablespoons soy sauce, sugar and sherry back into the wok. Stir and serve immediately.

Maureen Berkman
Scarsdale, New York

BOBOTIE

A traditional South African recipe.

Serves: 6

2 medium onions, chopped
2 tablespoons margarine
2½ pounds ground lean beef
1¼ cup non-dairy creamer (½ liquid creamer and ½ water)
3 eggs
2 slices white bread, cubed
¼ cup finely chopped dried apricots
1 apple, peeled and grated
¼ cup seedless raisins
¼ cup blanched almonds
2 tablespoons sugar or apricot jam
1 tablespoon curry powder
2 tablespoons lemon juice
2 teaspoons salt
¼ teaspoon pepper
¼ teaspoon tumeric
6 bay leaves or fresh lemon leaves

- Preheat oven to 350 degrees. Lightly grease an 8-inch x 12-inch oven-proof dish.
- In a large skillet, sauté the onion in hot margarine, until golden. Add the meat and stir until the meat loses its redness. Remove from heat.
- In a large bowl, mix together ¼ cup of non-dairy creamer, 1 egg and bread cubes, mashing the bread with a fork. Add the apricots, apples, raisins, almonds, sugar or jam, curry, lemon juice, salt and pepper, and mix until well blended. Add the meat mixture and mix lightly with a fork.
- Turn into the oven-proof dish and spread evenly. Press leaves into top of meat mixture. Bake uncovered for 30 minutes. Remove dish from oven. Pour topping over meat and bake 10 minutes or until the topping is set.

Topping

- Beat the remaining two eggs with the remaining cup of non-dairy creamer and tumeric until just blended.
- Serve with rice and chutney.

Taubene Hoppenstein
Mamaroneck, New York

BREAST OF VEAL

Yield: Serves 6 to 10, depending on size of veal breast.

2 to 4 onions, sliced
2 red peppers, sliced into strips
4 to 5 cloves garlic, sliced
⅓ bunch of celery, coarsely chopped
1 breast of veal
1 cup white wine
⅓ cup oil
Paprika, pepper, rosemary and tarragon to taste

- Preheat oven to 325 degrees. Use a large roasting pan.
- In a roasting pan, place onions, peppers, garlic and celery. Place veal on top of this layer. Pour wine and oil over meat. Season to taste with paprika, pepper, rosemary and tarragon. Bake for 3 to 3½ hours until very tender.

Note: This is one of those "whatever you like" recipes. The quantity of vegetables will depend on the size of veal. You can add carrots, omit celery. The vegetables flavor the meat and will not be served (although I think they're the best part). Veal can tolerate seasoning, so don't be timid.

Len Feiman
White Plains, New York

BRISKET OF BEEF WITH PEARS AND PRUNES

An unusual variation of a traditional dish.

Serves: 8

5 pounds brisket
Salt and pepper to taste
1 teaspoon ginger
¼ cup oil
2 large onions, chopped
2 cloves garlic
1 cup beef stock
¼ cup lemon juice
¼ cup brown sugar
¼ cup Lyles Golden syrup (made in England)
8 potatoes, peeled and halved
2 yams, peeled and cut into quarters
4 carrots, peeled and sliced
6 firm pears, unpeeled
½ pound prunes

- Preheat oven to 350 degrees. Use a large roasting pan.
- Sprinkle meat liberally with salt, pepper and ginger.
- Brown meat in hot oil; add onions and brown slightly.
- Place brisket, onions, garlic and stock in pan, cover and roast for 2 hours. Add extra stock or boiling water when necessary.
- Add lemon juice, brown sugar and syrup and cook for another 15 minutes.
- Add potatoes, yams, carrots, whole pears and prunes. Cook another hour before serving.

Maureen Berkman
Scarsdale, New York

CHILI

Hot and spicy!

Serves: 4

2 cups onions, sliced
3 cloves garlic, put through garlic press
¼ cup oil
2 pounds ground beef
2 (19-ounce each) cans kidney beans, drained
2½ cups canned tomatoes
4 tablespoons chili powder
2 tablespoons crushed red pepper flakes
¾ tablespoon oregano
1 tablespoon salt, or to taste

- In a large pot, sauté onion and garlic in oil for 10 minutes. Add the ground beef and brown, stirring a few times.
- Add remaining ingredients and simmer, covered, over low heat for 30 minutes.

Ann Jacobson
Purchase, New York

COUNTRY SHORT RIBS

Serves: 4 to 6

5 to 6 (about 5 pounds) short ribs
1 large onion, sliced

- Preheat oven to 350 degrees. Use a covered 2 quart casserole.
- Arrange short ribs in casserole. Top with onion.

Sauce

½ cup ketchup
2 tablespoons brown sugar
1 tablespoon red wine vinegar
1½ teaspoons chili powder
1 teaspoon salt
¼ teaspoon pepper
½ cup Burgundy wine
½ teaspoon Worcestershire sauce

- Combine ingredients. Pour over meat, cover and bake for 2 hours or until tender. Skim and discard any fat from sauce before serving.

Debbie Simon
Scarsdale, New York

GLAZED CORNED BEEF

Easy and delicious!

Serves: 6

6 to 7 pounds first cut corned beef
1 clove garlic
2 bay leaves
4 cloves
4 peppercorns

• Place corned beef and spices in a large pot. Cover with water and bring to a boil. Simmer for 3 to 4 hours, covered.

Glazing

¼ cup orange juice
¾ cup brown sugar
2 tablespoons corned beef stock
1 teaspoon Dijon-style mustard

• Preheat oven to 400 degrees. Place beef in a roasting pan.
• In a saucepan blend and heat all glazing ingredients. Pour over beef and place in oven for 30 minutes, basting occasionally.

Elaine Satuloff
Harrison, New York

LAMB SHISH KABOB

This is wonderful for a summer barbeque.

Serves: 10

Prepare ahead

Marinade (Yield: 1¾ cups)

¾ cup oil
6 tablespoons soy sauce
2 tablespoons Worcestershire sauce
1 clove garlic, minced
2 tablespoons plus 1 teaspoon lemon juice
¼ cup wine vinegar
½ tablespoon pepper
1¼ teaspoons salt
1 tablespoon dry mustard

Kabobs

5 pounds lamb from neck or shoulder, cut into 1½ inch cubes
3 medium green peppers, cut into 1½ inch flat squares
3 medium onions, cut into eighths
1 pound medium-size mushrooms
1 pint cherry tomatoes

- Marinate lamb at least 12 hours in refrigerator or overnight.
- Place on skewer: pepper, onion, meat, mushroom, tomato. Repeat so as to have four pieces of meat on each skewer.
- Grill about 15 minutes on each side.

Sandy Butwin
Upper Saddle River, New Jersey

MARINATED CUBED LAMB IN PITA A LA ALLEN FOR BARBECUE

We use this recipe all year round, not only in the summer, but on our skiing trips. It truly is wonderful and our guests love it.

Serves: 6

3 pounds lamb, trimmed of fat, and cubed

Marinade

1 (8-ounce) jar old fashioned coarse grain mustard
2 cups olive oil
2 tablespoons Herbs de Provence
Salt and pepper to taste

- In a large bowl mix all ingredients thoroughly. Put the lamb in the mixture and marinate for 1 hour, turning occasionally. Prepare the mayonnaise mixture.

Mayonnaise Mixture

1 cup green olive oil
2 tablespoons mayonnaise
⅓ cup red wine vinegar
1 teaspoon Dijon style mustard
2 teaspoons Herbs de Provence
Salt and pepper to taste

- Mix thoroughly and set aside.

½ head lettuce, shredded
2 cucumbers, or 1 long hot-house variety, finely chopped
2 medium tomatoes, finely chopped
1 small red onion, finely chopped
1 (12-ounce) jar hot or sweet red peppers
Hot sauce, optional
3 large pitas, cut in half, or 6 small size

- In separate bowls, place mayonnaise mixture, lettuce, cucumbers, tomatoes, onions and peppers. Have the hot sauce and pita ready for use.
- Close to barbecue time, have the grill ready and the coals very hot. Place the lamb on skewers and cook on each side for 5 minutes, basting each side frequently.
- Place the cooked lamb in individual pita breads. Top each one with lettuce, cucumber, onion and tomato. Your guests have the option to use pepper and hot sauce. Spoon the mayonnaise sauce on, as the last topping.

Blanche Gutstein
New York, New York

MARINATED LONDON BROIL

Serves: 5 to 6

1½ pounds London broil trimmed of fat

Marinade

2 cloves garlic, crushed
4 tablespoons oil
2 tablespoons soy sauce
2 tablespoons lemon juice

- Mix all ingredients thoroughly and pour over flank steak. Marinate for 25 minutes.
- Broil, basting with the marinade until desired degree of doneness.

Note: This recipe can also be done on an outside grill. Three to 4 chicken breasts, cut in half, can be substituted for the meat.

Flora Dominus
Harrison, New York

Variation:

¼ cup soy sauce
3 tablespoons honey
2 tablespoons vinegar
1½ teaspoons garlic powder
¾ cup salad oil
½ teaspoon ground ginger

- Combine all ingredients and marinate steak for 5 hours or overnight.
- Barbecue 5 to 7 minutes on each side. Slice diagonally.

Eleanor Weiner
Livingston, New Jersey

NAVARIN OF LAMB

A festive one meal dish.

Serves: 6 to 8

4 pounds lamb, trimmed, cut into small pieces
Flour for dredging
Salt and pepper to taste
4 tablespoons each olive oil and margarine
2 tablespoons sugar

• Lightly dredge the prepared meat in the flour after seasoning it with salt and pepper. Heat the margarine and oil in a large skillet and sauté the meat pieces after shaking off all excess flour. Sauté until golden brown, then sprinkle sugar over all. Toss the meat and sugar together until the sugar is golden brown and melted. Transfer to a heavy warm Dutch oven with a tight-fitting lid.

Add to pot:

2 to 3 cups canned beef bouillon
3 tomatoes, peeled and chopped
2 tablespoons tomato paste mixed with 1 tablespoon beef extract
2 cloves garlic, pressed
½ teaspoon dried rosemary
½ teaspoon thyme
2 bay leaves

• Cover and bake for 30 minutes in a 350 degree oven.

After 30 minutes, add:

16 small red-skinned new potatoes, either peeled or not
6 white turnips, peeled and quartered
6 to 8 carrots, peeled and cut into chunks

• Recover pot and bake for another 30 minutes.

16 small white onions, peeled
Salt and pepper, if needed

• Add the white onions to the pot with additional salt and pepper if needed after the second 30-minute period. Recover the pot and bake another 20 to 30 minutes (a total baking time of about 1½ hours). At this point, remove the bay leaves and add:

1 pound fresh green beans, cut French style
1 pound fresh shelled peas

• Do NOT mix the green vegetables through. Leave on top of the stew, recover the pot and cook until the green vegetables are just barely done, approximately 10 to 15 minutes.

Sherry Lieb
Livingston, New Jersey

RACK OF LAMB QUO VADIS

Serves: 6

2 racks of lamb
Margarine
Pepper to taste
4 small carrots, minced
2 medium onions, minced
2 tablespoons margarine
2 cups chicken broth
½ cup soft bread crumbs
½ cup minced parsley

- Preheat oven to 500 degrees. Use a shallow roasting pan.
- Wrap ends of rib with aluminum foil.
- Rub meat with margarine and sprinkle with pepper.
- Spread carrots and onions over bottom of roasting pan. Dot with margarine. Place lamb fat side down on vegetables. Roast for 20 minutes. Reduce heat to 400 degrees. Turn lamb over and add 1 cup of broth. Roast for 15 to 20 minutes. Sprinkle lamb with bread crumbs and parsley and slide under broiler for 4 to 5 minutes. Transfer to a hot platter.
- Add remaining broth to pan. Purée vegetables and stock in blender and serve as sauce with lamb.

Sherry Lieb
Livingston, New Jersey

ROAST RACK OF SPRING LAMB

This is a recipe brought home from a Lyonnais restaurant in Paris.

Serves: 2

1 rack of lamb
Salt and pepper
2 cloves garlic
3 to 4 tablespoons dried rosemary (rolled and crushed between your hands)
¾ cup beef bouillon or/beef bouillon cube dissolved in ¾ cup hot water
2 to 3 tablespoons dry red wine
1 to 2 teaspoons lemon juice
1 tablespoon margarine

- Preheat oven to 400 degrees.
- Split one clove of garlic into fine slivers and insert under the skin of each chop. Crush the other clove of garlic and rub on the top (fat side) of the roast. Sprinkle the entire surface of the roast with the crushed rosemary, salt and pepper.
- Place in small roasting pan, fat side up and bake for 40 minutes. Turn heat off and place roast on an oven-proof platter and let it remain in the hot oven.
- To the drippings in the roasting pan, which is now placed on stove on medium to high heat, add the bouillon, cooking a couple of minutes to reduce the amount. Add the wine and lemon juice and cook a bit longer, stirring constantly. Turn heat off and swirl in the margarine, correct seasoning and pour a little of this sauce over the roast. When sliced, the meat should be pale pink; don't ruin it by overcooking.

Gen Vergari
Yonkers, New York

ROAST VEAL

Serves: 8 to 10

5 pounds shoulder veal, rolled
3½ tablespoons shortening
Flour for dredging
1 medium onion, chopped
1 clove garlic, chopped
1 tablespoon parsley, chopped
¼ cup celery, chopped
1 tablespoon tomato paste
¾ teaspoon pepper
1 cup chicken broth
¾ cup wine
1 teaspoon Dijon-style mustard, or to taste
½ pound sliced mushrooms, sautéed

- Preheat oven to 450 degrees. Use a roasting pan.
- Melt 2 tablespoons shortening in a roasting pan in oven. Flour meat and place in pan. Brown on all sides. Remove from pan. Discard shortening and return veal to pan. Lower oven to 300 degrees.
- In one tablespoon shortening, sauté onions, garlic, parsley and celery until onions are transparent. Add tomato paste, pepper, chicken broth, and wine. Mix thoroughly. Pour over veal. Bake 2 hours, turning occasionally.
- Remove veal from pan. Skim fat from gravy and put all, including vegetables, into a blender. Add mustard and purée. Set aside.
- When veal is at room temperature slice and return to pan. Cover with mushrooms and gravy.
- Bake in a 350 degree oven ½ to 1 hour before serving.

Florence L. Greenberg
Great Neck, New York

SAVORY VEAL RAGOUT

A hearty robust stew!

Serves: 4

Oil or margarine
1 medium onion, chopped
1 clove garlic, minced
2 pounds stewing veal, cubed
1 large carrot, sliced
1 rib celery, sliced
1 small green pepper, cored and cubed
½ pound fresh mushrooms, sliced
1 teaspoon salt
Freshly ground pepper, to taste
½ teaspoon dried basil or 1 teaspoon fresh basil
½ teaspoon thyme
1 teaspoon dried parsley or 1 tablespoon fresh parsley, chopped
1½ cups tomato sauce, more if needed
1 small zucchini, cubed, or 1 small eggplant, peeled and cubed
½ cup dry white wine

- Preheat oven to 350 degrees. Use a 2½-quart covered casserole.
- In a large skillet, sauté onion and garlic until soft in oil or margarine. Add meat and brown lightly. Add carrot, celery, green pepper and mushrooms. Season with salt, pepper and herbs. Add wine and tomato sauce. Remove to casserole, cover and bake for ½ hour, add zucchini or eggplant. Add more tomato sauce, if needed. Bake another ½ hour or until meat is tender.

Marilyn Wilkes
Armonk, New York

STEAK DIANE

Effortless as well as delicious!

Serves: 3 to 4

3 to 4 shallots, minced
2 to 3 tablespoons margarine
1 large steak or 3 to 4 individual steaks, approximately ½ pound per person
Sprinkling of A-1® steak sauce, Worcestershire sauce and chopped chives
1 to 2 tablespoons fresh parsley, minced

- In an electric skillet, sauté the shallots in melted margarine, until golden in color. Add the meat and sprinkle with half the A-1® sauce, Worcestershire sauce, chives and parsley. Cook 5 to 10 minutes on one side; turn and sprinkle the other side with remaining seasonings. Cook 5 to 10 minutes longer. Serve immediately.

Judy Tallarico
Bel-Aire, California

STUFFED VEAL ROAST

A most innovative recipe.

Serves: 6 to 8

Prepare ahead

Veal

4 to 5 pounds veal loin roast or boned leg of veal, pounded flat
Lemon juice to taste
Garlic powder to taste

- Sprinkle veal with lemon juice and garlic powder and place in refrigerator for a few hours or overnight.

Stuffing

1 Bermuda onion chopped
2 tablespoons vegetable oil
2 large carrots, shredded
2 medium zucchini, shredded
1 stalk celery, diced
1 green pepper, diced
¼ pound mushrooms, sliced
1 (8-ounce) can water chestnuts, drained and sliced
1 egg, lightly beaten
¼ cup matzah meal or 3 slices toasted challah, soaked in water and squeezed dry.

- Sauté onion in oil until lightly browned and soft. Add remaining vegetables and stir for about 5 minutes.
- Add egg and either matzah meal or challah and mix well.

Topping

Salt and pepper to taste
1 cup white wine
1 tablespoon chicken stock

- Preheat oven to 350 degrees. Use a large roasting pan.
- Place stuffing on veal, roll up, tie with string and place in pan. Add salt, pepper, wine and chicken stock.
- Bake for 1½ hours covered. Remove cover and bake for another ½ hour.
- Cool slightly and slice.

Note: Place sliced onions and carrots around roast while baking, if you wish.

Lee Goldman
Miami Beach, Florida

SWEET AND SOUR MEATBALLS

Serves: 4 to 6

1 large onion, chopped
1 tablespoon margarine
¼ cup raisins
¾ cup dark brown sugar, firmly packed
2 pounds chopped meat
2 slices white bread, soaked in water and squeezed dry
Salt and pepper to taste
1 (8-ounce) can tomato sauce
1 (16-ounce) can sauerkraut
3 ginger snaps

- Preheat oven to 350 degrees. Use a Dutch oven for this recipe.
- Brown the onion in margarine. Add raisins, brown sugar and cook until sugar melts.
- In a large bowl, mix the meat, bread, salt and pepper to taste. Form into tiny meatballs; drop into pot. Add tomato sauce, sauerkraut and ginger snaps diluted in a little warm water.
- Bake for 1½ to 2 hours.

Marsha Pollack
Short Hills, New Jersey

SWEET AND SOUR MEATBALLS

Morris' all time favorite and always a hit with the grandchildren.

Serves: 6 to 8

4 (8-ounce) cans tomato sauce
4 to 5 tablespoons brown sugar
Juice of 2½ lemons
⅔ cup raisins
1 clove, optional
1 bay leaf, optional
1 medium-size onion, cut into quarters
1 clove garlic
Sprinkling of paprika
Salt to taste
2 slices white bread, toasted, soaked in water and then drained
2 pounds chopped meat
1 large egg

- In a saucepan, put tomato sauce, sugar, lemon juice and raisins. Add clove and bay leaf, if desired. Cook over low heat for 10 minutes.
- In a food processor or blender, put the onion, garlic, paprika and salt. Mince to medium-fine pieces. Add the bread and mix only until blended into mixture. Remove mixture from food processor or blender and add to the chopped meat. Add egg and blend thoroughly. Correct seasoning.
- With wet hands make small balls. Add to the sauce. Cook covered over low heat for 1 hour. Remove clove and bay leaf before serving.

Rose Segal
Brooklyn, New York

SWEET AND SOUR POT ROAST

Different from a standard pot roast recipe.

Serves: 6

5 pounds brisket of beef
1 tablespoon chicken fat
4 large onions, diced
3 cloves garlic, minced
2 cups water
3 bay leaves
4 tablespoons lemon juice or vinegar
2 tablespoons brown sugar
6 tablespoons ketchup
½ cup white raisins
Pinch of salt

- In a large pot, brown the meat in hot chicken fat on all sides. Add the onions and garlic, cooking until brown. Add water and bay leaves. Cover pot and simmer for 1 hour. Add lemon juice and brown sugar. Simmer for another hour in covered pot. Add ketchup, raisins and salt. Cover and cook ½ hour longer. Slice and serve with gravy.

Harriet Mattikow

VEAL CHOPS WITH WALNUTS AND RAISINS

Serves: 6

½ cup sugar
½ cup cider vinegar or sherry vinegar
6 veal chops, well trimed of fat
½ cup walnut pieces
½ cup vegetable oil
½ cup dry sherry
½ cup chicken broth
½ cup golden or dark raisins or currants

- Combine sugar and vinegar and marinate the chops for about 30 minutes.
- In a skillet, sauté the walnuts in 2 tablespoons oil, being careful not to let them burn. Cook until golden in color. Set aside.
- In a large skillet sauté the chops in remaining oil until caramelized and brown on both sides. Remove the chops and deglaze pan with sherry. Add the chicken broth and reduce sauce by ½. Put the chops back in pan and simmer for about 10 to 15 minutes or to desired degree of doneness.
- Add walnuts and raisins and serve.

Susan Berenson
Armonk, New York

VEAL MARSALA

Serves: 8

Salt and pepper to taste
Wondra flour for dredging
3 pounds veal cutlet, thinly sliced
4 to 6 ounces margarine
1 small onion, minced
1 clove garlic, minced
1 pound fresh mushrooms, sliced
1 cup beef broth
1 cup sweet Marsala wine

- Blend salt and pepper with flour. Sprinkle each cutlet with seasoned flour, shaking off excess.
- In a large skillet, melt margarine and sauté each cutlet briefly. Remove meat from pan. Sauté onion, garlic and mushrooms. Add broth and wine and boil briefly. Return meat to pan and heat about 5 minutes. Serve immediately.

Susan Berenson
Armonk, New York

VEAL PAPRIKASH

Serves: 3 to 4

1½ pounds veal, cut into large cubes
2 medium-size onions, diced
1 tablespoon chicken fat or other substitute
Paprika, garlic powder, salt and pepper to taste
1 (8-ounce) can tomato sauce

- Rinse veal and pat dry. In a large pot, simmer the diced onions in melted chicken fat (or substitute). Sprinkle paprika over the onions and cook until they are golden. Do not burn. Add the veal, garlic powder, salt and pepper to taste. Simmer for 15 to 20 minutes over low heat, then add the tomato sauce. Cover pot and simmer for 1½ hours or until tender.

Terry Berger
New York, New York

VEAL PICCATA

Serves: 4

1 pound thin veal scaloppine (lightly pounded)
4 tablespoons flour
½ teaspoon salt
½ teaspoon pepper
3 tablespoons margarine
½ lemon, sliced
½ cup dry white wine
Fresh parsley sprigs

- Wipe veal scaloppine with damp paper toweling. Combine flour, salt and pepper. Coat veal well with mixture. Heat margarine in a medium skillet until it sizzles. Add half of the veal slices and cook over high heat until well browned on both sides. Remove from pan. Repeat with rest of veal. Return all veal to skillet, add lemon slices and wine. Cook over low heat, covered, for 5 minutes. Garnish with parsley sprigs. Serve immediately.

Corrine Katz
White Plains, New York

Bay Basil Savory Coriander Sage Rosemary Parsley Mint Coriander Sage Rosemar
Sage Rosemary Parsley Mint Cinnamon Marjoram
MOLDS
nnamon Marjoram Thyme Juniper Bay
Bay Basil Savory Coriander Sage Rosemary Parsley Mint Cinnamon Parsley
Sage Rosemary Parsley Mint Cinnamon Marjoram Thyme Juniper Coriander Sage Rosemar
nnamon Marjoram Thyme Juniper Bay Basil Savory Coriander Bay Basil

PERTINENT PARTICULARS

- Grease mold with vegetable oil unless recipe states otherwise. To spread oil easily, use waxed paper, paper towel, or a pastry brush.

- Before unmolding any mold, run a thin sharp knife around the entire edge. Place serving plate on top of mold, center mold and then invert. If mold does not release, place a slightly dampened hot towel on the mold.

- Wash strawberries before removing stems to prevent berries from becoming soggy. Do not wash until ready to use.

- Wash and thoroughly dry blueberries before freezing.

- Italian plums freeze well. Wash, split in half, take pit out and place in freezer bag or container.

APRICOT MOLD

Very special for all occasions.

Prepare ahead

Serves: 10 to 12

2 (6-ounce) packages apricot gelatin
4 cups boiling water
1 pint sour cream
1 quart vanilla ice cream, slightly softened
2 (1-pound) cans whole peeled apricots, drained and mashed

- Lightly grease a 10-cup mold with vegetable oil.
- Dissolve gelatin in water and let soft set in refrigerator for 20 minutes.
- Fold in sour cream, ice cream and apricots.
- Beat with electric mixer on medium speed for 2 minutes or blend in food processor.
- Pour into mold and refrigerate until firm; at least 8 hours or overnight.

Note: The center of the mold may be filled with melon balls or strawberries when ready to serve.

Hope Hirschhorn
Harrison, New York

BAKED CRANBERRIES

Tart and tangy.

Serves: 18

2 (12-ounce) packages fresh cranberries
1 cup nuts, chopped and toasted, your choice
2½ cups sugar
1 cup orange marmalade
Juice of 1 lemon

- Preheat oven to 350 degrees. Use a 2½-quart baking dish.
- In a large bowl, mix all ingredients. Pour into dish and cover tightly with aluminum foil. Bake for 1 hour.
- Serve hot or cold.

Susan Katz
Teaneck, New Jersey

BAKED CURRIED FRUIT

An excellent accompaniment.

Serves: 12

Prepare one day ahead

1 (16-ounce) can cling peach halves
1 (20-ounce) can pineapple slices
1 (16-ounce) can pear halves

⅓ cup butter
¾ cup light brown sugar, tightly packed
4 teaspoons curry powder

- Preheat oven to 325 degrees. Use a 1½-quart round glass casserole.
- Drain fruits and *dry well* on paper towels.
- Arrange attractively in casserole.
- Melt butter; add sugar and curry powder. Blend well, stirring until sugar dissolves. Spoon liquid over fruits and bake 1 hour, uncovered. Cool, then refrigerate.
- One half hour before serving, reheat casserole at 325 degrees.

Note: 1 (16-ounce) can apricot halves may be added or substituted. For 20 servings the following amounts will be needed and the fruit baked in a 2-quart casserole.

2 (1 pound, 13-ounce) cans peach halves
1 (20-ounce) can pineapple slices
1 (1 pound, 13-ounce) can pear halves

½ cup butter
1 cup light brown sugar
6 teaspoons curry powder

Len Feiman
White Plains, New York

BAVARIAN CHEESE RING

Pretty and refreshing.

Prepare ahead

Serves: 10 to 12

Bottom Layer

1 (6-ounce) package raspberry gelatin
1 cup boiling water
1 (1-pound, 4-ounce) can crushed pineapple with juice, do not drain
1 (10-ounce) package frozen raspberries, defrosted

- Lightly grease a 10-cup mold with vegetable oil.
- Dissolve the gelatin in boiling water and soft set. Add the remaining ingredients and pour into the mold. Refrigerate until firm.

Middle Layer

1 (6-ounce) package lemon gelatin
½ cup boiling water
1 (3-ounce) package cream cheese, room temperature
½ pint heavy cream, whipped

- After the bottom layer is set proceed with the next layer.
- Dissolve the gelatin in water and soft set. Add cream cheese and beat with an electric mixer. Fold in whipped cream. Pour on top of first layer. Refrigerate until firm.

Top Layer

- Repeat the bottom layer. Refrigerate until firm and ready to serve.

Note: This can be made by omitting the top layer and using a 6-cup mold.

Hope Hirschhorn
Harrison, New York

BLACK CHERRY MOLD

Prepare ahead

Serves: 12 to 14

2 (6-ounce) packages black cherry gelatin
4½ cups boiling water
2 (16-ounce) cans pitted black cherries, with juice
1 (3-ounce) package lemon gelatin
1¼ cups boiling water
1 pint sour cream

- Lightly grease a 12-cup mold with vegetable oil.
- To *one* package black cherry gelatin, add 2¼ cups boiling water. Stir and add *1* can black cherries with juice. Stir. Pour into the mold and refrigerate until firm and set.
- Add 1¼ cups boiling water to the lemon gelatin. Cool briefly and slowly fold in sour cream. Stir until smooth. Pour over the first layer. Chill until firm.
- Prepare the third layer by repeating procedure of first layer. Pour over second layer.
- Refrigerate until third layer sets.

Sylvia Orenstein
Great Neck, New York

BLUEBERRY MOLD

Prepare ahead

Serves: 10 to 12

1 (16-ounce) can blueberries, drained, reserve liquid
2 (3-ounce) packages raspberry gelatin
1 (16-ounce) can crushed pineapple, drained, reserve liquid
2 (3-ounce) packages lemon gelatin
1 pint sour cream

- Lightly grease a 10-cup mold with vegetable oil.
- Add enough boiling water to blueberry liquid to make 3 cups. Pour into raspberry gelatin, stir and add blueberries. Pour into a mold and chill until set.
- Add enough boiling water to the pineapple liquid to make 3 cups. Pour into lemon gelatin; stir, and add crushed pineapple and sour cream. Spoon over chilled blueberry layer. Refrigerate until ready to serve.

Elinore Skalet
White Plains, New York

CRANBERRY MOLD

Prepare ahead

Serves: 24

Bottom Layer

1 cup light sweet cream
½ cup sugar
1 package unflavored gelatin
2 tablespoons hot water
½ pint sour cream
½ cup hot water
1 teaspoon vanilla

- Lightly grease a 16-cup mold with vegetable oil.
- In a saucepan heat sweet cream and sugar until it boils. Remove from heat and set aside.
- Soak gelatin in 2 tablespoons water and combine with the cream and sugar mixture. When cooled, add sour cream, ½ cup hot water and vanilla.
- Pour into mold and refrigerate until completely set.

Top Layer

2 (6-ounce) packages, raspberry, cherry, or strawberry gelatin
1½ cups boiling water
1 (1-pound, 4-ounce) can crushed pineapple with juice
2 (1-pound) cans whole cranberries
1 cup chopped walnuts

- Dissolve gelatin in water; add pineapple and cranberries, stirring until cranberries are completely dissolved.
- Cool completely and pour on top of the first layer.
- Place in refrigerator and partially set.
- Remove from refrigerator; add nuts and refrigerate until firm.

Fern Bindelglass
White Plains, New York

CRANBERRY MOLD

A Thanksgiving treat.

Prepare ahead

Serves: 10 to 12

2 (6-ounce) packages raspberry gelatin
3 cups hot water
1 cup pineapple juice
1 cup orange juice
1 (1-pound) can crushed pineapple, drained, reserve juice
2 (1-pound) cans whole cranberries
Grated orange and lemon rinds from 1 orange and 1 lemon
¾ cup chopped walnuts

- Lightly grease a 10-cup mold with vegetable oil.
- Dissolve gelatin in hot water and let soft set.
- Stir in remaining ingredients.
- Place in mold and chill until firm.

Hope Hirschhorn
Harrison, New York

HOT FRUIT COMPOTE

Serves: 10 to 12

1 (11½-ounce) package coconut cookies, grated
1 (1-pound, 13-ounce) can purple plums, pitted and drained
1 (1-pound, 13-ounce) can bing cherries, pitted and drained
1 (1-pound, 13-ounce) can peach halves, drained
1 (1-pound, 4-ounce) can pineapple chunks, drained
½ cup Grand Marnier or Apricot Brandy

- Preheat oven to 350 degrees. Use a 2½ to 3 quart greased heatproof casserole.
- Grate the cookies in a blender or food processor. Set aside.
- Alternate the cookie crumbs with each of the four fruits in layers until all are used. End with crumbs.
- Pour brandy over the fruit mixture. Bake for 30 to 40 minutes.
- Serve warm.

Hope Hirschhorn
Harrison, New York

LEMON MOLD

A layered lemon delight.

Prepare ahead

Serves: 5 to 6

1 (3-ounce) package lemon gelatin
1¾ cups boiling water
1 (6-ounce) can frozen lemonade, thawed
1 (4-ounce) container Birds Eye® Cool Whip® Non-Dairy Whipped Topping

- Lightly grease a 3-cup mold with vegetable oil.
- In a large bowl, put lemon gelatin, add the boiling water and mix thoroughly until completely dissolved. Add the lemonade to the gelatin mixture. Stir until well-blended. Let cool but do not let it set.
- Using a hand held electric beater or wire whisk, beat in the Birds Eye® Cool Whip® Non-Dairy Whipped Topping.
- Pour mixture into the mold and refrigerate overnight.

Note: Recipe can easily be doubled.

Micki Hoffman
Rye, New York

LEMON MOLD

Delicious and beautiful!

Prepare ahead

Serves: 6

1 (6-ounce) package lemon gelatin
2 tablespoons sugar
⅛ teaspoon salt
3 cups boiling water
2 cups light cream (or half and half)
1 teaspoon vanilla
1 cup sour cream

- Grease a 6-cup mold with vegetable shortening.
- Dissolve gelatin, sugar and salt in boiling water. Stir in cream, vanilla and sour cream. Chill until slightly thick.
- Beat until smooth and pour into a mold. Chill until firm.

Joanne Skemer
Scarsdale, New York

ORANGE MOLD

Prepare ahead

Serves: 12

6 (3-ounce) packages orange gelatin
6 cups water (3 boiling, 3 cold)
2 pints orange-pineapple or mandarin orange yogurt
2 (11-ounce) cans mandarin oranges, drained

- Lightly grease a 12-cup mold, with vegetable oil.
- Dissolve gelatin in boiling water. Add the cold water. Beat in the yogurt. Pour into the mold. When slightly thickened, fold in drained oranges. Chill until firm.

Variations:
1. Lime gelatin, lemon yogurt and crushed pineapple (drained).
2. Strawberry gelatin, strawberry yogurt and 2 packages of frozen strawberry halves in syrup (thawed and drained).

Micki Hoffman
Rye, New York

ORANGE SHERBET MOLD

Prepare ahead

Serves: 8

1 (6-ounce) package orange gelatin
1¾ cups boiling water
1 pint orange sherbet
1 (11-ounce) can mandarin oranges, sliced and drained

- Lightly grease a 6-cup mold with oil.
- Dissolve gelatin in boiling water; set aside to cool. Combine gelatin with sherbet and mix.
- Place the mandarin orange slices on bottom of the mold, add the gelatin and sherbet mixture. Return to refrigerator to set.

Marsha Pollack
Short Hills, New Jersey

PUNCH BOWL MOLD

Colorful, pretty and refreshing.

Yield: 30 cups

Start 3 days ahead

1st Layer

1 (6-ounce) package lime gelatin
1 (15½-ounce) can sliced pineapple, drained
Cherries

- You will need a 28 or 30 cup bowl, clear glass; if it has a pedestal base so much better!
- Mix gelatin according to directions on package. Pour some into the bottom of a punch bowl and let set to thicken in refrigerator.
- Arrange slices of pineapple over the gelatin and place 1 cherry in the center of each slice. Return to refrigerator to set again.
- Pour remainder of gelatin over fruit.
- After the first layer has set and before adding the next layer let gelatin stay out of refrigerator for 5 minutes.

2nd Layer

1 (6-ounce) package orange gelatin
2 scant cups boiling water
1 pint orange sherbet
1 (11-ounce) can mandarin oranges, drained

- Stir gelatin into boiling water. Add sherbet. Hand whip with a wire whisk to blend. Add oranges.
- Cool to room temperature.
- Add to first layer. Place in refrigerator to set.

3rd Layer

1 (6-ounce) package cherry gelatin
1 (16-ounce) can fruit cocktail, drained, reserve liquid

- To the fruit juice add enough boiling water to make 3½ cups liquid. Pour into cherry gelatin, stir to dissolve. Add the fruit cocktail.
- Cool to room temperature.
- After second layer has rested outside refrigerator for 5 minutes, pour the cherry gelatin on top of it and return to refrigerator.

4th Layer

1 envelope unflavored gelatin
½ cup boiling water
1 cup light sweet cream
½ cup sugar
1 cup sour cream

- Dissolve gelatin in boiling water.
- Scald the light cream and add the sugar. Add gelatin to the mixture. Cool for ½ hour. Add sour cream and beat by hand until smooth.
- After 3rd layer has rested outside refrigerator for 5 minutes, pour mixture on top.
- Return to refrigerator to set. When firm remove from refrigerator for 5 minutes before pouring in next layer.

5th Layer

1 (6-ounce) package lemon gelatin
2 cups hot water
1 (16-ounce) can blueberries in syrup

- Dissolve gelatin in hot water. Add blueberries and syrup. Cool to room temperature. Pour over fourth layer. Refrigerate to set. When firm, remove from refrigerator and let rest for 5 minutes before proceeding to 6th layer.

6th Layer

1 (6-ounce) package strawberry gelatin
2 cups boiling water
1 cup crushed pineapple, drained, save juice
1 cup frozen strawberries, thawed, save juice
1 pint heavy cream
Birds Eye® Cool Whip® Non-Dairy Whipped Topping, for topping
Whole fresh strawberries, for topping

- Dissolve gelatin in 2 cups boiling water. Add pineapple juice and chill until slightly thickened.
- Add strawberries and the crushed pineapple. Mix thoroughly.
- After the gelatin is slightly thickened, whip the cream and fold into the fruit mixture. Pour over 5th layer. Refrigerate to set.
- Top with Birds Eye® Cool Whip® Non-Dairy Whipped Topping and whole strawberries before serving.

Ellen Bloom and Alice Kent
Livingston, New Jersey

SAUTÉED OR "FRIED" APPLE RINGS

Serves: 6

6 large, tart, well-flavored apples
3 to 4 tablespoons butter
½ to ¾ cup brown sugar
⅛ teaspoon salt
½ teaspoon cinnamon
1 tablespoon lemon juice

- Pare the apples, and use an apple corer to remove their centers. Cut into 1 to 1½ inch slices. Melt butter in a heavy skillet over medium heat. When it is hot, place apple slices in and gently turn so they are well-coated. Cover them until they are steaming.
- Mix the brown sugar, salt and cinnamon together and pour this over apples, turning them gently and covering both sides with the sugar mixture. Sprinkle lemon juice all over the tops. Cook them covered over a gentle fire, only until partially tender. If the apples are dry, a little hot water may be added. Uncover them and cool until they are tender, but not mushy or broken apart. You can add additional butter as needed. When finished, they should be slightly caramelized, shiny and glazed.

Gen Vergari
Yonkers, New York

SPICED FRUIT

Prepare ahead

Serves: 12

1 (1-pound, 13-ounce) can peaches, halved or sliced
1 (1-pound, 13-ounce) can pears, halved or sliced
1 (1-pound, 13-ounce) can pitted apricots, halved
1 (1-pound, 13-ounce) can sliced pineapple or chunks
2 teaspoons whole cloves
1 stick cinnamon
½ cup molasses
⅓ cup white vinegar

- Use a 10-cup glass bowl.
- Drain syrup from the fruit into a saucepan. Put the drained fruit into a glass bowl.
- To the syrup add remaining ingredients and cook until reduced to 2 cups.
- Pour over fruit and refrigerate overnight.

Grace Heller
White Plains, New York

STRAWBERRY NUT MOLD

Prepare ahead

Serves: 8

2 (3-ounce) packages gelatin (1 lemon, 1 strawberry)
1 cup boiling water
2 (10-ounce) packages frozen strawberries, thawed
1 (7-ounce) can crushed pineapple, do not drain
3 medium sized bananas, mashed
1 cup chopped walnuts
1 pint sour cream

- Grease a 10-cup mold with vegetable oil.
- Dissolve gelatin in water. Fold in fruit and nuts.
- Place half of the mixture into the mold and chill for 1½ hours. Spoon on sour cream and chill another half hour.
- Gently spoon remaining half of fruit and nut mixture over the chilled half. Refrigerate until firm.

Margo Ruddy
Short Hills, New Jersey

PASSOVER
Bay Basil Savory Coriander Sage Rosemary Parsley Mint Coriander Sage
Sage Rosemary Parsley Mint Cinnamon
Marjoram Thyme Juniper Bay
Bay Basil Savory Coriander Sage Rosemary Parsley Mint Cinnamon Parsley
Sage Rosemary Parsley Mint Cinnamon Marjoram Thyme Juniper Coriander Sage
Marjoram Thyme Juniper Bay Basil Savory Coriander Bay Basil

PERTINENT PARTICULARS

- The following may not be used for Passover: cornstarch, confectioners sugar, baking powder, baking soda, yeast, dried beans, peas, legumes, grains, grain alcohol.

- Kosher Substitutions Include the Following: For Milk; use half Coffee Rich® and half water. For Cream; use the non-dairy product Coffee Rich®. For Whipping Cream; use "Hellers Whirl Whip." It is available at kosher butcher stores.

- Flour Measurements for Passover: 1 cup all purpose flour equals ¼ cup matzah cake meal and ¾ cup potato starch. ½ cup all purpose flour equals 2 tablespoons matzah cake meal and 6 tablespoons potato starch.

- A Kosher substitute for milk or cream: use ½ cup chicken stock mixed with 1 egg yolk and 1 teaspoon cornstarch for each ½ cup of milk or cream.

APRICOT CANDY BALLS

A lovely hostess gift.

Yield: Approximately 24

Prepare one week ahead

1 pound best quality apricots, cut into squares
½ cup sugar
1 teaspoon lemon juice
½ teaspoon lemon extract
½ teaspoon vanilla
¼ pound unsalted pistachio nuts, shelled

- Rinse apricots and finely chop ½ in food processor. Add remaining apricots and chop. Add sugar, lemon juice, lemon extract, and vanilla, mixing well. Process until mixture leaves sides of bowl and begins to form a ball.
- Shape into 1-inch balls, forming each around one whole pistachio. Sugar palms of hands from time to time to facilitate procedure. Roll apricot balls in sugar and place on cookie sheet to dry. Insert 1 whole pistachio into center of each candy.
- Let dry for one week. Place in Petit Four cases.

Betty Laboz
Brooklyn, New York

Editor's Note: If you prefer this less sweet, use just ⅓ cup sugar.

BAKED BROILERS WITH MATZAH-NUT STUFFING

Serves: 4 to 6

1 cup minced onion
1 cup minced celery
½ cup coarsely chopped nuts
6 tablespoons margarine
5 matzahs finely broken
½ teaspoon salt
⅛ teaspoon pepper
2 teaspoons paprika
1 egg, slightly beaten
1 cup canned chicken broth condensed, undiluted
2 broilers, split in half

- Preheat oven to 350 degrees. Grease a large baking dish or roasting pan.
- Sauté onion, celery and nuts in the margarine until the onion is tender but not browned. Add broken matzahs and toss lightly. Combine seasonings, egg and condensed broth and add to matzah mixture. Spread in prepared baking dish or roasting pan. Place broiler halves on top. Brush with melted margarine and sprinkle with salt and pepper.
- Bake for 1 to 1½ hours, or until tender and golden brown.

Estelle Silverstone
Harrison, New York

BAKED GEFILTE FISH MOLD

Excellent, well worth the effort!

Serves: 6 to 8

2 pounds fish fillets, (whitefish, pike, turbot or mixed fish)
1 onion, chopped
1 carrot, grated
1 teaspoon oil
1 tablespoon sugar
2 teaspoons salt
Dash of pepper
2 eggs, beaten
½ cup cold water
2 tablespoons oil
Green pepper rings
Small slices of onion

- Preheat oven to 350 degrees. Brush bottom of a 9-inch x 5-inch x 3-inch loaf pan with oil.
- Put fish through food grinder with chopped onion, grated carrot, oil, sugar, salt, pepper, beaten eggs and cold water. Blend well.
- Place green pepper rings and onion slices across bottom of pan. Pour fish mixture into pan. Bake 1 hour, uncovered. Remove from oven, turn out upside down on platter. Slice; serve hot or cold.

Phyllis Fass
Scarsdale, New York

BANANA CAKE

Serves: 10

7 eggs, separated and at room temperature
1 cup sugar
1/4 teaspoon salt
1 cup mashed bananas (about 2 large ripe ones)
3/4 cup Passover cake flour
1/4 cup potato starch

- Preheat oven to 325 degrees. Use an ungreased 9-inch tube pan.
- In a large mixing bowl, beat the egg yolks with sugar until creamy and light in color.
- Combine salt, mashed bananas, cake flour and potato starch. Add this to the egg yolk mixture.
- Beat egg whites until stiff and gently fold this into the batter.
- Pour the cake mixture into the pan and bake for 50 minutes or until a cake tester comes out clean.
- Invert pan onto a wire rack and let cool completely before removing.

Eve Ebenhart
Delray Beach, Florida

BEACON HILL COOKIES

Yield: 30 cookies

2 egg whites
1/8 teaspoon salt
3 tablespoons sugar
1/2 teaspoon vinegar
1/2 teaspoon vanilla
1/2 heaping cup chopped coarse walnuts
1 heaping cup chocolate chips, (melted)
1/2 cup coconut, unsweetened (buy in health food store)

- Preheat oven to 350 degrees. Grease a cookie sheet.
- Beat egg whites; add salt. Add sugar gradually and beat well. Add vinegar and vanilla and continue to beat well until egg whites hold their form and peak. Fold in nuts, chocolate and coconut. Mix carefully until all the egg whites have disappeared.
- Drop by teaspoonful 1/2-inch apart. Bake for 8 minutes. *Do not* remove cookies from cookie sheet for 15 minutes.

Note: This recipe freezes well. Do not limit this to Passover only; it is wonderful all year long!

Eve Ebenhart
Delray Beach, Florida

CHEESE MATZAH

Served in South Africa for breakfast, lunch or afternoon tea.

Serves: 6 to 8

4 to 6 matzahs, moistened in milk
1 pound cream cheese
¼ pint cream
2 tablespoons sugar
1 egg, beaten
Cinnamon and sugar for topping

- Preheat oven to 325 degrees. Lightly grease a jelly roll pan.
- Moisten the matzahs in milk but do not soften them. Place on prepared pan.
- Mix cream cheese, cream, sugar and egg together and spread the matzahs thickly with cheese mixture. Sprinkle the cinnamon and sugar lightly over the top.
- Bake until golden brown and lightly set.
- Cut into required sizes while warm.

Note: These can also be made on small matzah crackers.

Maureen Berkman
Scarsdale, New York

DESSERT SOUFFLÉ

This will become a holiday favorite.

Serves: 8

8 eggs, separated, room temperature
8 teaspoons sugar
6 cups fresh fruit, cut into pieces
LeRoux Kirsch, enough to sprinkle over fruit
4 tablespoons brandy

- Preheat oven to 350 degrees. Use a 7½-inch x 12-inch oval oven proof casserole.
- Beat yolks until lemon colored; slowly add the sugar.
- Beat egg whites until stiff. Fold gently into the yolk mixture.
- Place the fruit into casserole and spoon meringue over the top, sealing it in.
- Bake for 15 minutes or until top is lightly browned.
- Heat brandy in a saucepan and pour over meringue. Ignite before serving.

Note: This is one of my favorite dessert recipes for Passover.

Fern Bindelglass
White Plains, New York

GEFILTE FISH

Yield: 12 to 14 pieces

White fish
Yellow pike
Winter carp, omit if not fresh

• The ratio of the above fish can be adjusted according to the availability, but the total amount of fish must equal 5 pounds.

1 extra carp head (if fresh) for the pot, to make the gravy gel
2 extra large onions, sliced (for the pot)
4 carrots, sliced
Salt and pepper to taste
2 large onions, quartered
2 eggs
½ cup cold water

• In large pot, place all the fish bones. Add the two extra large sliced onions along with the carrots, salt and pepper. Add enough cold water so that you will be able to cover half of each piece of fish. Bring to a boil. Remove foam as it rises to the surface.
• Have your fish store grind the fish or use a food processor.
• In a wooden bowl chop the fish. Add 2 quartered onions, eggs, water, salt and pepper. Continue chopping until the fish mixture stands up in peaks. This will require 15 to 20 minutes, minimum. With wet hands form into oval shapes.
• Place fish carefully, one at a time, into boiling water. When it returns to a boil, reduce heat, cover and simmer for 3 hours. Check at 2½ hours; uncover, reduce amount of liquid (if you have to by ¾'s). Be sure you have enough gravy for the fish.
• Remove fish and carrots. Strain remaining liquid and add to fish.
• Refrigerate.

Editor's Note: The secret to excellent gefilte fish is lengthy chopping until mixture is light and fluffy. Aerate as you chop.

HONEY PASSOVER COOKIES

A very special holiday cookie.

Yield: 30 cookies

1 egg
1 tablespoon safflower oil
Water
1 box Passover Honey Cake Mix
1 tablespoon instant powdered coffee
1 cup walnuts, coarsely chopped
1 cup raisins or chocolate chips

- Preheat oven to 350 degrees. Generously grease 3 cookie sheets.
- In a measuring cup, put egg, oil and enough water to measure ½ cup.
- Pour mixture into a mixing bowl and beat with a wire whisk.
- Add coffee and cake mix to the egg mixture. Stir with a fork until blended. *Do not beat.*
- Add the nuts and raisins or chocolate chips and blend thoroughly.
- Drop by a teaspoon onto a cookie sheet, 2½ inches apart. They will spread.
- Bake for 10 minutes. Remove from oven and cool slightly. While still warm, carefully remove to a wire rack to cool.

Editor's Note: Use 1 tablespoon instant powdered espresso coffee.

Fredya Simon
Englewood Cliffs, New Jersey

MATZAH APPLE PUDDING

A favorite for this holiday.

Serves: 10 to 12

8 sheets matzah, broken into small pieces
6 eggs, beaten
1 cup sugar
½ teaspoon salt
2 tablespoons lemon juice
2 tablespoons orange juice
Rind of 1 lemon and 1 orange, grated
½ cup chopped walnuts
1 cup raisins
4½ cups Granny Smith or McIntosh apples, peeled, cored, and thickly sliced, about 8 or 9 apples.
¼ cup sugar mixed with 1½ tablespoons cinnamon
¼ cup melted margarine

- Preheat oven to 350 degrees. Grease a 9-inch x 13-inch baking pan.
- Place crushed matzah in a large bowl, and pour boiling water over to just soften. Squeeze out all the water and drain.
- Beat eggs until foamy. Add sugar, beating well. Stir in the drained matzah, salt, juices, rinds, walnuts and raisins. Spread half of this mixture into the baking pan.
- Coat the sliced apples with the sugar and cinnamon mixture. Place half the apples over the matzah mixture. Spread the remaining matzah mixture over the apples, then cover with the remaining apples.
- Pour the melted margarine over the top.
- Bake for 30 minutes, covered. Remove cover and bake an additional 20 minutes or until lightly browned.

Hope Hirschhorn
Harrison, New York

MATZAH MEAT PIE

A Mid-Eastern dish from my Sephardic family.

Serves: 4 to 6

1 large onion, peeled and chopped
3 tablespoons oil
1½ pounds ground lamb or beef
1 teaspoon cinnamon
½ teaspoon allspice
2 tablespoons or more dark raisins
2 tablespoons pine nuts or walnuts may be substituted
1 cup beef bouillon
5 to 6 matzahs
1 egg, lightly beaten

- Preheat oven to 375 degrees. Use a 9-inch pie plate or equivalent.
- In a large skillet, sauté the onion in 2 tablespoons oil until golden. Add ground meat and spices. Stir and cook about 10 minutes until meat has browned but is still moist. Add raisins. Remove from stove and set aside.
- In a small skillet, fry nuts in 1 tablespoon oil.
- Place bouillon in a shallow, large rectangular pan. Soak matzahs, one at a time, pressing them gently to absorb the liquid.
- Press 2 or 3 softened matzahs into the pie pan. (You may have to tear matzah to cover bottom of dish). Place meat filling on top of matzah and use remaining matzah to cover.
- Brush top with beaten egg and bake about ½ hour or until top is golden.

Note: This recipe is not as difficult to prepare as it may appear. It does not take very long and can be made a day ahead. To warm, cover with aluminum foil and place in a 325 degree oven until reheated.

Paula Lustbader
Greenwich, Connecticut

MERINGUE SURPRISES

A winning recipe.

Yield: 22 to 24 cookies

2 egg whites
1/8 teaspoon salt
1 teaspoon vanilla
1/2 cup sugar
6 ounces chocolate chips

- Preheat oven to 300 degrees. Grease a cookie sheet.
- Beat egg whites until foamy. Add salt and continue beating until stiff, but not dry. Add vanilla and gradually beat in sugar, beating until stiff and satiny. Fold in chocolate chips.
- Drop by teaspoonful on a greased cookie sheet. Bake for 22 to 25 minutes.

Mary Rosenblatt

Variations: Omit chocolate chips and use one of the following:
1 cup finely chopped pecans or
1 cup chopped dried fruit or
1 cup raisins

Marilyn Sherman
Scarsdale, New York

ORANGE ROAST BRISKET

Serves: 6

3 medium onions, sliced
3½ to 4 pounds lean beef brisket (first cut)
½ cup red wine
1 cup orange juice
2 to 3 tablespoons tomato sauce
1 teaspoon sugar
Salt, pepper, paprika and garlic to taste

- Preheat oven to 325 degrees. Use a covered roasting pan.
- Place the onions on bottom of roasting pan. Place brisket on top, fat side up.
- Combine the wine, orange juice, tomato sauce and sugar. Pour over the meat. Add the spices and roast in covered pan for 2½ hours. Raise heat to 350 degrees and roast for ½ hour uncovered.
- When brisket has cooled, slice thinly against the grain.

Corrine Katz
White Plains, New York

PASSOVER APPLE CAKE

A very special dessert.

Serves: 10 to 12

6 eggs
1 cup sugar
1½ cups cake meal
⅔ cup oil
1 tablespoon cinnamon
1 cup raisins
1 cup chopped nuts
8 Granny Smith apples, peeled and sliced

- Preheat oven to 350 degrees. Use a large greased 9-inch x 13-inch pan.
- In a large mixing bowl mix the eggs, sugar and cake meal together. Add oil and mix very well. Batter will be very thick.
- Combine the cinnamon, raisins, nuts and sliced apples.
- Spread half the batter in the baking pan. Spread half of the apple mixture over the batter. Spread remaining batter over apples (mixture may not cover completely). Cover with rest of apples. Sprinkle on topping and bake for 1½ hours. Let cool. Slice in squares to serve.

Topping

⅔ cup chopped walnuts or pecans
1 cup sugar
4 teaspoons cinnamon

- Mix all ingredients together. Sprinkle over top of cake.

Joan Carroll
Short Hills, New Jersey

Editor's Note: The batter is thick; spread bottom layer thinly. Check after 1 hour. Cake may be done.

PASSOVER CANDY

Yield: 70 pieces; 1½-inch x 1½-inch squares

1 pound honey
1 pound walnuts, coarsely chopped
½ teaspoon lemon juice
1 tablespoon matzah meal

- You will need a 2 to 3 quart white enamel pan, wooden spoon and a wooden square board.
- Bring honey to a boil over low heat. Cook until it turns a reddish golden color (about 10 minutes). Watch carefully, otherwise it will boil over. Add walnuts, lemon juice and matzah meal. Lower heat and stir constantly with wooden spoon. Cook until thick, about 10 minutes or more.
- Turn mixture out on the wooden board which has been wet down with cold water and with wet palms of your hands pat out to ¼ to ½-inch thickness making a large, even square about 13-inch x 13-inch. Mixture is very hot-keep wetting hands. Cool completely, 3 hours or more. Cut into even sized squares, using a dampened sharp knife. Place in one layer on a plate and refrigerate.
- Before serving, bring to room temperature.

Note: This recipe can be frozen using freezer paper, shiny side, between layers.

Sally Katz

PASSOVER EGG NOODLES

Serves: 6 to 8

4 eggs
4 tablespoons cold water
1 tablespoon potato starch
Dash of salt

- Use a 8-inch crêpe pan and a linen tea towel.
- In a bowl, beat eggs slightly, adding the rest of ingredients to make a very thin batter. Beat until smooth. Pour ⅛ cup batter in a thin stream onto a well-greased crêpe pan, starting at the center and tilt pan to distribute evenly. Cook over moderate heat until lightly browned on under side. Turn out on a tea towel, bottom side up. Continue in this manner, stirring batter each time, until all the batter is used. Roll up each pancake and cut into thin strips for noodles.
- Drop into hot chicken soup just before serving.

Sally Katz

PASSOVER MATZAH STUFFING

Yield: Enough for a 10 to 12 pound turkey

½ cup boiling water
3 matzahs broken into small pieces
2 tablespoons vegetable oil
1 medium to large onion, diced
3 to 4 stalks celery with green leaves, diced
1 tablespoon fresh minced parsley
½ teaspoon salt (optional)
Dash fresh ground pepper
¼ teaspoon sugar
1 large Granny Smith apple, peeled, cored and grated
2 eggs, beaten

- Using a large mixing bowl, add water to the broken matzah pieces and let stand.
- Heat a large skillet, place oil, and when hot add onions, celery and parsley. Cook until onions are golden in color and celery is fairly soft.
- Add salt, pepper, sugar, and grated apple to the matzah. Add onion, celery and parsley mixture. Beat eggs and add, mixing well with two forks.

Note: In place of Granny Smith apple, green seedless grapes may be used.

Corrine Katz
White Plains, New York

PASSOVER NUT CAKE

Successful for years and years.

Serves: 10 to 12

9 eggs, separated
½ cup sugar
½ cup orange juice
Finely grated rind of one orange
1½ heaping cups ground walnuts
¾ cup Passover cake flour

- Preheat oven to 350 degrees. Grease a 9-inch tube pan; lightly dust with cake flour.
- Beat egg whites with ¼ cup sugar until glossy and stiff. Beat egg yolks with remaining ¼ cup sugar until light and frothy. Add orange juice and rind to egg yolk mixture.
- Add walnuts to cake flour. Mix half of cake flour into egg mixture. Fold remaining flour into egg whites. Mix each thoroughly and when well-mixed combine both mixtures.
- Pour into tube pan and bake for 1 hour on a rack in the middle of oven.
- Cool completely on cake rack before removing from pan.

Sally Katz

PASSOVER PINE NUT COOKIES

Light and delicate.

Yield: 30 to 32 cookies

½ heaping cup toasted pine nuts
¼ pound margarine or sweet butter, room temperature

Sift together

½ cup cake meal
½ cup potato starch

½ cup granulated sugar (use ¾ cup sugar when doubling recipe)
1 egg yolk
1 teaspoon vanilla

- Preheat oven to 300 degrees. Grease a cookie sheet and flour with cake meal.
- Roast pine nuts until light golden in color. Set aside to cool.
- In a bowl, cream together butter and sugar until creamy. Beat in the egg yolk, vanilla, cake meal and potato starch. Blend thoroughly. Fold in the pine nuts and blend again.
- Drop batter by teaspoonful onto a cookie sheet. Bake 20 to 25 minutes or until pale golden. *Do not* overbake. Let set a minute or so, but while still warm, carefully remove with a spatula to a cake rack and let cool completely. Cookie is very delicate and must be handled carefully.

Note: Freezes well.

Corrine Katz
White Plains, New York

PASSOVER SPONGE CAKE

Serves: 10

9 large eggs, separated
1½ cups sugar
⅓ cup orange or lemon juice
1 tablespoon orange or lemon rind, grated
6 tablespoons cake meal
6 tablespoon potato starch
1 teaspoon salt

Topping

Juice of 1 orange or 1 lemon, ⅓ cup
½ cup superfine sugar

- Preheat oven to 300 degrees. Use a 10-inch angel food pan (tube).
- In a large bowl, beat egg whites until stiff. Add ¾ cup sugar.
- In another bowl, combine cake meal, potato starch, and salt.
- Beat egg yolks until thick and lemon colored. Add rest of sugar to yolks. Add juice and rind to yolks. Fold into egg whites alternating yolk and cake meal mixture, starting and ending with cake meal. Bake for 1 hour and 15 minutes. Invert pan to cool.
- Pour juice of orange or lemon mixed with sugar over cake, if desired.

Debbie Simon
Scarsdale, New York

PASSOVER VEGETABLE PUFFS

A holiday favorite from a secret recipe.

Yield: 32 puffs

2 onions chopped
1 pound fresh mushrooms, coarsely chopped
4 tablespoons vegetable oil
4 (10-ounces each) packages frozen chopped spinach, defrosted and drained
8 carrots, peeled and grated

8 eggs, lightly beaten
Salt to taste
½ teaspoon black pepper
4 tablespoons Passover chicken soup mix
1½ cup matzah meal

- Preheat oven to 350 degrees. Three greased muffin tins, (12 cups each) or a 9-inch x 13-inch baking dish.
- In a skillet, sauté onions and mushrooms in oil. Set aside.
- To the eggs, add the spinach, carrots, onions, mushrooms, salt, pepper, soup mix and matzah meal, mixing thoroughly after each addition.
- Put mixture into muffin tins and bake for 45 minutes. Remove from oven and with a spatula release the puffs. Serve warm.

Note: You can put mixture into baking dish and cut into squares to serve. Can be prepared ahead and frozen.

Editor's Note:
- Sprinkle each cup with matzah meal for easier release of the puffs.
- Substitute 2 pounds zucchini for spinach.

PEACH FARFEL FOR PASSOVER

Serves: 12

1 pound farfel
Hot water
7 beaten eggs
¾ pound melted margarine
1 cup sugar
2 cups peach juice (drained from canned peaches)
1 teaspoon vanilla
¾ teaspoon salt
3 (16-ounce) cans peaches, sliced
Cinnamon to taste
Sugar to taste

- Preheat oven to 350 degrees. Grease a 3-quart Pyrex dish.
- Soak farfel in hot water to soften, then drain. Place in a large bowl.
- Beat the eggs and margarine together until light. Add to farfel and mix. Add sugar, peach juice, vanilla and salt and blend well.
- Spoon half the mixture into the baking dish. Add a layer of sliced peaches. Add rest of mixture and layer the remainder of peaches. Sprinkle with lots of cinnamon and sugar.
- Bake for 1 hour.

Penny Weill
Scarsdale, New York

QUICK PASSOVER CHEESE CAKE

Add this to your holiday entertaining

Serves: 12

Crust

¼ cup margarine, melted
12 crushed Passover egg kichel
½ cup sugar
½ teaspoon cinnamon

- Use a 9-inch x 13-inch baking pan.
- Pour the margarine over the bottom and sides of baking pan. Mix together the kichel, sugar and cinnamon. Pat over the bottom and sides of the pan.

Filling (All ingredients at room temperature)

4 eggs
1 pound cream cheese, cut into eighths
1 pound creamed cottage cheese
3 cups sour cream
2 tablespoons melted butter or margarine
Grated rind and juice of 1 orange
Grated rind and juice of 1 lemon
1½ cups sugar
1 tablespoon potato starch
1 tablespoon Passover cake meal

- Preheat oven to 400 degrees.
- In the large bowl of an electric mixer, place the eggs, cream cheese, cottage cheese, sour cream, melted butter, rind and juice of orange and lemon. Beat until smooth.
- Combine the sugar, potato starch and cake meal in a bowl and slowly add to the creamed mixture until well-mixed.
- Pour into the crumb lined pan. Bake for 5 minutes. Reduce heat to 325 degrees and bake for 50 minutes more or until cake is set and slightly browned around the edges. Cool in the pan.

Note: This recipe can also be divided between two 9-inch square or two 8-inch round pans. Baking time at 325 degrees is about 40 minutes for the two pans.

Ruth Alpert
Stamford, Connecticut

RASPBERRY MOUSSE

Prepare ahead

Serves: 12

3 (10-ounce) packages frozen raspberries, defrosted and drained on paper towel
1 extra package for garnish
2 teaspoons sugar
2 tablespoons LeRoux Kirsch
2 tablespoons LeRoux apricot brandy
2 egg whites, room temperature
8 ounces Birds Eye®, Cool Whip®, Non-Dairy Whipped Topping, defrosted

- Purée 3 packages raspberries in a blender or food processor. Strain with a wooden spoon to remove the seeds.
- In a large bowl, combine the seedless purée with 1 teaspoon sugar and liqueurs. Set aside.
- Beat egg whites until peaks form. Slowly add 1 teaspoon of sugar and continue beating until stiff.
- Fold the egg whites into the purée with a rubber spatula. When incorporated, fold in the Cool Whip®. Mix carefully and thoroughly.
- Pour into individual dessert size ramekins and top with extra raspberries. Cover with plastic wrap and then foil. Freeze until solid. Remove from freezer 20 minutes before serving.

Note: Fresh strawberries may be used as a topping.

SOUTH AFRICAN ROAST TURKEY

A unique way to roast a turkey.

Serves: 10 to 12

14 to 16 pound turkey
4 sticks celery
2 large carrots
2 cups tomato juice
1 cup dry sherry
1 tablespoon paprika
2 tablespoons salt
¼ teaspoon black pepper
4 cups water

- Preheat oven to 350 degrees.
- Place turkey in a large deep roasting pan. Stuff with celery and carrots.
- Mix all other ingredients together and pour over the turkey. Bake uncovered for 3 hours turning the turkey over every half hour. Must use oven mitts.
- Gravy is served separately.

Note: The skin will be crisp and the meat moist.

Maureen Berkman
Scarsdale, New York

WALNUT TORTE

Serves: 10 to 12

12 eggs, separated, at room temperature
2 cups sugar
¼ teaspoon salt
1 pound walnuts, finely ground
4 tablespoons matzah meal

- Preheat oven to 350 degrees. Butter three 9-inch round cake pans. Line the bottoms with parchment paper and butter the paper. Sprinkle with matzah meal.
- In a small mixing bowl, beat egg yolks and combine with sugar. Beat until thick and lemon colored. Add the ground nuts.
- In a large bowl beat egg whites and salt until stiff and satiny.
- Fold half the nut mixture into the egg whites, alternating with the matzah meal. Fold in the remaining nut mixture.
- Divide the batter among the three pans. Bake for 45 minutes or until a cake tester comes out clean when inserted into the center of the torte.
- Invert pans on a rack, but do not remove until they are completely cooled. When cool, cut around edges, invert, remove the pans and papers, invert again to finish cooling right side up.

Filling

8 ounces heavy cream sweetened with 1 tablespoon superfine sugar
1 tablespoon of vanilla, brandy, cognac, or sherry
1 (12-ounce) jar jam or preserves, melted (currant, raspberry, or strawberry)
1 pint fresh strawberries

To Assemble

- Add flavoring to the whipped cream.
- Spread the bottom layer with half the jam or preserves, and top with one third the whipped cream. Repeat this procedure with the next two layers. Cover the top with whipped cream and decorate with whole strawberries.

Variation:

- This torte can be baked in a 10-inch springform pan (size is important) in a 325 degree oven for 1 hour and 15 minutes or until top springs back when lightly touched. Invert to cool as it may sink in the middle. Remove from pan when completely cooled.
- Spread top with layer of jam or preserves (your choice of flavor). Cover the top with ½ pint of whipped cream flavored as stated in ingredients.

Note: Cake freezes well. *Do not* put the final topping on until you are ready to use.

Debbie Simon
Scarsdale, New York

PASTA,
RICE, &
POTATOES
Bay Basil Savory Coriander Sage Rosemary Parsley Mint Coriander Sage Rosemary
Rosemary Parsley Mint Cinnamon Marjoram
Marjoram Thyme Juniper Bay
Bay Basil Savory Coriander Sage Rosemary Parsley Mint Cinnamon Parsley
Sage Rosemary Parsley Mint Cinnamon Marjoram Thyme Juniper Coriander Sage Rosemary
Marjoram Thyme Juniper Bay Basil Savory Coriander Bay Basil

PERTINENT PARTICULARS

- A little lemon juice cooked with boiled rice will keep grains separate and white.
- Cook pasta or rice in chicken broth or stock instead of water for added flavor.
- When cooking pasta, add 2 tablespoons of vegetable oil to the water. This prevents noodles from sticking together.
- Rinse cooked pasta with warm water to keep it from sticking together.

FAVORITE PASTA

Always a hit!

Serves: 6 to 8

½ cup finely chopped parsley
1 garlic clove, minced
2 medium onions, minced
4 radishes, minced
2 carrots, minced
1 large leek, minced
⅓ cup basil (fresh) or 1 teaspoon dried
3 tablespoons butter
3 tablespoons oil
1 cup finely chopped cabbage (radicchio is good)
4 tomatoes, peeled and diced
2 small zucchini, sliced
1 cup clear vegetable broth
½ cup sliced green pepper
1 pound linguine, cooked according to package directions, "al dente" or fresh
Freshly grated cheese

- Combine parsley, garlic, onions, radishes, carrots, leek and basil.
- Heat the butter and oil in a large pot. Add vegetable mix and simmer until soft. Add the cabbage, tomatoes, zucchini and broth. Simmer, covered, for ½ hour. Add the green pepper and simmer a few minutes more.
- Serve heated over hot linguine with lots of freshly grated cheese.

Note: Sauce is superb made a day in advance.

Marcia Rosenthal
Pittsburgh, Pennsylvania

PASTA WITH RICOTTA

Serves: 6 to 8

2 (10-ounce) packages frozen chopped spinach
1 pound ricotta cheese
3 eggs, lightly beaten
⅔ cup Parmesan cheese, grated
½ cup fresh parsley, chopped
2 teaspoons salt or to taste
½ teaspoon pepper
3 to 4 cups marinara sauce
1 pound tube-like pasta (elbows or penne)

- Preheat oven to 375 degrees. Use a 3 quart casserole.
- Cook spinach according to package directions and drain. Combine all ingredients, except pasta, mixing well.
- Cook pasta "al dente;" drain. Add to other ingredients, pour into 3 quart casserole and bake for 30 minutes. Serve with additional Parmesan cheese, if desired.

Myrna Lehr
Maplewood, New Jersey

PASTA WITH UNCOOKED TOMATO SAUCE

A delicious way to use your garden tomatoes.

Serves: 4 to 6 as a main course
or 10 to 12 as a side dish

Prepare ahead

2 pounds fresh tomatoes, cut in half
¾ cup virgin olive oil
¼ cup fresh basil, chopped
Salt and freshly ground pepper to taste
2 cloves garlic, finely chopped
Pinch red pepper flakes
6 to 8 ounces mozzarella cheese, diced
1 pound fusilli pasta, cooked according to package directions, "al dente"
½ cup black oil-cured olives

- Gently squeeze seeds out of tomatoes and cut into small pieces. Place in a nonmetallic container and add the oil. Toss gently. Add the herbs, seasonings and cheese, toss very lightly. Refrigerate for at least 3 hours.
- Place the pasta in a large bowl and toss with 1 tablespoon oil to keep it from sticking. Add the cold sauce and drained olives. Serve immediately or keep at room temperature until ready to serve. Garnish with fresh basil leaves.

Aileen Karp
Mamaroneck, New York

PERCIATELLI PUTANESCA

Serves: 3 to 4

Olive oil, as needed
3 cloves garlic, minced
1 tablespoon dried basil, crumbled
½ cup chopped fresh parsley
A few crushed red pepper flakes
1 (28-ounce) can Italian plum tomatoes, drained and chopped
2 tablespoons capers, rinsed and drained
2 (3-ounce) cans black olives, pitted, drained and sliced
Salt and freshly ground pepper to taste
1 pound perciatelli pasta, "al dente," cooked according to package directions
Freshly ground Parmesan cheese

- Coat a large skillet with olive oil, and heat. Sauté garlic, basil, parsley and pepper flakes for 2 minutes. Add tomatoes and heat gently for 5 minutes. Stir in capers and olives and add salt and pepper to taste. Remove from heat.
- When you are ready to start boiling the water for perciatelli, return sauce to heat and simmer. Drain the cooked pasta, arrange a serving on each plate, spoon the heated sauce over top and sprinkle with cheese.

Judy Bianco
New York, New York

PORCINI MUSHROOM FETTUCCINE

Rich and delicious.

Serves: 6 as an appetizer
3 to 4 as an entrée

1½ ounces dried Porcini mushrooms. If not available use Shittake. If bought fresh, use about 6 to 8 ounces
3 to 4 tablespoons sweet butter
1 pint heavy cream
1½ cups freshly ground Parmesan or Locatelli cheese (preferably the imported varieties)
Ground pepper to taste
1 pound fettuccine, fresh or dry packaged

- If using dried mushrooms, soften in warm water; drain. If fresh, just slice and set aside.
- Using a skillet, sauté the mushrooms in butter. Cook until wilted, then remove and set aside. Into the same skillet, add the cream and grated cheese, stirring slowly over a low heat, creating a sauce. Add pepper to taste. Blend the mushrooms into the sauce. Keep warm until ready to serve.
- Prepare pasta. Cook fresh variety about 2 minutes in boiling water until "al dente". If packaged, cook about 7 minutes. Drain.
- Pour the entire sauce over the pasta either individually portioned out or in a large casserole. Serve hot. Add extra cheese if needed.

Morton Metzger
New York, New York

QUICK PASTA PRIMAVERA SURPRISE

- The crudités you made for company that seemed to multiply no matter how much your guests ate. You now have all the vegetables to make Pasta Primavera.

- Just boil your favorite pasta "al dente" and before the last 4 minutes of cooking, add all your vegetables (except pea pods—they take 1 minute). When ready, pour all ingredients (pasta and vegetables) into a colander and drain. Put into a large bowl and toss with your favorite sauce or dressing.

- Serve hot or at room temperature.

Corrine Katz
White Plains, New York

SPINACH LASAGNE

Serves: 8

2 pounds fresh, loose spinach, or 2 packages (20 to 24 ounces total)
1 medium onion, chopped
½ pound fresh mushrooms, sliced
1 tablespoon oil or butter
1 pound ricotta cheese
2 eggs
¼ pound freshly grated Parmesan cheese
½ pound mozzarella cheese, sliced
1 pound lasagne noodles
1½ quarts homemade tomato sauce

- Preheat oven to 350 degrees. Grease a 9-inch x 13-inch baking pan.
- Wash spinach but do not dry. Cook in a covered saucepan, with only the water remaining on leaves, until wilted. Set aside.
- Sauté onion and mushrooms in butter or oil. Set aside.
- In a large bowl, combine ricotta cheese, eggs, Parmesan cheese, spinach, onions and mushrooms. Mix all ingredients thoroughly.
- Cook lasagne according to package directions, "al dente". Rinse in cold water.

To Assemble

- Layer of tomato sauce.
- Layer of lasagne (overlapping each noodle slightly).
- Layer of ricotta mixture. Cover evenly. Spread with a thin metal spatula.
- Thin slices of mozzarella cheese.
- Continue in this way until all ingredients are used and the top layer is lasagne noodles and tomato sauce.
- Cover with aluminum foil and bake 30 minutes. Remove the foil and bake another 5 to 10 minutes. Let set for about 5 to 10 minutes before cutting to serve.

Jeffrey Katz
Beverly Shores, Indiana

CHINESE FRIED RICE "Á LA CYNTHIA"

A sure fire hit!

Serves: 12 to 16

4 tablespoons corn oil
4 eggs
1 pound mushrooms, sliced
1 pound onions, chopped
6 to 8 scallions, chopped
2 red peppers, sliced
1 (2-pound) box Uncle Ben's® Long Grain Rice
6 tablespoons soy sauce
½ pound pea pods, left whole, blanched
Freshly ground pepper to taste
5 to 6 drops red hot sauce

- Heat oil in a large saucepan.
- Mix eggs and scramble in oil until they become golden brown. Remove from pan with a slotted spoon (drain). Set aside.
- Brown all vegetables, except peas pods, in oil (drain).
- Bring 4 quarts of water to a boil and cook rice for 2 to 3 minutes. Remove from heat, drain and rinse with cold water.
- Heat a 6-quart deep pot until very hot. Pour drained rice into pot with soy sauce and brown, stirring continually until rice is lightly browned.
- Stir all vegetables including pea pods into rice. Add pepper, hot sauce and eggs. Mix thoroughly and heat over low flame until hot.

Paula Lustbader
Greenwich, Connecticut

DELICIOUS RICE

Serves: 6

¼ pound margarine
5 onions, chopped
½ pound fresh mushrooms, sliced
1½ cups Uncle Ben's® Rice
1 (4-ounce) can blanched, slivered almonds, toasted
1 (11½-ounce) can beef consommé
1 can water
1 (8-ounce) can water chestnuts, sliced
¼ cup chopped green pepper
1 cup snow peas, sliced diagonally
Salt and pepper to taste

- Preheat oven to 350 degrees. Use an ungreased 2 to 2½-quart casserole.
- In a large skillet, sauté onions in margarine until golden. Sauté mushrooms, then rice. Add remainder of ingredients except snow peas and mix thoroughly.
- Pour into casserole and bake for 40 minutes. Add snow peas and bake 10 minutes more.

Hope Hirschhorn
Harrison, New York

KASHA WITH EGG BOWS

(Kasha Varnishkes)
Not just for a holiday.

Serves: 6 to 8

3 large onions, sliced
2 (4-ounce) jars mushrooms, drained and sliced, or
½ pound fresh mushrooms, sliced
Oil for sauté
Salt, pepper, paprika to taste
1 cup kasha (medium grain)
1 egg
1 cup boiling water
Dash salt
1 (1-pound) box egg bows

- Sauté onions and mushrooms in oil. Season with salt, pepper and paprika and set aside.
- In a large skillet, mix the uncooked kasha with egg and fry in 1 to 2 tablespoons oil until each grain is separate and dry, stirring constantly with a wooden spoon. Remove from skillet and put into a pot containing the boiling water and salt. Lower heat and simmer until tender. Add a small amount of water if necessary. Add onions and mushrooms.
- Boil bow knots according to package directions until tender. Drain and mix with the other ingredients. Serve hot.

Pearl Resnick
New York, New York

MAJADENAH ARABIC RICE AND LENTIL DISH

Serves: 4 to 6

Prepare ahead

1 large onion, finely chopped
2 tablespoons oil
3½ to 4 cups boiling water, depending on desired tenderness
1 cup white rice
1 cup brown lentils (soak overnight)
Salt and pepper to taste

- Fry the onion in oil until soft and golden brown. Add the other ingredients. Cover tightly and simmer for 20 minutes until rice and lentils are soft and water has boiled away.
- Serve hot or cold.

Menucha Shrier
Johannesburg, South Africa
Now residing in Stamford, Connecticut

RICE DISH

Serves: 10

3 cups cold cooked rice
¼ cup butter or margarine
2 (10-ounce) packages frozen peas
2 bunches scallions with tops, chopped
1 (8-ounce) can sliced water chestnuts, cut in half
1 pound fresh mushrooms, sliced (optional)

- Preheat oven to 350 degrees. Grease a 2½-quart baking dish.
- In a large skillet, brown rice in butter. Add peas and stir. Add scallions and water chestnuts to the mixture and mix together. (Add more butter or margarine if the mixture gets too dry). Bake 20 minutes.

Note: If adding mushrooms, sauté briefly in 2 tablespoons butter. Discard liquid and add to rice mixture.

Rita Schwartz
Roslyn, New York

SPECIAL HERBED RICE

Serves: 4 as a main course;
10 as a side dish

1 (6-ounce) box long grain and wild rice mix
1 cup white rice, uncooked
3 cups water
1 onion, chopped
¼ green pepper, chopped
1 pound ground veal
⅛ pound margarine
1 (5-ounce) can water chestnuts, sliced
¼ teaspoon marjoram
2 teaspoons sesame seeds

- Preheat oven to 350 degrees. Grease a 2-quart cassrole with margarine.
- Combine wild rice mix (retain seasoning packet) and white rice in saucepan. Cover with the water and bring to a rolling boil. Boil for 8 minutes; drain and rinse with cold water. Return rice to pan, replace on stove. Cover and let sit for 10 minutes.
- Sauté onion, green pepper, and veal in 1 tablespoon margarine. Add mixture to cooked rice along with water chestnuts, marjoram, sesame seeds and seasoning mix in envelope. Blend well and add melted margarine. Pour into the casserole and bake for 25 minutes.

Debbie Simon
Scarsdale, New York

WILD RICE CASSEROLE

This gets raves!

Serves: 6 to 8

2 cups wild rice
½ cup olive oil
2 tablespoons margarine
2 tablespoons chopped onion
2 tablespoons chopped chives
3 tablespoons chopped green pepper
4 cups hot chicken broth
¾ cup sliced toasted almonds
½ cup sliced mushrooms (optional)
Salt and pepper to taste

- Preheat oven to 350 degrees. Grease a 2½-quart casserole.
- Wash and drain rice.
- Heat oil and margarine; brown onions, chives and green pepper. Add rice; cook and stir until rice turns yellow, about 10 minutes. Add broth, almonds and mushrooms and season with salt and pepper.
- Place in casserole, cover and bake 1¼ hours.

Betty Laboz
New York, New York

APRICOT SWEET POTATOES

Serves: 8

2 pounds sweet potatoes, peeled
1 cup dried apricots
1 cup light brown sugar, firmly packed
¼ cup butter, melted
1 teaspoon grated orange rind
¼ cup apricot liquid (see recipe)
¼ cup chopped walnuts

- Preheat oven to 375 degrees. Grease a 2-quart baking dish and set aside.
- Parboil sweet potatoes. Drain and slice.
- In a saucepan, place apricots. Add enough water to cover. Boil until apricots puff up. Drain and retain apricot liquid. Slice apricots.
- Layer sliced potatoes in the baking dish; add a layer of apricots and place over the potatoes. Sprinkle with some brown sugar, then a mixture of melted butter, grated orange rind and apricot liquid sprinkled over the layers. Repeat until potatoes and apricots are used up. Pour remainder of liquid over top.
- Bake uncovered for 40 minutes, top with nuts, then bake 5 minutes longer.

Elaine Satuloff
Harrison, New York

HORSERADISH POTATOES

An unusual surprise taste awaits you!

Serves: 6 to 8

6 to 8 medium potatoes, peeled and cut into shoestrings

- Let potatoes stand in water while preparing sauce.

Sauce

2 tablespoons butter
2 tablespoons flour
2 cups heavy cream
3 tablespoons prepared white horseradish
1 tablespoon finely chopped parsley
½ teaspoon caraway seeds
Salt and pepper to taste
2 tablespoons unflavored bread crumbs

- Preheat oven to 350 degrees. Grease an 8-inch x 12-inch baking dish.
- In a heavy skillet, over low heat, melt butter and flour stirring until smooth. Add cream slowly and stir until thickened. Add remaining ingredients except bread crumbs.
- Place drained potatoes into prepared dish, pour sauce over potatoes and sprinkle with bread crumbs. Bake for 45 minutes or until potatoes are tender.

Marianne Beyl
Greenwich, Connecticut

NANCY'S POTATO SALAD

The best you ever tasted.

Serves: 8

6 large potatoes, peeled, cooked, and diced
6 hard-boiled eggs, diced
3 stalks celery, diced
1 small green pepper, diced
1 small red pepper, diced
1 large red or white onion, chopped
6 small sweet pickles, chopped
1 tablespoon white vinegar
¼ cup sweet pickle juice
1 tablespoon sugar
1 tablespoon Dijon-style mustard
Salt and pepper to taste
1 cup mayonnaise

- Boil potatoes until fork-tender. Set aside to cool. Dice potatoes and place in a large bowl. Add all other ingredients and mix well.
- Refrigerate until ready to serve.

Nancy Thompson
Bridgeport, Connecticut

POTATO CHEESE PUFFS

Yield: 10 to 12 puffs

1½ cups mashed potatoes, hot or cold
3 tablespoons hot milk
½ cup grated Cheddar cheese
¼ teaspoon paprika
½ teaspoon celery salt
1 small onion, grated
1 teaspoon minced parsley
2 eggs, separated
Melted butter

- Preheat oven to 350 degrees. Grease a cookie sheet.
- In a bowl, mix potatoes with milk and grated cheese. Add paprika, celery salt, onion and parsley. Stir.
- Beat egg yolks and add to mixture. Beat egg whites until stiff and fold into mixture.
- With a large spoon, drop into separate mounds onto cookie sheet. Brush tops with melted butter. Bake 20 minutes.

Ruth Abromowitz
Short Hills, New Jersey

POTATO ONION CHEESE BAKE

Serves: 6 to 8

6 large potatoes, peeled
1 pound Swiss or Jarlesberg cheese, grated coarsely
2 (2.8-ounce) cans french fried onions
Salt, pepper and garlic powder to taste

- Preheat oven to 350 degrees. Grease a 7½-inch x 11¾-inch baking dish.
- Boil potatoes for about 15 minutes. They should be firm. Cool and grate coarsely.
- Layer potatoes, cheese and onions; dot with butter. Repeat once, making sure to end with onions.
- Bake covered for 45 minutes. Uncover and bake another 15 minutes.

Hope Hirschhorn
Harrison, New York

POTATO PANCAKES

Serves: 4 to 6

6 potatoes, peeled and grated
1 medium onion, finely chopped
3 eggs, lightly beaten
1 to 2 tablespoons fine bread crumbs
Salt and pepper to taste
Oil for frying

- In a mixing bowl, combine potatoes and onion. Stir in eggs, bread crumbs and seasoning to taste.
- Coat a skillet with oil and when sizzling hot, drop in mixture by tablespoonful. Cook until brown and crisp on both sides.

Jeanne Quinn
White Plains, New York

POTATO PUDDING

Serves: 8 to 10

4 onions, quartered
4 eggs
1 cup melted chicken fat
3 tablespoons flour
12 potatoes, grated
2 carrots, grated
Salt and pepper to taste

- Preheat oven to 425 degrees. Generously grease a 9-inch x 13-inch baking dish or use individual custard cups.
- Combine the onions, eggs, chicken fat and flour in a blender and mix thoroughly.
- Squeeze the water out of potatoes, place in a large bowl; add carrots and blended ingredients. Add salt and pepper to taste. Stir to mix, pour into prepared dish and bake for 1 hour.

Note: These ingredients can also be used to make potato pancakes by omitting the carrots and chicken fat.

Hope Hirschhorn
Harrison, New York

PRUNE AND POTATO CASSEROLE

(Tzimmes)

Serves: 6 to 8

1 pound brisket
2 teaspoons salt or to taste
1 tablespoon chicken fat
1 onion, sliced
5 sweet potatoes, peeled and cut into thick slices
½ pound prunes
2 tablespoons flour
⅓ to ½ cup honey or 4 to 5 tablespoons brown sugar
½ teaspoon cinnamon
Dash of nutmeg

- Preheat oven to 350 degrees. Grease a 3-quart casserole.
- Sprinkle meat with salt and brown in fat with onion. Add enough water to cover and cook covered for 1 hour.
- Place meat in center of casserole and surround with potato slices. Add prunes and water in which the meat was cooked, adding more if necessary, to cover the contents.
- Brown the flour lightly in a frying pan, stirring to prevent scorching. Remove from heat and stir in honey or brown sugar, ½ cup of meat broth and spices. Stir until smooth.
- Pour into casserole and stir to distribute evenly. Cover and bake for 2 hours or until meat is tender.
- Bake last 30 minutes without cover for a golden brown top.

Ruth Turim
Brooklyn, New York

SWEET POTATO CASSEROLE

Serves: 8 to 10

Margarine, as needed
6 medium-size apples, Granny Smith or any hard apple, peeled and cored (if desired, leave skin on), sliced or cut into ⅛ths
Lemon juice
6 sweet potatoes, peeled and quartered
1 (1-pound, 4-ounce) can pineapple, slices or chunks, retain juice
1 (1-pound, 1-ounce) can bing cherries, pitted and drained, discard juice
Cinnamon, as desired

- Preheat oven to 350 degrees. Coat bottom and sides of casserole with margarine.
- Sprinkle apple slices with lemon juice to prevent browning.
- Place sweet potatoes, apples, pineapple with juice and cherries in casserole.
- Sprinkle cinnamon liberally over top. Dot with margarine over entire surface. Bake for 1 to 1½ hours.

Note: Sweet potatoes can be parboiled to cut cooking time.

Daisy Dwyer
Spanish Town, West Indies

APRICOT NOODLE PUDDING

A very tasty treat!

Serves: 10 to 12

1 (16-ounce) package wide noodles
¾ cup butter, melted
6 apples, diced
1 cup white raisins
1 (8-ounce) box dried apricots, cut in half
1½ cups sugar
Juice of 1 lemon
Juice of 1 orange
6 eggs, beaten

- Preheat oven to 350 degrees. Grease a 9-inch x 13-inch baking dish.
- Cook noodles according to package directions. Pour butter over drained noodles.
- Add fruits, sugar, juices and mix well.
- Add eggs and blend thoroughly.
- Pour into prepared dish and spread topping over all. Bake for 1 hour.

Topping

½ cup sugar
¼ to ½ cup corn flake crumbs

- Mix and spread on top. Dot with butter.

Bobbi Sloate
Scarsdale, New York

GOURMET NOODLE PUDDING

One of the very best!

Serves: 10

½ pound wide noodles
6 eggs
¼ cup sugar
1 pound cottage cheese
½ pound cream cheese
¼ cup milk
1 pint sour cream or yogurt
¼ pound butter, melted
1 cup raisins, optional
1 teaspoon vanilla

- Preheat oven to 350 degrees. Butter a 9-inch x 13-inch baking dish.
- Boil noodles in boiling salted water. When cooked, drain, rinse under cold water and drain again.
- Beat eggs with sugar. Mash cream cheese with milk. Put noodles in a bowl and add all the ingredients. Blend well and pour mixture into baking dish.

Add Topping As Follows:

8 ounces corn flakes
¼ pound butter, melted
1 cup brown sugar

- Crumble the corn flakes, add brown sugar and melted butter, mixing thoroughly. Spread mixture over pudding. Bake for about 40 minutes.

Pearl Firestone
New Rochelle, New York

NOODLE PUDDING

Anne Pochapin has made this for many of our luncheons for the Westchester Chapter.

Serves: 12

1 pound medium size noodles
4 eggs, separated
1 cup sugar
1 pound cottage cheese
1 pint sour cream
¾ cup butter, melted
½ teaspoon salt
¼ teaspoon cinnamon
1 teaspoon vanilla
1 (28-ounce) can sliced peaches or apricots

- Preheat oven to 350 degrees. Butter a 9-inch x 13-inch baking pan.
- Boil noodles in salted water until almost tender and drain.
- Beat egg whites until stiff and place in refrigerator.
- Place the noodles in the baking pan. Mix the remaining ingredients except fruit in a large bowl. Fold egg whites into mixture and pour over noodles. Place fruit over top.
- Bake for 45 to 60 minutes. Raise heat for the last few minutes to brown top. Cut into squares.

Anne Pochapin
New Rochelle, New York

NOODLES AND SPINACH

Serves: 10

1 pound narrow noodles
½ pound butter, melted
2 (10-ounce) packages frozen chopped spinach, thawed and drained
6 eggs, beaten
1 pint heavy sweet cream or 1 pint sour cream
2 envelopes onion soup mix

- Preheat oven to 350 degrees. Grease a 9-inch x 13-inch baking dish.
- In a large pot of boiling water, cook noodles as directed, "al dente". Drain well.
- Place noodles in a large bowl and stir in butter. Add remaining ingredients and mix thoroughly.
- Pour into prepared casserole and bake, uncovered for 45 minutes.

Note: If doubling the recipe, use only 3 packages of onion soup mix.

Lucille Wagner
Scarsdale, New York

SPICY COLD NOODLES

Try chop sticks for this one.

Serves: 4

Water
1 tablespoon peanut oil
½ pound Chinese egg noodles
1 tablespoon sesame seed oil
1 cup mung bean sprouts

- Boil water, adding enough for the noodles. Add the peanut oil to the boiling water and boil noodles for 3 to 5 minutes. Stir occasionally. Drain and rinse in cold water. Cut noodles into 6-inch pieces. Mix noodles with sesame seed oil, set aside.
- Rinse bean sprouts, drain on paper towel to dry. Set aside.

Sauce

2 tablespoons sesame seed paste
2 tablespoons dark soy sauce
1 tablespoon brewed tea
½ tablespoon red vinegar
½ tablespoon chili oil (hot oil)
½ tablespoon sesame seed oil
½ teaspoon sugar
1 clove garlic, minced
1 teaspoon ginger root, freshly ground
2 scallions, white and green part, chopped

- In a bowl, mix sesame seed paste, soy sauce and tea and blend thoroughly. Add vinegar, sesame and chili oils, sugar, garlic, ginger and scallions. Combine all ingredients well.
- When ready to serve, add bean sprouts to the noodles. Mix sauce once again and pour over noodles. Toss until coated. Serve immediately and at room temperature.

Variations: Substitute 1 cup sliced chicken (white part only), for bean sprouts. Substitute all sesame paste for equal parts of sesame paste and peanut butter. Blend both together thoroughly.

Mark Katz
Chevy Chase, Maryland

POULTRY
Bay Basil Savory Coriander Sage Rosemary Parsley Mint Coriander Sage
Sage Rosemary Parsley Mint Cinnamon
Marjoram Thyme Juniper Bay
Bay Basil Savory Coriander Sage Rosemary Parsley Mint Cinnamon Parsley
Sage Rosemary Parsley Mint Cinnamon Marjoram Thyme Juniper Coriander Sage
Marjoram Thyme Juniper Bay Basil Savory Coriander Bay Basil

ARTICHAUTS-POULET CASSEROLE

A wonderful combination!

Serves: 6

3 pounds chicken pieces (breasts and thighs)
1½ teaspoons salt
½ teaspoon paprika
¼ teaspoon pepper
6 tablespoons margarine
1 (8-ounce) can whole mushrooms, drained or ½ pound fresh
2 tablespoons flour
1 cup chicken broth
¼ cup sherry (dry) or dry white wine (I like Vermouth)
1 (14-ounce) can artichoke hearts (drained)

- Preheat oven to 375 degrees. Use a casserole large enough to hold the chicken in a single layer.
- Season chicken with salt, paprika and pepper. In a large skillet brown on all sides in margarine.
- Place chicken in a single layer in casserole.
- Sauté mushrooms in drippings remaining in skillet. Blend in flour and cook for a minute or so. Add chicken broth and wine and cook until thickened. Place artichokes in casserole on top of chicken. Pour sauce over all. Bake uncovered for 45 minutes.

Denise Korngold
Nantucket, Massachussets

Editor's Note: This recipe worked well adding ½ teaspoon thyme and-or ½ teaspoon tarragon.

BELGIAN CHICKEN

Quick, easy and delicious.

Serves: 4

4 boned chicken breasts, pounded thin
4 tablespoons dry mustard
2 tablespoons dry white wine
4 medium shallots, minced
Pepper to taste
2 teaspoons basil or tarragon (optional)
1 cup bread crumbs, unseasoned
2 tablespoons margarine, melted

- Broil chicken breasts 4 minutes on each side; cool. Mix mustard, white wine, shallots, pepper, basil or tarragon. Dip chicken breasts in mustard sauce, coat with bread crumbs. Place coated breasts on broiling rack; drizzle with margarine. Broil for 2 to 3 minutes until brown and crisp.

Mark Katz
Chevy Chase, Maryland

CHICKEN BREAST TERIYAKI

An Oriental delight.

Serves: 4 to 6

Prepare ahead

Teriyaki Sauce

½ cup dry sherry
½ cup soy sauce
1 tablespoon Worcestershire sauce
1 teaspoon A-1® steak sauce
2 teaspoons chopped parsley
½ teaspoon finely minced garlic
¼ teaspoon dry mustard
1 teaspoon sugar
1 tablespoon honey
¼ teaspoon ginger

- Combine all ingredients. This may be used for lamb, steak or chicken.
  4 to 6 whole chicken breasts, split in half.
  1 pound small, whole mushrooms.
- Marinate chicken in teriyaki sauce overnight, turning a couple of times.
- Sauté mushrooms in margarine about 5 minutes. Set aside.
- Cook chicken on outdoor grill or in broiler. Slice and serve with mushrooms and warmed peaches.

Peach Accompaniment

1 (28-ounce) can peach halves
Brown sugar

- Preheat oven to 350 degrees. Line a cookie sheet with aluminum foil and place peach halves on foil. Place ½ teaspoon brown sugar in each half. Bake for 10 minutes or until heated through thoroughly.

Roxene Feinberg
Scarsdale, New York

CHICKEN CACCIATORE

Serves: 4

4 pound frying chicken, cut into serving pieces
5 tablespoons olive oil (to cover pan bottom)
2 medium onions, diced
1 clove garlic, minced
1 cup sliced mushrooms
1 green pepper, sliced
½ cup canned tomatoes, drained
1 teaspoon oregano
¼ teaspoon basil
¾ cup dry wine (red or white)
½ teaspoon hot pepper flakes

- In a large saucepan, brown chicken pieces in oil. When done remove from pan.
- Place all the vegetables and seasonings on the bottom of pan, add chicken and wine.
- Simmer, covered, for 40 minutes.

Anita Newman
Scarsdale, New York

CHICKEN COLOMBIANA

A great dish for entertaining.

Serves: 24

10 chicken breasts, or 4 chickens (3 pounds each) cut bite size
½ pound flour (or enough to coat chickens)
8 tablespoons margarine
8 tablespoons vegetable shortening
3 cups chopped onions
3 cloves garlic, minced
2 cups chopped green pepper
2 cups diced carrots
2 cups diced celery
4 tablespoons salt, or to taste
2 teaspoons pepper
4 teaspoons crushed cumin
8 cups Italian plum tomatoes
3 cups chopped stuffed olives
3 cups raw corn kernels, cut from cob

- Preheat oven to 325 degrees. Use a 12-inch x 17-inch casserole or roasting pan.
- Dredge chicken in flour and brown on all sides in margarine and shortening, then transfer to a casserole. Add onions, garlic, green pepper, carrots and celery to skillet in which chicken cooked. Cook briefly, stirring constantly.
- Spoon vegetables over chicken; add salt, pepper, cumin, tomatoes, olives and corn.
- Bake for 45 minutes to 1 hour.

Note: If this dish is to be made for a party, omit the olives and corn, when preparing a day before. On day of party, reheat, adding the corn and olives.

Ruth Greer
Rye, New York

CHICKEN FRANÇAIS

The best you ever tasted!

Serves: 2

2 whole chicken breasts, cut thin and pounded for scaloppine
Flour for dredging
2 eggs, beaten with 2 tablespoons water
Salt and pepper to taste
Peanut or blended vegetable oil

- Dip chicken in flour, then in egg, season to taste with salt and pepper. Brown in hot oil until golden brown. Drain on paper towels. Keep warm.

Sauce

1 cup dry sherry
6 tablespoons margarine
2 teaspoons lemon juice
2 tablespoons fresh parsley, chopped

- Boil sherry for 3 minutes in a saucepan. Add margarine and when it has dissolved add lemon juice and parsley. Boil for 10 seconds. Pour hot sauce over chicken when ready to serve.

Note: May be prepared ahead and frozen with or without sauce. The amount of sauce may be increased if desired.

Gloria Hendler
Bernardsville, New Jersey

CHICKEN IMPERIAL

Serves: 4 to 6

4 small chicken breasts, split
1½ teaspoons salt
¼ cup margarine
⅓ cup dry sherry
½ teaspoon garlic powder
2 teaspoons Worcestershire sauce
1 teaspoon oregano
½ teaspoon dry mustard
1 teaspoon curry powder
¼ teaspoon paprika
⅛ teaspoon Tabasco sauce
Spiced peaches and parsley for garnish

- Preheat oven to 350 degrees. Use a large shallow baking pan.
- Sprinkle chicken with salt.
- In a small saucepan, combine margarine, sherry and seasonings. Stir over medium heat until margarine melts and mixture is smooth. Remove from heat and brush generously over chicken. Bake for 1 hour and 20 minutes or until tender; turn and baste every 10 to 15 minutes.
- Serve garnished with spiced peaches and parsley.

Debbie Simon
Scarsdale, New York

CHICKEN KIEV

Always a winner.

Serves: 6

Prepare ahead

¼ pound margarine, chilled and firm
6 whole chicken breasts, boned, skinned and flattened
Salt and pepper to taste
1 bunch chopped scallions
Flour for dredging
2 eggs, lightly beaten
1 cup fresh bread crumbs
vegetable oil

- Cut margarine into six lengthwise pieces. Place a piece in center of each breast, sprinkle with salt, pepper and scallions. Roll up envelope fashion being sure sides overlap.
- Dredge each roll in flour, dip in beaten eggs and roll in bread crumbs. Refrigerate for at least 1 hour before frying.
- Fill a pot with enough oil to cover the breasts completely. Heat until hot, then lower heat. Add chicken gradually and brown on all sides. Cook about 10 to 15 minutes. Drain on paper towels.

Mark Hirschhorn
New York, New York

CHICKEN-SPICY SZECHUAN NOODLES

Serves: 4

6 cups boiling water
2 large chicken breasts
6 ounces fine egg noodles
1 teaspoon plus 1 tablespoon sesame oil
¼ cup sesame paste
3 tablespoons water
1 to 2 teaspoons hot chili oil (optional)
3 tablespoons light soy sauce
2 tablespoons red wine vinegar
¼ cup peanut or corn oil
2 tablespoons garlic, finely chopped

- In a large pot, bring 6 cups water to a boil, add chicken breasts. Do not add salt. When water returns to a boil, turn heat down and simmer for 10 minutes. Remove breasts, reserving the broth. Bring broth back to boil and add noodles. Cook, stirring occasionally, for 3 minutes. Drain and rinse under cold water until chilled. After thorough draining, put into mixing bowl; add 1 teaspoon sesame oil and toss.
- Cut or pull the chicken into fine shreds. Set aside.
- Mix 3 tablespoons water with the sesame paste, stirring. Add the chili oil, if desired, soy sauce, vinegar, peanut oil, garlic and remaining tablespoon of sesame oil and blend.
- To serve; arrange noodles on a serving dish. Cover with the chicken and spoon the sauce over top.

Carol Bockner
Scarsdale, New York

Editor's Note: This is a very attractive dish when surrounded with blanched snow peas, steamed asparagus or broccoli, and cubes of red pepper.

CHICKEN VERONIQUE

Serves: 6

12 chicken breasts
Salt to taste
Paprika to taste
½ cup margarine, divided
1 onion, finely chopped
1 clove garlic, minced
¼ pound mushrooms, sliced
4 tablespoons flour
1 cup chicken bouillon
2 tablespoons lemon juice
1 cup white, seedless grapes

- Sprinkle chicken pieces with salt and paprika.
- In a large skillet, melt ¼ cup margarine over medium heat. Add chicken and brown well on all sides. Remove chicken. Add remaining margarine to the skillet. Add onion and garlic cooking over low heat 5 minutes, stirring occasionally. Add mushrooms and cook 2 minutes longer.
- Blend in flour, chicken bouillon and lemon juice. Cook, stirring constantly, until mixture comes to a boil and is thickened. Add chicken pieces and cover tightly. Lower heat and simmer 30 minutes or until chicken is tender. Add grapes last 5 minutes.
- Arrange chicken on a warmed serving platter and pour sauce over top.

Susan Berenson
Armonk, New York

CHICKEN WITH CUMIN-MEXICAN STYLE

A zesty creative touch to a gourmet recipe.

Serves: 4 to 5

* *Seasoning Mixture*

1 teaspoon salt
1 teaspoon black pepper
1 teaspoon white pepper
1 teaspoon red pepper
2 tablespoons cumin

6 chicken breasts, halved
4 cloves garlic, finely minced
Juice of 3 limes
5 tomatoes, coarsely chopped

***Seasoned Flour*

1 cup flour
½ teaspoon salt
½ teaspoon black pepper
½ teaspoon white pepper
½ teaspoon red pepper

1 tablespoon chopped parsley
¼ cup vegetable oil
4 medium onions, thinly sliced
½ cup dry white wine

- Prepare * Seasoning Mixture and set aside.
- Prepare ** Seasoned Flour and set aside.
- Preheat oven to 375 degrees. Use a 9-inch x 13-inch baking pan.
- Wash and pat dry the chicken breasts. In a large bowl, mix the chicken with half the garlic, half the * Seasoning Mixture, and half the lime juice, and marinate for ½ hour.
- In another bowl, mix the tomatoes, the remainder of the garlic, other half of * Seasoning Mixture, remainder of the lime juice, and parsley.
- Heat 2 tablespoons oil in a large skillet, and sauté the onions over medium heat until soft, but not yet browned. Place the onions in the bottom of the large baking pan. In the same skillet, add oil and heat over medium flame.
- Dredge the chicken in the ** Seasoned Flour, and sauté on both sides until brown. Add more oil if necessary. Place the browned chicken pieces over the onions in the pan and cover with the seasoned tomatoes. Pour wine over the top. Cover and bake for 45 minutes.

Note: Red pepper may be reduced or eliminated, depending on how spicy you want this recipe to be.

Robert Gold, M.D.
Boca Raton, Florida

CHINESE CHICKEN WITH CASHEWS

Serves: 2

Sauce

3 tablespoons hoisin sauce
2 tablespoons dry sherry
2 tablespoons lite soy sauce

- Stir together and set aside.

2 egg whites
1 tablespoon sherry
1 tablespoon cornstarch
1 pound chicken cutlet, or more, cut into cubes
1 cup and 1 tablespoon peanut oil
1 to 2 bunches scallions, minced
¼ pound raw cashews per pound of meat, leave whole

- Beat the egg whites, sherry and cornstarch until fluffy.
- Marinate the chicken cubes in this mixture for 5 minutes. (If refrigerated, remove 15 minutes before cooking.)
- Heat 1 cup oil in wok. (The oil should be very hot.) Stir-fry chicken until golden. Remove from wok, drain excess oil from chicken and set aside.
- Drain all oil from wok. Add the tablespoon fresh oil to wok, wait until hot, then stir-fry scallions and raw cashews. Add chicken and sauce and serve immediately.

Judy Tauber
Riverdale, New York

Editor's Note: ½ pound of any fresh vegetable may be added for color and crunch.

COQ AU VIN

A foolproof recipe.

Serves: 4 to 6

12 small white onions, whole, peeled
¼ cup margarine
4 to 5 pound chicken, cut up, or 4 whole chicken breasts and 8 legs
Salt, pepper, paprika to taste
½ pound mushrooms, sliced
2 cloves garlic, crushed
1½ cups burgundy wine
¼ cup parsley, minced
½ teaspoon Bouquet Garni
½ to 1 cup chicken stock
Kneaded margarine (2 tablespoons margarine, room temperature and 1 teaspoon flour mixed together)

- In a large skillet, sauté whole onions in margarine until soft, stirring back and forth so they do not burn. Remove onions and set aside.
- Add chicken pieces to pan and brown on all sides. Sprinkle with salt, pepper and paprika. Add mushrooms, cook until they are soft and stir in crushed garlic.
- Return onions to pan and cook for 1 minute. Slowly add wine while stirring, raise heat to reduce liquid, then lower heat again. Add parsley and Bouquet Garni. Stir in chicken stock and cook until sauce begins to boil. Remove chicken pieces to a serving platter.
- Using a wire whisk, stir in the kneaded margarine, blending until smooth. Pour over chicken and serve immediately.

Annette Kranich
Pittsburgh, Pennsylvania

EASY SWEET AND SOUR CHICKEN

A different combination of flavors.

Serves: 4 to 6

2 chickens, 3 to 3½ pounds each, cut into quarters or eighths
1 (8-ounce) bottle chili sauce
1 (8-ounce) jar apricot preserves
1 (8-ounce) can sauerkraut, undrained

- Preheat oven to 375 degrees. Use two 9-inch x 13-inch pans or 1 large roasting pan.
- Mix chili sauce, apricot preserves and sauerkraut together.
- Place chickens in pans in a single layer. Pour mixture over the top. Bake uncovered for 1¼ hours.
- If chicken does not brown enough, place under the broiler for a few minutes. Watch carefully so it does not burn.

Susan Fischer
Pound Ridge, New York

ESCALOPES RATATOUILLE

Serves: 4 to 6

½ cup all-purpose flour
1 teaspoon salt
¼ teaspoon pepper
6 whole boneless chicken breasts, split
½ cup olive oil
2 large onions, sliced
2 zucchini, sliced
2 large tomatoes, sliced
2 green peppers, in strips
1 small eggplant, diced
2 cloves garlic, crushed
Salt to taste
1 teaspoon crumbled thyme
½ teaspoon pepper

- Preheat oven to 350 degrees. Use a 9-inch x 13-inch baking pan.
- In a bowl mix flour, salt and pepper. Dip cutlets into mixture, shake off excess, and chill in refrigerator.
- In a large skillet, heat the oil and sauté cutlets until they appear to be fairly done. Remove from pan and drain on paper towels. Add onions, zucchini, tomatoes, peppers and eggplant to pan drippings. (More oil may be needed.) Sprinkle with garlic, salt, thyme and pepper. Cover and cook stirring occasionally for 10 minutes. Remove from heat and place in the baking pan. Top with the cutlets. Bake for no more than ½ hour.

Note: Can be frozen before baking. Entire recipe freezes well.

Alice Kent
Livingston, New Jersey

HONG KONG DUCK

Looks elegant, tastes superb!

Serves: 2

1 fresh duckling
2 whole oranges
1 heart of celery
Salt to taste
1 bunch parsley (for garnish)

- Preheat oven to 400 degrees. Use a 3-inch deep roasting pan.
- Wash and dry duck, salt inside and out, and fill with one whole orange and celery heart. Place in a pan, without the rack, and roast for 45 minutes.

Marinade

Giblets
2 stalks celery, cut into large pieces
1 orange, cut into quarters
6 black peppercorns
2 carrots, cut into large pieces
1 teaspoon oregano
1 tablespoon dried parsley
2 cups water
1 bottle dry, red wine (3/4 liter)

- Place all marinade ingredients, except wine, in a heavy pot and bring to a boil. Simmer covered for 45 minutes.
- Remove duck from oven (it will stick to the pan). Reduce heat to 375 degrees.
- Pour off all fat and return duck to oven for 45 minutes. Add wine to marinade and bring to boil. Simmer uncovered for 45 minutes. Remove duck from oven and again drain off fat.
- Baste with some marinade. Return to oven and roast for 1 hour, basting every 10 minutes, using all of the marinade. The duck will appear as if lacquered, deep red brown with dark flecks.
- Remove from oven and allow to sit for 10 to 15 minutes. While still in pan, carve with small sharp pointed knife. Carefully remove leg and thigh in one piece with skin intact and place on heated platter. Cutting down to breastbone, remove each whole breast fillet in one piece with skin intact. Place on heated platter or individual serving plates.
- Allow 1 whole leg and breast per person.
- Garnish with orange slice, fresh parsley or watercress, if desired.

Judy Resnick
Rye, New York

MICKI'S CHICKEN

Serves: 10 to 12

Prepare ahead

12 chicken breasts
1 (12-ounce) jar apricot preserves
1 (12-ounce) jar pineapple preserves
4 tablespoons teriyaki sauce
Juice of 2 fresh lemons
2 tablespoons garlic powder

- Place chicken breasts skin side up in a shallow baking pan.
- Mix remaining ingredients, pour over chicken and allow to marinate several hours or overnight.
- Bring to room temperature and bake in 325 degree oven for 1 hour.

Micki Hoffman
Rye, New York

PARTY CHICKEN CUTLETS

A special treat for your guests.

Serves: 6

8 whole chicken cutlets (if very large cut them in half)
Salt and pepper to taste
3 beaten eggs
3 cups chopped walnuts
1 cup bread crumbs
3 tablespoons margarine
2 tablespoons corn oil

- Season cutlets with salt and pepper. Combine walnuts and bread crumbs.
- Dip the cutlets into eggs, then coat with nut-crumb mixture.
- Heat the oil and margarine together in a large skillet and fry on both sides. May then be refrigerated. Before serving, heat in preheated 400 degree oven for 15 minutes.
- Serve with plum sauce.

Plum Sauce

1 (1-pound) can plums, drain, reserve juice, remove pits
1 (6-ounce) jar plum preserves
2 tablespoons margarine
6 ounces chicken broth
¼ cup sherry
1½ teaspoons lemon juice

- Purée the plums in a blender. Add juice, a little at a time, until purée measures 1½ cups.
- Combine all ingredients in a saucepan and cook over low heat for 30 minutes. May be thickened with cornstarch.

Sondra Eichel
Scarsdale, New York

POULET AUX APRICOTINES

(Cornish Hens with apricot glaze and wild rice stuffing)

Serves: 6

6 Cornish Game hens
Salt, pepper, ginger and lemon juice to taste
½ pound melted margarine or oil
3 cups cooked, wild rice
1 (1-pound) can apricots, drained

Sauce

2 (1-pound) cans apricots (puréed in food processor)
Juice and rind of 1 orange
2 tablespoons golden syrup
1 teaspoon ginger, ground
1 teaspoon soy sauce
1 tablespoon lemon juice

- Combine the puréed apricots with other ingredients. Bring to boil. Set aside.

- Preheat oven to 400 degrees. Use a baking pan or casserole.
- Season hens with salt, pepper, ginger and lemon juice. Place breast side up in baking pan or casserole just large enough to hold hens side by side. Spoon the margarine or oil over the hens and place in oven. Baste every 5 to 10 minutes. After 30 minutes, remove the pan from oven and loosely pack the rice into the hens' cavities. Sew or cover with foil.
- Pour approximately ½ to ¾ of apricot sauce over the hens and return to the oven. Baste again every 5 to 10 minutes, adding more sauce if necessary. Cook for 20 to 30 minutes, reducing heat to 350 degrees, if necessary. Remove from oven.
- Serve decorated with apricot halves.
- Extra sauce can be heated and served separately.

Maureen Berkman
Scarsdale, New York

POULET RÔTI AUX CERISES

(Roast Chicken With Cherries)

Serves: 4 to 6

Prepare ahead

2 broilers, cut into eighths
1 (8-ounce) bottle French style dressing

- Marinate chicken in dressing for 2 to 4 hours in refrigerator.
- Preheat oven to 350 degrees
- Place chicken in a roasting pan, skin side up, and roast uncovered for 1½ hours.

Sauce

½ (6-ounce) jar red currant jelly
1 tablespoon cornstarch
1 (16-ounce) can black bing cherries, pitted, drained; reserve juice
4 tablespoons frozen orange juice concentrate
6 tablespoons Cherry Herring liqueur

- Melt jelly in saucepan over low heat. Blend cornstarch and cherry juice; add orange juice and Cherry Herring liqueur to jelly. Heat together until hot and sauce is clear and somewhat thickened. Pour over chicken and bake 15 to 20 minutes more.
- Add cherries at the last minute of baking.

Marylyn Castros

ROAST DUCKLING MONTMORENCY

Serves: 4

1 (4 to 5 pound) duck, quartered (the butcher will do this for you)
Salt, pepper, garlic powder and paprika to taste

Sauce

1 large can black bing cherries, pitted and drained, reserve juice
2 tablespoons cornstarch
1 large navel orange, reserve peel
¼ cup brown sugar
¼ cup Madeira or Port wine
2 tablespoons ginger marmalade or preserves

- Drain the cherries and set aside. Place the juice in a large saucepan. Dilute corn starch in a small amount of cherry juice and stir into saucepan. Remove skin from orange with tip of sharp knife and thinly julienne the orange peel. Add to pan. Juice orange and add with brown sugar, wine and marmalade. Stir and cook sauce until it comes to boil and thickens. After boiling a few minutes, remove from heat and stir in the cherries. Use to baste duck.

- Preheat oven to 400 degrees. Use a large roasting pan.
- Season the duck pieces with salt, pepper, garlic powder and paprika after carefully removing all fat you can get to with a knife. Lay the duck pieces on a rack in pan and place in oven. Add a small amount of hot water (about 1 inch) to the bottom of pan. This prevents the hot fat from splattering and smoking in the oven. Roast duck for about 20 minutes, then turn it and roast for another 20 minutes. Remove duck from oven after it is quite brown and crisp on both sides. Transfer the pieces to another tray and pour off all the fat that has accumulated in the bottom of pan. Wipe the pan out with a paper towel. Replace rack and put duck pieces back on the rack. Add a small amount of water to bottom of pan again. Reduce heat to 350 degrees. Return duck to oven, baste with sauce and roast 30 minutes. Turn duck, baste other side and roast another 30 minutes. By this time duck should be fork tender and ready to eat.

STIR-FRY CHICKEN CURRY

A wonderful stir-fry recipe.

Serves: 4 to 6

1 pound whole boneless chicken breasts, cut in squares
Margarine or oil as needed
1 teaspoon cinnamon
3 tablespoons mild curry powder
Black pepper to taste
3 scallions, chopped
2 cloves garlic, crushed
1 green pepper, diced
Other chopped vegetables, such as 1 pound mushrooms, sliced; 1 pound zucchini, cubed; or any other combination.
1 cup chicken stock
1 teaspoon salt
1 teaspoon paprika
1 tablespoon flour, more if necessary

- Using a wok, stir-fry chicken in margarine until almost cooked. Add cinnamon, curry powder and black pepper. Stir-fry for a few minutes. Add scallions, garlic, green pepper and vegetables of your choice. Continue to stir-fry for 5 to 10 minutes or until vegetables are done. Add chicken stock and salt. Simmer 5 to 10 minutes longer. Add paprika.
- Add flour to thicken sauce; continue adding more if necessary, tablespoon by tablespoon.
- Serve immediately over hot rice.

Elizabeth Waymire

SUNNY CHICKEN

Serves: 4

1 chicken, cut into serving pieces
½ cup orange juice
¼ cup soy sauce
¼ cup ketchup
¼ cup honey
1 teaspoon salt
1 teaspoon basil
¼ teaspoon pepper

- Preheat oven to 350 degrees. Place chicken pieces in a large shallow baking pan.
- Mix remaining ingredients and pour over chicken.
- Bake, uncovered, for 1 hour.

Susan Abrams
Katonah, New York

SWEET AND SOUR WALNUT CHICKEN

Sweet, spicy and delicious.

Serves: 6

Sauce

½ cup ketchup
4 tablespoons soy sauce
1 teaspoon Worcestershire sauce
3 tablespoons sugar
2 teaspoons sesame oil
Cayenne to taste
½ cup chicken broth

- Combine all ingredients. Set aside.

Ingredients For Chicken

2 tablespoons cornstarch
5½ teaspoons sugar
¼ teaspoon salt
3 whole boneless, skinless chicken breasts cut into ¾-inch cubes
1 cup plus 3 tablespoons peanut oil
1 cup walnuts
1 tablespoon minced peeled ginger
1 tablespoon minced garlic
2 tablespoons minced scallion
2 red bell peppers cut into 1-inch triangles
2 carrots cut into julienne strips
¾ pound snow peas
1 bunch watercress (stems discarded)

- In a large bowl combine cornstarch, ½ teaspoon sugar and salt. Add the chicken which has been patted dry. Toss the mixture to coat the chicken well.
- Heat the wok, add the peanut oil until hot but not smoking. Add the chicken in batches separating the pieces as they are added. Stir-fry for about 1 minute until pale golden. Transfer to a bowl with a wire strainer.
- Cook walnuts in oil remaining in the wok for 10 to 15 seconds, transfer to a small bowl with wire strainer. Sprinkle walnuts with 5 teaspoons sugar. Toss well, discard remaining oil in wok.
- Add remaining 3 tablespoons oil in wok, stir-fry ginger, garlic and scallions for 30 seconds. Add peppers, carrots and stir-fry for 45 seconds. Add chicken, snow peas and watercress. Stir-fry until chicken is hot.
- Add sauce, cook mixture over high heat, stirring until sauce comes to boil and stir in walnuts.

Maureen Berkman
Scarsdale, New York

WALNUT CHICKEN

Serves: 3 to 4

1 teaspoon cornstarch
1 tablespoon water
1 egg white
3 tablespoons pepper sauce, optional
2 whole chicken breasts boned, skinned, and cubed
3 tablespoons soy sauce
1 tablespoon Bourbon or Scotch
Dash sugar, optional
4 tablespoons oil
3 green onions, diced
1½ cups broccoli flowerets
½ cup asparagus tips
¾ cup any fresh vegetable of your choice
1 green pepper, sliced
1 clove garlic, minced
2 teaspoons powdered ginger or 2 slices fresh, minced
1 cup walnuts

- Mix together the cornstarch, water, egg white and pepper sauce. Add the chicken and toss.
- In a small bowl, mix the soy sauce, Bourbon or Scotch, and sugar.
- Heat wok with 2 tablespoons of oil. Stir-fry the chicken until cooked through (3 to 4 minutes). Remove from wok.
- Add remaining 2 tablespoons oil to wok. Stir-fry all vegetables, garlic and ginger for 1 to 2 minutes. Add chicken and stir for 1 minute. Add soy-Bourbon mix and stir-fry quickly until sauce is thick. Add walnuts. Stir and serve immediately.

Marcia Rosenthal
Pittsburgh, Pennsylvania

SALADS
Bay Basil Savory Coriander Sage Rosemary Parsley Mint Coriander Sage Rosemary
Sage Rosemary Parsley Mint Cinnamon Marjoram
Cinnamon Marjoram Thyme Juniper Bay
Bay Basil Savory Coriander Sage Rosemary Parsley Mint Cinnamon Parsley
Sage Rosemary Parsley Mint Cinnamon Marjoram Thyme Juniper Coriander Sage Rosemary
Cinnamon Marjoram Thyme Juniper Bay Basil Savory Coriander Bay Basil

ASIAN SALAD WITH TOFU

An exotic combination of ingredients.

Serves: 4 to 6

Vinaigrette Dressing

¼ cup red wine vinegar
⅛ cup sesame oil
¼ cup soy sauce

• Mix together and pour over salad.

1 head romaine lettuce
½ pound mushrooms, sliced
½ pound tofu, cubed
¼ cup sesame seeds, unhulled

• Prepare lettuce and mushrooms for salad. Place on individual salad plates; place chunks of tofu over salad. Sprinkle with sesame seeds and vinaigrette.

Cynthia Hogan
Chevy Chase, Maryland

BEAN SALAD

Serves: 8

Prepare ahead

1 (15-ounce) can wax beans, drained
1 (15-ounce) can red kidney beans, drained
1 (15-ounce) can chick peas, drained
1 (15-ounce) package cut green beans, frozen, cooked according to directions on package
1 medium onion, chopped
1 green pepper, chopped

- Mix all ingredients together in a large salad bowl.

Dressing

½ cup sugar
⅔ cup wine vinegar
½ cup oil
½ teaspoon salt
½ teaspoon pepper
½ teaspoon Worcestershire sauce
¼ cup chopped parsley

- Mix all ingredients except parsley together and pour over bean mixture. Marinate in refrigerator for 24 hours. Sprinkle with parsley before serving.

Penny Weill
Scarsdale, New York

CAESAR SALAD

Serves: 6 to 8

2 to 3 cloves garlic, crushed
¾ cup olive oil
2 heads romaine lettuce
1½ teaspoons Worcestershire sauce
1 teaspoon salt
Freshly ground pepper
1 egg, coddled (cooked for 1 minute)
¼ cup lemon juice
¼ cup grated Parmesan cheese
2 cups croutons, toasted
1 flat can anchovies (optional)

- Add the garlic to the oil and let stand for several hours.
- Tear the lettuce into bite-size pieces. Put in a large bowl with oil and seasonings.
- Open the egg onto the greens, sprinkle with lemon juice, add cheese and toss all together.
- Add croutons and serve immediately.

Roger Hirschhorn
Harrison, New York

CARROT SALAD

A simple salad with a touch of class.

Serves: 6 to 8

1 cup mayonnaise (preferably homemade)
½ cup sour cream
½ cup duck sauce
1 packet rich brown seasoning and broth mix
¼ teaspoon pepper

- Combine all ingredients in a large bowl. Set aside.

2 bunches carrots, grated
2 shallots, minced
1 red onion, minced
Minced parsley
Finely shredded lemon peel

- Add to dressing and mix well. Serve garnished with minced parsley and finely shredded lemon peel.

Len Feiman
White Plains, New York

CHICKEN SALAD WITH WILD RICE

Great for a special luncheon.

Serves: 4 main courses
8 buffet servings

Prepare ahead

½ cup wild rice
1½ cups water
Salt
2 cups diced poached chicken (1 cup chicken equals 1 breast)
½ cup thinly sliced green onion
½ cup diced celery
½ cup toasted blanched almonds, chopped
1 cup watercress leaves

- Rinse rice under running water. Bring 1½ cups salted water to rapid boil in medium saucepan over high heat. Stir in rice and return water to rapid boil.
- Stir rice with fork and reduce heat so water simmers gently. Cover and cook until grains puff open and white interior of rice appears, about 25 to 35 minutes.
- Rinse rice under cold water; drain well. Transfer to a large bowl.
- Add chicken, green onion, diced celery and chopped almonds.
- Add watercress 1 to 2 hours before serving.

Tarragon Vinaigrette

½ cup olive oil
¼ cup white wine vinegar (Tarragon)
1 tablespoon chopped fresh tarragon or 1 teaspoon dried, crumbled
1 teaspoon coarse salt
½ teaspoon freshly ground pepper

- Whisk oil into vinegar in medium bowl 1 drop at a time. Stir in tarragon, salt and pepper.
- Pour small amount of vinaigrette over chicken salad and toss gently, adding more vinaigrette, a little at a time, until evenly coated. Serve slightly chilled.

Note: Mix all ingredients the day before except for watercress.

Variation: Substitute 2 cups sliced fresh mushrooms for chicken.

Harriet Meyers
White Plains, New York

CHINESE CHICKEN SALAD

Crunchy and fresh tasting.

Serves: 6

4 ounces rice sticks
2 to 4 cups oil for deep frying
2 boneless skinned chicken breasts, halved
½ teaspoon salt
2 tablespoons light soy sauce
1 small head lettuce, shredded
1 Chinese cabbage, shredded
½ cup preserved red ginger, chopped

- Preheat oven to 350 degrees. Use a shallow roasting pan.
- Deep-fry rice sticks quickly, a few at a time, in very hot oil until they puff, about 1 second. Drain and remove.
- Rub chicken breasts with salt and soy sauce. Place in pan, pour 1 tablespoon oil over chicken and roast for 30 minutes. When chicken cools, break meat apart with hands into shreds. Do not cut. Set aside.

Sauce

½ cup sesame seed oil
¼ teaspoon salt
2 teaspoons sugar
½ cup white wine vinegar
½ cup light soy sauce
2 scallions, chopped fine

- Combine all the sauce ingredients in a bowl. Mix well and add scallions.
- In a large clear serving bowl, place lettuce, Chinese cabbage and chicken; toss well. Add the sauce and toss again, carefully. Arrange rice sticks on top and serve cold.

Optional ingredients to add:

1 cup water chestnuts, sliced
1½ cups snow pea pods, washed and trimmed
½ cup peanuts, unsalted
½ cup cashew nuts, unsalted

Debbie Simon
Scarsdale, New York

COLD NOODLES AND CHICKEN ORIENTALE

Serves: 4 to 6

4 cups fine egg noodles
1 tablespoon salad oil
2 cups cooked chicken, diced
½ pound (2½ cups) fresh bean sprouts
1 cucumber, peeled, seeded, and cut into julienne strips
½ cup slivered or shredded radishes
¼ cup sliced green onions

- Cook noodles according to package directions. Rinse in cold water and drain well. Toss the noodles in a large bowl with oil; cover and chill.

Sauce

⅓ cup warm water
¼ cup creamy peanut butter
2 cloves garlic, crushed
¼ cup soy sauce
¼ cup sesame or salad oil
2 tablespoons wine vinegar
4 teaspoons sugar
1 teaspoon salt
½ teaspoon ground red pepper

- Mix water and peanut butter in a small bowl until smooth. Add remaining ingredients and mix well.
- To serve, add chicken and bean sprouts to noodles. Add sauce and toss. Garnish with cucumber, radishes and green onions.

Debbie Simon
Scarsdale, New York

COLE SLAW

A new twist for an old favorite.

Serves: 18 to 24

Prepare ahead

1 medium-large green cabbage, shredded
1 small red cabbage, shredded
1 bunch carrots, peeled and shredded
1 bunch celery, finely diced
2 green peppers, finely diced
1 red pepper, finely diced
1½ cups ketchup
1½ cups prepared mild mustard
½ cup mayonnaise
¾ cup apple cider vinegar
¾ cup sugar

- In a large bowl, combine all vegetables.
- Mix remaining ingredients in a blender. Add to cabbage mixture stirring until well-blended. Refrigerate until ready to serve.

Rona Cutler
Scarsdale, New York

CRAZY TUNA SALAD

Adults will love this too.

Serves: 6

1 head lettuce, torn into bite-size pieces
2 (12½-ounce) cans tuna fish, drained
1 (5-ounce) can chow mein noodles
1 large red onion, sliced into thin rings

- Combine all ingredients in a large bowl and refrigerate.

Dressing

⅔ cup mayonnaise
⅔ cup sour cream
1 tablespoon sugar
1 tablespoon lemon juice

- In a separate bowl, mix the ingredients until smooth. Refrigerate. When ready to serve, combine with salad ingredients.

Brenda Siegler
White Plains, New York

GAZPACHO MOLD

Cool and refreshing!

Prepare ahead

Serves: 10 to 12

1 green pepper, cored and seeded, finely chopped
1 cucumber, peeled and seeded, finely chopped
3 ribs celery, finely chopped
½ red onion, finely chopped
1 (46-ounce) can tomato juice
1 tablespoon red wine vinegar
1 teaspoon chopped garlic
1 teaspoon Worcestershire sauce
3 envelopes unflavored gelatin
Salt to taste

- Lightly oil an 8-cup ring mold with vegetable oil.
- In a saucepan, pour the tomato juice, vinegar, chopped garlic, Worcestershire sauce, gelatin and salt and bring to a boil. Add the chopped vegetables to the hot tomato mixture.
- Stir to blend. Pour into mold and refrigerate until firm.

Note: The center of the mold may be filled with cottage cheese when ready to serve.

Susan Berenson
Armonk, New York

HEALTH SALAD

The flavor continues to improve.

Serves: 12

Prepare recipe a few days ahead

1 green cabbage
2 peeled cucumbers, sliced
2 carrots, sliced thin
1 green pepper, diced
2 red onions, thinly sliced
¾ cup sugar
¾ cup white vinegar
⅛ teaspoon salt
½ cup water
¾ cup vegetable oil
3 cloves garlic, sliced
1 tablespoon garlic powder, optional
1 tablespoon oregano
1 tablespoon celery seeds

- Shred cabbage in a large bowl. Add remaining ingredients and mix thoroughly.
- Refrigerate and keep covered, until ready to serve.

Note: Salad will keep in refrigerator for two weeks.

Susan Katz
Teaneck, New Jersey

HEARTS OF PALM, ARTICHOKE HEARTS, ENDIVE AND WALNUT SALAD

Serves: 6

1 (14-ounce) can artichoke hearts, drained and quartered
1 (7½-ounce) can hearts of palm, drained and sliced into julienne strips
4 endive, cut off bottom and discard; slice remainder into long strips
1 cup walnuts

Tehini Vinaigrette

1 cup olive oil
⅓ cup apple cider vinegar
2 cloves garlic
2 teaspoons Dijon-style mustard
½ teaspoon salt
1 tablespoon tehini

Blend in food processor all ingredients, except tehini. Just before serving add 1 tablespoon tehini to the vinaigrette. Blend all ingredients together. Pour over salad.

Beryl Levitt
Larchmont, New York

MOTHER'S RUSSIAN SALAD

An old-fashioned favorite.

Serves: 3 to 4

2 potatoes peeled, boiled, and diced
1 tomato, diced
2 hard-boiled eggs, diced
1 (10-ounce) package frozen peas, thawed
1 sour pickle, diced, or 1 teaspoon India relish, drained
1 cucumber, peeled and diced
1 bunch scallions, chopped
Salt and pepper to taste
2 tablespoons mayonnaise or to taste

- Mix all ingredients together. Serve on lettuce.

Harriet Mattikow

PASTA SUPREME

Serves: 6 to 8

4 fresh asparagus spears, cut diagonally in 1-inch pieces
1 large or 2 small zucchini, halved and cut into julienne strips
½ cup fresh shelled peas
1 cup broccoli flowerets
¾ pound thin spaghetti
¼ pound (1½ cups) sliced mushrooms
2 cups tomatoes, cut into ½-inch cubes
3 tablespoons fresh basil, chopped
¼ cup fresh parsley, chopped
1½ cups mayonnaise
2 teaspoons garlic, finely minced
2 tablespoons white vinegar
Salt and pepper to taste
½ cup toasted pine nuts (pignoli)

- Boil or steam the four green vegetables until crisp tender. Set aside.
- Cook spaghetti about 7 minutes or until just tender. Drain. Rinse with cold water, drain again. Toss with vegetables, mushrooms, tomatoes and herbs.
- Combine mayonnaise, garlic and vinegar, add to spaghetti mixture and toss. Add salt and pepper. Garnish with nuts.
- Serve at room temperature.

Penny Weill
Scarsdale, New York

PICKLED MUSHROOMS

A zesty combination.

Serves: 4

Prepare Ahead

In a jar shake:

1 envelope dry Italian dressing
⅓ cup tarragon vinegar
2 tablespoons water

Add:

⅔ cup oil
1 tablespoon sugar
6 drops Tabasco

• Shake all of the above thoroughly.

Pour dressing over:

1½ pounds mushrooms, cleaned and sliced
1 medium onion, sliced in rings
4 cloves garlic, crushed
1 (drained weight 6 ounces) can pitted black olives, sliced

• Refrigerate at least 3 hours or overnight.

Penny Weill
Scarsdale, New York

PICKLED RELISH

Wonderful to munch on.

Serves: 8

Prepare ahead

1 small cauliflower, cut into flowerets
2 carrots, cut into 2-inch strips
2 stalks celery cut into 1-inch strips
1 green pepper cut into 2-inch strips
1 (4-ounce) jar pimiento
1 (3-ounce) jar pitted green olives
¾ cup wine vinegar
½ cup oil
2 tablespoons sugar
2 teaspoons salt
½ teaspoon oregano
¼ teaspoon pepper
¼ cup water

- Combine all ingredients. Bring to a boil stirring occasionally.
- Reduce heat and cover. Simmer for 5 minutes.
- Cool. Refrigerate 24 hours.
- Drain and serve with toothpicks.

Marilyn Fields
Delray Beach, Florida

SESAME RICE STICK SALAD

Serves: 6

1 cup salad oil
2 ounces rice sticks
4 cups thinly shredded Chinese cabbage

- Heat the oil to 375 degrees in a wok or a deep heavy skillet. Add rice sticks, a few at a time. As soon as they are puffed, remove with a wire strainer. Drain on paper towels. Toss with Chinese cabbage.

Sesame Seed Dressing

6 tablespoons vinegar
2 tablespoons soy sauce
2 tablespoons sugar
2 tablespoons sesame oil
2 tablespoons dry sherry
2 teaspoons finely chopped fresh ginger
2 teaspoons toasted sesame seeds
2 drops Tabasco sauce (optional)

- Place all ingredients in a covered jar and shake well. Mix with shredded cabbage and rice sticks.

SEVEN LAYER SALAD

You will want to make this again and again. It is truly wonderful!

Serves: 20 for a buffet
Serves: 6 to 8 for a main luncheon course.

Prepare one day ahead

½ head iceberg lettuce or romaine, shredded
1 medium size green, red and yellow pepper, coarsely chopped
1 large red onion, coarsely chopped
3 stalks celery, coarsely chopped
1 package Birdseye® Deluxe Tender Tiny Peas, defrosted, but not cooked
1 pint mayonnaise
1 (8-ounce) package shredded Cheddar cheese
Vegetable bacon bits
A 9-inch x 4½-inch clear glass bowl

- The ingredients of the vegetables may vary in amounts, depending on the size of the glass bowl.
- Using a clear pretty bowl, layer ingredients in order listed above, leaving out bacon bits. Spread mayonnaise evenly over the top. (A metal spatula used to ice a cake is helpful.)
- Cover very tightly with plastic wrap and refrigerate overnight.
- Just before serving, sprinkle vegetable bacon bits over the top.

Note: Other combinations of vegetables may be used, or more of the same ingredients used above. Tomatoes or cucumbers are not recommended.

Variations: Radishes, sliced or chopped; zucchini, chopped; carrots, grated; yellow summer squash, chopped; water chestnuts, sliced; jicama thinly sliced, and cut into small cubes, or hard boiled eggs coarsely chopped or sliced.

Margot Sider
Boca Raton, Florida

SPINACH SALAD

An old favorite and still popular.

Serves: 6 to 8

1½ pounds fresh spinach
½ pound fresh mushrooms, sliced
3 hard cooked eggs, sliced
1 red onion, thinly sliced
½ cup vegetable bacon bits

- Wash spinach twice; spin dry thoroughly. Cut off and discard stems. Tear leaves into small pieces. Place in a clean pillowcase and put in refrigerator overnight. (This makes the spinach very crisp).
- Remove spinach from refrigerator as close to the time you are going to use it as possible. Place in large salad bowl; add remaining ingredients. Toss with salad dressing just before serving.

Salad Dressing

3 tablespoons oil
1 tablespoon vinegar
¼ teaspoon Dijon-style mustard
Salt and pepper to taste
1 clove fresh garlic, minced

- Mix all ingredients together, beat well and pour over spinach salad.

Anita Roe
Scarsdale, New York

SPINACH SALAD

Serves: 6 to 8

Dressing

⅔ cup olive oil
⅓ cup red wine vinegar
2 teaspoons Dijon-style mustard
2 teaspoons grated onion
½ teaspoon fresh lemon juice
Salt and pepper to taste

• Combine all ingredients and mix well.

Salad

1 pound spinach, washed, dried and stemmed
2 bunches watercress, leaves only
2 oranges, peeled and sectioned
1 avocado, peeled and sliced
1 green apple, peeled and sliced
¼ cup chopped walnuts

• Place in a large salad bowl. Pour dressing over salad ingredients, toss lightly. Sprinkle with chopped nuts.

Sylvia Weinsier
Rancho Mirage, California

SUNBURST SALAD

Serves: 6 to 8

Dressing

3 tablespoons cold pressed oil
1½ teaspoons lemon juice
½ teaspoon garlic powder
1 tablespoon vegetable powder

• Combine all ingredients in blender and pour over salad before serving.

Small head romaine lettuce
6 to 8 leaves Boston lettuce
½ carrot, grated
½ raw beet, peeled and grated
6 (2-inch) slivers of raw yellow squash
½ ripe avocado, cut into wedges
6 plum tomatoes, quartered

• Break the lettuce into a large bowl. Mound the grated carrot and beet in the center of greens. Arrange squash slivers star-fashion from outside edges of grated vegetables to edge of bowl. Between slivers place wedges of avocado. Place tomatoes around edge of bowl. Drizzle dressing over all.

Fae Boczko
New Rochelle, New York

SWISS GREEN PEA SALAD

An exceptionally flavorful combination.

Serves: 10 to 12

1 cup mayonnaise
2 teaspoons sugar
1 teaspoon nutmeg
2 teaspoons Dijon-style mustard
1 medium-size head iceberg lettuce, coarsely chopped
7 tablespoons vegetable bacon bits
8 ounces Swiss cheese, cut into matchstick size pieces
30 ounces frozen peas, thawed
1 red onion, thinly sliced

- In a bowl, combine mayonnaise, sugar, nutmeg and mustard; set aside.
- In a salad bowl mix together lettuce, 5 tablespoons vegetable bacon bits, cheese, peas and onion.
- Pour dressing over salad and toss gently to coat evenly.
- Season with salt and pepper if desired.
- Garnish with remaining vegetable bacon bits.

Linda Altman
Harrison, New York

SZECHUAN CUCUMBER SALAD

Serves: 4

2 cucumbers, peeled, halved lengthwise and seeded
1 carrot, thinly sliced
1 tablespoon rice vinegar
1 teaspoon sugar
1 teaspoon soy sauce
Freshly grated ginger to taste
1 teaspoon sesame oil
½ teaspoon salt (optional)

- Slice cucumbers into ¼-inch slices. Toss with rest of ingredients.
- Chill until ready to serve.

Carol Goldstone
Portchester, New York

TABOULE

Wonderful flavors from the Middle-East.

Serves: 4

½ cup fine bulgur (cracked wheat)
1 cup warm water
2 tablespoons oil
1 bunch parsley, finely chopped
1 bunch scallions, chopped
2 tomatoes, seeded and chopped
1 teaspoon cumin
1 teaspoon fresh mint leaves, minced or ½ teaspoon dried
1 teaspoon salt
Juice of 1 lemon

- Place bulgur in a large bowl with water. Let sit ½ hour. Drain well, squeezing out as much water as possible. Add oil and the remaining ingredients. Mix well.

Betty Laboz
Brooklyn, New York

TURKEY PASTA SALAD PRIMAVERA

Serves: 4 to 6

Prepare ahead

8 ounces thin spaghetti, cooked according to package directions, and drained
¾ cup herbed vinegar and oil salad dressing
2 cups cubed roasted breast of turkey
⅓ cup mayonnaise
2 medium tomatoes, diced
1 cup fresh mushrooms, sliced
½ cup frozen peas, thawed
1 green or red pepper, diced
¼ cup sliced green onions
2 tablespoons minced parsley
½ cup seasoned croutons, (optional)

- In a large bowl, toss hot spaghetti with salad dressing. Cover and chill for 2 hours.
- When ready to serve, combine turkey with mayonnaise. Toss with pasta and vegetables. Sprinkle with parsley and croutons.

Morton Metzger
New York, New York

TORTELLINI SALAD

Serves: 12

2 pounds tortellini (stuffed with cheese), cooked according to directions on package
½ pound small shell macaroni, cooked according to directions on package
2 (8½-ounce) cans artichoke hearts, drained and sliced
1 (drained weight 6-ounces) can black olives, drained and sliced
2 red peppers, thinly sliced
1 cup sliced scallions
1 (2-ounce) jar pignoli nuts
¼ cup fresh dill, chopped
¼ cup fresh basil, chopped
¼ cup fresh parsley, chopped
½ cup grated Parmesan cheese, or to taste
6 radishes, sliced paper thin

Dressing

1 cup olive oil
½ cup wine vinegar
2 teaspoons Dijon-style mustard

- Mix ingredients thoroughly.

- Cook tortellini and small shells, drain and put into a large salad bowl. Add artichokes, olives, peppers, scallions and nuts.
- When ready to serve, add herbs, cheese, dressing and radishes.

Aileen Wolff
White Plains, New York

SAUCES

Bay Basil Savory Coriander Sage Rosemary Parsley Mint Coriander Sage Rosemary
Sage Rosemary Parsley Mint Cinnamon Marjoram
Marjoram Thyme Juniper Bay
Bay Basil Savory Coriander Sage Rosemary Parsley Mint Cinnamon Parsley
Sage Rosemary Parsley Mint Cinnamon Marjoram Thyme Juniper Coriander Sage
Marjoram Thyme Juniper Bay Basil Savory Coriander Bay Basil

PERTINENT PARTICULARS

- If sauce is too salty, add a whole peeled raw potato and cook gently to absorb the salt. Discard potato.

- In recipes for spaghetti or barbeque sauce, chopped apple may be substituted for sugar.

- To deglaze: pour off any fat before adding ¼ cup or more hot water or stock to pan juices. Cook on top of stove stirring and scraping the solidified particles until well-blended. The addition of wine or dry sherry hastens the deglazing process.

- To clarify butter: in a heavy saucepan, melt sweet butter over low heat without stirring. Do not brown. Skim off the white foam that rises to the top and discard. Carefully pour off the clear yellow liquid butter into a container, leaving remaining white particles in the pan.

ALFREDO SAUCE FOR LINGUINE

Yield: 1 cup

½ cup butter or margarine
⅓ cup half and half or light cream
1 egg yolk
¼ cup Parmesan cheese, grated

- In a saucepan, melt butter; add cream, egg yolk and cheese. Stir with whisk to blend. Heat slowly, stirring constantly until heated through.
- Pour over cooked linguine and mix together.

Sharon Strongin
Scarsdale, New York

BARBECUE SAUCE

Yield: 3½ cups

¼ cup vinegar
1½ cups water
¼ cup sugar
4 teaspoons prepared mustard
¼ teaspoon pepper
1 tablespoon salt or to taste
¼ teaspoon cayenne pepper
2 thick slices lemon
2 medium onions, sliced
½ cup margarine
1 cup ketchup or chili sauce
3 tablespoons Worcestershire sauce

- Combine all ingredients in a saucepan. Simmer uncovered for 20 minutes. Cover and cook for 40 minutes longer. Refrigerate. Reheat when ready to use.

Note: This is an old Southern recipe, and is perfect for chicken. The original recipe was used for barbecued chickens grilled outdoors, and given to me as a gesture of friendship from a Southerner to a Northerner.

Estelle Silverstone
Harrison, New York

CHICKEN FAT WITHOUT CHICKEN FAT

Tastes like the real thing.

Yield: 3 cups

1 (24-ounce) bottle peanut oil
6 large carrots, sliced
6 large onions, sliced

• Fry the carrots and onions in oil slowly until brown. Drain and cool. This takes on color and odor and consistency of real chicken fat.

Sondra Feinberg
Harrison, New York

CHOCOLATE FUDGE SAUCE

Don't count the calories on this one!

Yield: 2 cups

2 squares (1 ounce each) unsweetened chocolate
2 tablespoons butter
1 teaspoon vanilla
1 (16-ounce) can sweetened condensed milk

• Melt chocolate and butter in a double boiler. Remove from heat and cool slightly. Add vanilla and condensed milk to the chocolate mixture. Stir until smooth. If too thick, when ready to serve, add a small amount of boiling water stirring to desired consistency.

Carolyn Davis
Armonk, New York

CRANBERRY GLAZE

Yield: 2 cups

1 cup cranberry cocktail juice
1 cup light brown sugar, firmly packed
1 teaspoon dry mustard
¼ teaspoon ground cloves
¼ teaspoon allspice
1 teaspoon vinegar

- Combine all ingredients in a saucepan. Stir thoroughly and bring to a boil. Reduce heat to simmer and cook until thickened; about 20 minutes. Remove from heat
- Use as a glaze for chicken or corned beef.

Corrine Katz
White Plains, New York

CUMBERLAND SAUCE

Yield: 2 cups

1 cup red currant jelly
1 (6-ounce) can frozen orange juice concentrate, defrosted
4 tablespoons dry sherry
1 teaspoon dry mustard
⅛ teaspoon ground ginger
¼ teaspoon hot pepper sauce

- In a pot, combine all ingredients and simmer until smooth.

Note: This sauce is wonderful for baked or broiled chicken.

Lucille Scheer
Purchase, New York

GREEN GODDESS SALAD DRESSING

Yield: 1¼ cups

1 cup mayonnaise
1 clove garlic
3 tablespoons tarragon vinegar
1 flat can anchovies, drained
3 tablespoons scallions, chopped
1 cup parsley, chopped
1 tablespoon lemon juice
Salt and pepper to taste

- Mix all ingredients in a blender.
- Use on green salads or as a dressing for pasta salad.

Hope Hirschhorn
Harrison, New York

HERB MAYONNAISE FOR FISH

Yield: 1¼ cups

2 tablespoons finely chopped onion
2 tablespoons Dijon-style mustard
1 teaspoon Worcestershire sauce
¼ teaspoon Tabasco sauce
Salt and pepper to taste
2 teaspoons red wine vinegar
1 egg yolk
1 cup oil; peanut, corn or vegetable
1 tablespoon finely chopped chives
2 teaspoons finely chopped tarragon
1 tablespoon finely chopped parsley

- In a mixing bowl combine onion, mustard, Worcestershire sauce, Tabasco sauce, salt and pepper to taste, vinegar and egg yolk.
- Gradually add the oil beating constantly. When the mixture is thickened add the chives, tarragon and parsley.
- Spoon over poached fish when ready to serve.

Blanche Gutstein
New York, New York

HOT FUDGE SAUCE

A chocolate lovers delight!

Yield: 4 cups

8 ounces unsweetened chocolate
2 cups sugar
1 (13-ounce) can evaporated milk
1 teaspoon vanilla

- Melt chocolate in double boiler, add sugar and stir. Cook covered in double boiler for ½ hour on very low heat. Mixture will be thick. Add evaporated milk and vanilla; cook for 1 minute stirring to blend until smooth.

Hope Hirschhorn
Harrison, New York

LEMON CRÈME

Yield: 1 pint

¼ pound unsalted butter
1 cup sugar
¼ cup lemon juice
Grated rind of 1 lemon
2 eggs, well beaten

- In top half of double boiler put butter, sugar, lemon juice and rind. Cook over simmering water stirring until butter is melted.
- Add the eggs and continue cooking until thickened, stirring frequently. This should take about 15 minutes.
- Very versatile. Spoon over fruits, spread on toast or pound cake. Freezes well and defrosts almost immediately. Recipe can easily be doubled.

- *Variation:* Add 1 pint heavy cream, whipped, to Lemon Crème and serve as a dessert.

Len Feiman
White Plains, New York

MARINADE FOR STEAK OR LAMB

Yield: 1½ cups

Prepare ahead

1 (5-ounce) bottle soy sauce
½ cup sherry
½ cup brown sugar
1½ tablespoons garlic powder

- Mix all of the ingredients together and pour over meat. Marinate for at least 5 hours.

Amy Singer
Harrison, New York

MARSHMALLOW ICING

Yield: Enough for two 8-inch layers

2 egg whites, very cold
½ teaspoon cream of tartar
Slightly less than 1 cup of Karo light syrup
1 teaspoon vanilla

- Chill a large bowl and beaters.
- In a saucepan, heat syrup over a low flame; add vanilla. Cook until heated through.
- Beat egg whites until frothy. Add cream of tartar and continue to beat. Drip syrup very slowly into the egg whites. Beat until stiff and satiny.

Note: This is wonderful on chocolate cake.

MUSTARD HOLLANDAISE SAUCE

Yield: 1½ cups

3 tablespoons dry mustard
¼ teaspoon salt
½ teaspoon sugar
2 tablespoons water
½ pound butter
2 egg yolks
1 tablespoon water
1 tablespoon lemon juice

- Mix mustard, salt, sugar and water. Let stand for 10 minutes. Clarify butter by melting butter in 200 degree oven, using a one quart heatproof glass measuring cup.
- Skim top off melted butter with small spoon. Discard the white milky substance at the bottom.
- Pour ¾ cup of the clarified butter into a heavy saucepan and whisk in egg yolks. Cook over low heat whisking rapidly until mixture becomes thick and foaming like a custard, not more than 10 minutes. Remove saucepan from heat.
- Add remaining butter beating vigorously. Add lemon juice and stir in the mustard mixture.
- This sauce is good on breaded fish fillets.

Blanche Gutstein
New York, New York

Editor's Note: We found this tasty sauce especially good on steamed vegetables.

ORANGE SAUCE FOR ROAST DUCK

Yield: Enough for 2 ducks

Rind of 1 navel orange
Water to cover

- Peel the rind from the orange. Be sure not to have the white portion included. Cut the rind into thin julienne strips.
- Place in a saucepan and cover with water. Bring to a rolling boil. Drain. You will have about 1 tablespoon julienne of orange rind. Replenish water and repeat this process twice more to eliminate the bitter taste from the orange rind. Drain.

1 cup orange juice
½ (10-ounce) jar currant jelly
1 clove garlic, minced (optional)
3 tablespoons cornstarch
¼ cup cold water

- Mix orange rind, juice, jelly and garlic in a saucepan. Dissolve cornstarch in water and add. Cook and stir over low heat until sauce thickens.

Note: Sauce may also be used for Cornish hen or chicken.

Corrine Katz
White Plains, New York

RASPBERRY SAUCE

Yield: 1 cup

3 (10-ounce) packages frozen raspberries, drained
3 tablespoons sugar
2 tablespoons Frambois or Kirschwasser

- Drain raspberries, but save juice for another purpose. Purée in a blender and push through a fine sieve to remove seeds. Put the puréed berries into a small saucepan with the sugar and liqueur. Cook over low heat until well mixed and heated enough for sugar to melt.
- If the sauce seems too thick it can be thinned out with some of the raspberry juice.
- Chill and serve.

Sherry Lieb
Livingston, New Jersey

RAW RADISH SAUCE

Beautiful with raw vegetables!

Yield: 1 Pint

Prepare ahead

1 cup finely chopped radishes
1 (8-ounce) package cream cheese
1 garlic clove, minced
1 tablespoon fresh lemon juice
¾ teaspoon salt
½ teaspoon dried dillweed
Parsley for garnish

- Combine first 6 ingredients in food processor and mix well. Season with freshly ground pepper. Chill 4 hours to several days. Garnish with parsley. Serve with crudités.

Marcia Rosenthal
Pittsburgh, Pennsylvania

SWEET AND HOT MUSTARD

You will never buy mustard again!

Yield: 1 quart

Prepare ahead

4 ounces mustard powder
1 cup imported tarragon vinegar
½ cup sugar
¼ pound butter, room temperature
6 eggs
Juice of 1 lemon

- In top of double boiler put mustard powder and tarragon vinegar (do not blend). Let stand covered overnight.
- Uncover, blend and heat at a low temperature. Water should simmer.
- Add sugar and butter, stir until butter melts.
- Add eggs one at a time, stirring constantly.
- Let cook five additional minutes stirring constantly. Remove from heat.
- Add lemon juice and mix. Mixture will not look perfectly smooth.

Note: This will keep, refrigerated, for several weeks.

Len Feiman
White Plains, New York

* THEODORE SAUCE

Yield: 1½ cups

3 tablespoons butter or margarine
1 cup chili sauce
¼ cup white wine
1 tablespoon Worcestershire sauce
1 tablespoon parsley, chopped
Dash garlic powder

- Melt butter or margarine in saucepan. Add chili sauce, wine, Worcestershire sauce. Stir over low heat until all ingredients are smoothly blended. Add chopped parsley and garlic powder.
- Bring to boil, stirring constantly. Remove from heat immediately.

* Family cook for 40 years who apprenticed as a young boy from Georgia on the Florida East Coast railroads.

Diane Hallenbeck
White Plains, New York

THOUSAND ISLAND DRESSING

Yield: 4 cups

1 teaspoon dry mustard
1 teaspoon salt
1 teaspoon confectioners sugar
2 egg yolks
2 tablespoons white vinegar
1½ cups olive oil
2 tablespoons lemon juice
1 cup mayonnaise
⅓ cup chili sauce
2 tablespoons green pepper, chopped
1 tablespoon chives, chopped
1 tablespoon pimiento, chopped
½ cup sour cream

- Mix dry ingredients together. Add egg yolks and when well-beaten add ½ teaspoon vinegar. Gradually add oil, drop by drop, beating constantly. As the mixture thickens, dilute with remaining vinegar and lemon juice.
- To mayonnaise, add chili sauce, green pepper, chives and pimiento. Fold in sour cream. Combine both mixtures.

Joan Safir
Stamford, Connecticut

TOMATO AND ORANGE SAUCE

Yield: 3 cups

¼ cup margarine
1 cup onions, chopped
4 large tomatoes, peeled, seeded and chopped
1 cup orange juice
2 tablespoons orange concentrate
1 to 2 teaspoons salt or to taste
1 tablespoon brown sugar

- Melt margarine in medium size saucepan. Add onions and sauté until tender.
- Add tomatoes and simmer 10 minutes.
- Stir in orange juice, concentrate, salt and sugar. Simmer 5 minutes more.

Note: Use for fish or for basting baked chicken.

Rose Rabbino

TURKEY GRAVY

Yield: $1\frac{1}{2}$ quarts

6 cups water
Turkey giblets, neck and gizzard; omit liver
1 large onion, peeled and left whole
2 large carrots, peeled
4 stalks celery, with greens
1 large clove garlic
Salt and pepper to taste

- In a pot, put cold water and giblets. Bring to a boil and skim off the brown particles that form at the top. Add onion, carrots, celery, garlic and salt and pepper. Reduce heat and simmer for 1 hour.
- Remove the giblets from the pot and when cool enough to handle, carefully remove the meat from the neck and cut the gizzard in half.
- In batches, add the giblets, all vegetables and liquid to a food processor or blender and purée. Correct seasoning if necessary.
- When turkey is finished cooking, remove from roasting pan. Boil 1 to 2 cups water and add to the pan. Scrape all the particles that cling to the bottom. Pour liquid through a strainer and put into a container. Place in the freezer. This will cause the fat to rise and set. Skim fat off and add the remaining liquid to the gravy mixture. Stir thoroughly. Heat over low flame until hot.

Note: This makes a nice, fairly thick gravy without adding any flour.

Corrine Katz
White Plains, New York

VEGETABLE MARINADE FOR SALAD OR PASTA

An unusual tasty combination.

Serves: 4 as a salad
4 to 6 with pasta

Prepare ahead

1 (drained weight 6-ounces) can black olives, pitted and sliced
1 (14-ounce) can artichokes, sliced
2 small zucchini, sliced
1 (7½-ounce) can hearts of palm
1 small onion, sliced
1 envelope dry buttermilk dressing
1 small bottle Italian dressing
8 to 10 cherry tomatoes, sliced
1 (8-ounce) can bamboo shoots

- In a large salad bowl, mix all ingredients together. Cover and marinate in refrigerator for 12 hours or more. Stir occasionally. Marinade keeps well in the refrigerator.
- Serve on lettuce or mix with cooked pasta.

Shirley S. Goller
Mission, Kansas

SOUPS
Bay Basil Savory Coriander Sage Rosemary Parsley Mint Coriander Sage Rosemary
Rosemary Parsley Mint Cinnamon Marjoram
Marjoram Thyme Juniper Bay
Bay Basil Savory Coriander Sage Rosemary Parsley Mint Cinnamon Parsley
Sage Rosemary Parsley Mint Cinnamon Marjoram Thyme Juniper Coriander Sage
Marjoram Thyme Juniper Bay Basil Savory Coriander Bay Basil

PERTINENT PARTICULARS

- Soups made with meat, bones or chicken should be prepared a day ahead so that the fat can be skimmed off.

- To remove fat from soup, chill the soup. The fat rises and will solidify when cold. Use a paper towel floated over the top to absorb the fat. Any fat remaining may be removed with a spoon.

- Make an extra pot of chicken soup and freeze in ice cube trays. When frozen, remove from freezer trays and place in a heavy duty plastic bag and return to freezer. You will always have chicken cubes ready for any recipe requiring chicken stock.

CABBAGE SOUP

Yield: 5 quarts

Prepare ahead

3 pounds flanken or lean short ribs
3½ quarts water
6 beef bones
1 (3-pound) head cabbage, shredded
Salt to taste
1 (35-ounce) can whole tomatoes
2 onions, sliced
3 stalks celery, diced
Juice of 1 lemon
1 tablespoon sugar
2 tablespoons brown sugar
8 ginger snaps, broken in half

- In a large soup pot, cook meat and bones in enough water to cover. Cook for 15 minutes and skim the top. Add remaining ingredients.
- Simmer, covered, on low heat for 3 hours.
- Refrigerate overnight. When ready to serve, remove fat and reheat.

Hope Hirschhorn
Harrison, New York

CARROT SOUP

An interesting combination and easy to do.

Serves: 2

2 medium carrots, peeled and diced
1 cup chicken stock
¼ cup minced onion
Pinch salt
1 bay leaf
Pinch nutmeg or ginger
½ cup orange juice
Sprigs of mint

- Combine the carrots, stock, onion, salt, bay leaf, nutmeg or ginger and cook for 20 minutes.
- Remove carrots and onion and purée very well. Discard bay leaf. Return to pot and add orange juice. Reheat.
- Serve with a sprig of mint on top.
- May be served hot or cold. Recipe doubles and triples well.

Elaine Satuloff
Harrison, New York

CHICK PEA DITALINI SOUP

Serves: 4 to 6

Prepare ahead

1 cup ditalini macaroni
2 quarts water
2 to 4 bouillon cubes
1 medium onion, chopped
1 tablespoon oil
1 (19-ounce) can chick peas, plus liquid, or cannelini beans
1/8 teaspoon garlic powder or to taste
2 teaspoons dried parsley
Salt and pepper to taste

- Boil ditalini for 10 minutes in 2 quarts of water containing the bouillion cubes. Do not drain!
- In a skillet, brown the onion in oil. Add this to the ditalini, along with the chick peas and liquid. Season with garlic powder, salt, pepper, and parsley. Cook soup 5 more minutes. It is preferable to make this soup one day in advance to allow it to marinate and thicken; thin with water if necessary. Adjust seasoning and top with grated cheese.

Barbara Blau
Short Hills, New Jersey

CHICKEN SOUP

Yield: 4½ quarts

Prepare ahead

1 whole 6-pound roasting chicken, split in half
4 whole chicken breasts, split in half
5 pounds giblets; necks, backs, gizzards
8 celery stalks, cut in half
5 carrots, peeled, cut in half
2 onions, whole
Salt, pepper and garlic to taste
Parsley (optional)
4½ quarts water or enough to cover all ingredients in pot

- Use a 12 quart soup pot.
- Place all ingredients in pot and bring to a boil. Cover and cook on very low light for 3 hours.
- Remove chicken and carrots and set aside. Discard other ingredients. Strain soup into a large bowl and place in the refrigerator until all fat rises to the top; several hours or overnight. Remove fat.
- Mash carrots and add to the clear defatted soup. This adds flavor and color.
- Reheat soup when ready to serve or place in freezer containers and freeze.

Note: The giblets are the secret to good chicken soup. Use chicken for any recipe requiring cooked chicken.

Hope Hirschhorn
Harrison, New York

CHILLED FRESH TOMATO AND BASIL SOUP

A perfect beginning to your meal.

Serves: 4

Prepare ahead

4 tomatoes, peeled, seeded and quartered
½ cup olive oil
¼ cup wine vinegar
4 cloves of garlic
3 slices of white bread
3 cups tomato juice
15 leaves of basil
Salt and pepper to taste

- Put all the ingredients in a bowl and let stand in the refrigerator, for 24 hours.
- Put all ingredients in a food processor and mix well.
- Chill again for several hours before serving.

Goldie Feigert
Katonah, New York

COLD CUCUMBER SOUP

Prepare ahead

Serves: 2 to 3

2 cucumbers, peeled and seeded
1 to 2 garlic cloves, minced
⅔ cup sour cream
1 cup (8-ounces) plain yogurt
2 tablespoons plus 2 teaspoons fresh dill, for garnish
Salt and pepper to taste
1 tablespoon chopped walnuts

- Place cucumbers, garlic, sour cream and yogurt in a blender or food processor. Blend until smooth.
- Pour into a bowl and add dill, salt and pepper. Mix thoroughly and chill in refrigerator.
- Garnish with remaining dill and walnuts.

Renee Nussbaum
Boynton Beach, Florida

ESCAROLE AND CANNELINI BEAN SOUP

Incredibly quick, easy and delicious!

Serves: 4 to 6

1 pound escarole or spinach
½ cup water
1 (16-ounce) can of cannelini beans and juice
½ teaspoon salt
½ teaspoon pepper
½ teaspoon garlic salt
1 tablespoon butter
Grated Parmesan cheese

- Wash greens under cold water. Cook in a covered pot in ½ cup water for 10 to 15 minutes until thoroughly wilted. Add beans and juice. Season with salt, pepper, garlic and butter.
- Serve piping hot with grated cheese.

Barbara Blau
Short Hills, New Jersey

ESCAROLE AND RICE SOUP

Soup in sixteen minutes!

Serves: 6

3 tablespoons olive oil
¼ cup finely chopped onion
1 clove minced garlic
1½ pounds escarole, washed and chopped
8 cups chicken soup
¼ cup rice, raw
¼ teaspoon freshly ground pepper

- Heat the oil in a soup pot. Sauté onion and garlic until tender.
- Add escarole and cook for 3 minutes, stirring. Add 1 cup of broth, cover and simmer for 3 minutes until limp. Add rice, remaining soup and pepper. Simmer for 10 minutes.

Barbara Blau
Short Hills, New York

GAZPACHO

A summertime pleaser.

Prepare ahead

Serves: 8

1 cup chopped, peeled tomatoes
½ cup chopped green pepper
½ cup chopped celery
½ cup chopped cucumber
¼ cup chopped onion
2 teaspoons snipped parsley
2 teaspoons snipped chives
1 small garlic clove, minced
2 to 3 tablespoons tarragon wine vinegar
2 tablespoons oil
1 teaspoon salt
¼ teaspoon fresh ground pepper
½ teaspoon Worcestershire sauce
2 cups tomato juice
½ to 1 cup croutons
Chopped vegetables for garnish (your choice)

- Combine all the above ingredients except croutons and vegetables for garnishing.
- Purée in blender.
- Chill for 8 hours.
- Garnish with croutons and chopped vegetables of your choice.

Myra Goldberg
Los Angeles, California

GREEN SPLIT PEA SOUP

Your family will ask for this again and again.

Serves: 6

7 cups water
5 to 6 beef marrow bones
1 (16-ounce) package green split peas
1 large onion
4 whole carrots, peeled
4 stalks celery, cut into large pieces
2 medium turnips, peeled and left whole
2 large parsnips, peeled and left whole
1 large clove garlic, peeled, left whole
1 bay leaf
1 bunch Italian parsley
Salt and pepper to taste

- Put the water and bones in a large soup pot. Bring to a boil and simmer for about 10 to 15 minutes. Skim off as much of the foam as possible.
- Put the peas in colander and let hot tap water run over the peas for about 5 minutes. Remove any foreign substances and drain. (You can also boil 3 to 4 cups water, put peas in a bowl and let stand for 5 minutes. Drain before adding to soup pot.)
- Place peas and remaining ingredients in pot. Cover and bring to a boil. Reduce heat to a very low simmer and cook gently for 1 to 1½ hours or until split peas are tender and have dissolved. Be sure to stir from time to time. When soup is finished, remove bones and discard bay leaf.
- In a blender or food processor, purée the soup and remaining ingredients in several batches. Return the purée to soup pot and correct seasoning. Serve hot.

Note: Soup can be diluted with chicken stock or water. Freezes well.

Corrine Katz
White Plains, New York

INSTANT SUMMER SOUP

Serves: 1

1 tomato, peeled
1 dollop of sour cream
Salt and pepper to taste

- Place all ingredients in blender and blend until thick.

Note: I have also partially frozen this mixture and served it in a champagne glass. Decorate with a little sour cream and minced chives.

Barbara Blau
Short Hills, New Jersey

Editor's Note: 1 tablespoon fresh basil or ½ teaspoon dried plus a dash of Tabasco can also be added.

MINESTRONE SOUP

Serves: 12 to 14

1 quart water
½ cup dry navy beans
4 tablespoons margarine
1 cup fresh peas
1 cup diced unpeeled zucchini
1 cup diced potatoes
1 cup diced carrots
⅓ cup diced celery
2 tablespoons finely chopped onions
½ cup finely chopped leeks, using an inch or two of the greens
2 cups canned tomatoes, drained (save liquid in case you need extra in soup)
2 quarts chicken broth
1 bay leaf
Salt, pepper and parsley to taste
½ cup rice

- Bring 1 quart water to boil; add beans. Boil 2 minutes. Remove from heat and let soak 1 hour. Simmer for about another ½ hour or until slightly underdone. Drain and set aside.
- Melt margarine in a large skillet and sauté peas, zucchini, potatoes, carrots and celery for 2 to 3 minutes. Do not brown. Set aside.
- Cook onions and leeks in margarine until soft (slightly underdone).
  Put the onions and leeks into a large pot with vegetables, tomatoes, chicken stock and seasonings. Bring to boil.
- Add beans and rice. Cook until rice is tender (about 20 minutes).
- Remove the bay leaf and parsley before serving.

Carol Solomon
New York, New York

SWEET AND SOUR BEET SOUP

(Hot Borscht)

Serves: 8 to 10

3 tablespoons oil
1 onion, chopped
2 cloves garlic, finely minced
4 to 5 large beets, raw, peeled and coarsely grated
1 (8-ounce) can tomato purée
¼ cup red wine vinegar or to taste
1 teaspoon sugar or to taste
8 cups beef stock, preferably home made
½ cabbage, coarsely shredded
Salt and pepper to taste
Minced fresh dill, optional

- Heat oil in a large stock pot; add onion and cook until softened. Add garlic and cook, stirring until onions are just browned. Add beets, tomato purée, vinegar, sugar and 4 cups stock. Bring to boil, lower heat and simmer about 20 minutes. Add cabbage and remaining stock. Continue to simmer 15 to 20 minutes. Correct seasonings, adjust sugar-vinegar ratio.
- Serve hot with minced dill.

Len Feiman
White Plains, New York

TURKEY SOUP

Don't throw that turkey carcass away-make soup!

Yield: 2 to 2½ quarts

1 turkey carcass plus bones (carcass may have to be broken in half)
8 cups water
1 large onion, left whole
4 carrots, peeled and left whole
4 stalks celery with tops, cut in half
1 bunch Italian parsley
1 (6-ounce) package vegetable soup mix with mushrooms
1 clove garlic, peeled
Salt and pepper to taste

- Put all the ingredients in a large soup pot except for the small packet in the soup mix.
- Bring to a boil and then reduce heat to simmer. Cover and cook for 1¼ hours stirring occasionally. Add the packet and cook for another 15 minutes.
- When soup is finished, remove carcass. When cool enough to handle, remove meat from bones and return meat to soup. Carefully remove any bones remaining in the pot. Slice the carrots and return to soup. Serve hot.

Corrine Katz
White Plains, New York

VEGETABLE SOUP

Thick and delicious!

Yield: 7 quarts

Prepare ahead

3 pounds lean flanken or lean short ribs
6 beef bones
5 quarts water
1 cup barley, put into a colander and thoroughly rinsed
1 cup navy beans
1 cup yellow split peas
1 cup green split peas
1 cup small dried lima beans
2 medium onions, quartered
3 stalks celery, sliced diagonally into 1-inch pieces
4 carrots, sliced diagonally into 1-inch pieces
2 large potatoes, peeled and cut into eighths
1 small head cabbage, shredded
1 (35-ounce) can tomatoes, do not drain
1 teaspoon sugar
Salt, pepper and garlic powder to taste
1 (10-ounce) package frozen mixed vegetables

- Place the meat, bones and water in a 12 quart pot. Bring to a boil and simmer for 15 minutes. Skim the surface.
- Add the remaining ingredients, except the frozen vegetables. Simmer over low heat for 3 hours.
- Add frozen vegetables during the last ten minutes of cooking.
- Remove meat, discard marrow bones, and refrigerate meat and soup overnight.
- When ready to serve, remove all fat. Reheat soup with meat and serve.

Note: Any other vegetables of your choice may be added; peas, corn, green beans, mushrooms.

Hope Hirschhorn
Harrison, New York

ZUCCHINI SOUP

A summer or autumn delight.

Yield: 1½ quarts

2 tablespoons margarine
1 large onion, sliced
1 leek, white part only, sliced
½ teaspoon curry powder
4 cups chicken broth
6 medium-size potatoes, peeled and cut into large cubes
6 medium zucchini, cut into cubes, do not peel

- Melt the margarine in a soup pot. Add the onion and leek. Cook for 5 minutes. Add curry powder, stirring for 2 minutes. Add chicken broth and potatoes. Cook for 10 minutes. Add zucchini and cook for 15 minutes. Set aside and let cool for 10 minutes.
- In batches, place all ingredients in a blender or food processor and purée. Reheat just before serving.

Note: You can add 1 cup of very small boiled elbow macaroni (cooked "al dente") to the soup.

Eve Ebenhart
Delray Beach, Florida

Bay Basil Savory Coriander Sage Rosemary Parsley Mint Coriander Sage
Sage Rosemary Parsley Mint Cinnamon
Mayoram Thyme Juniper Bay
Bay Basil Savory Coriander Sage Rosemary Parsley Mint Cinnamon Parsley
Sage Rosemary Parsley Mint Cinnamon Mayoram Thyme Juniper Coriander Sage
Mayoram Thyme Juniper Bay Basil Savory Coriander Bay Basil

VEGETABLES

PERTINENT PARTICULARS

- Place a slice of brown bread on top of cabbage when cooking. This eliminates the cabbage odor.
- To peel shallots, place in boiling water for 1 to 2 minutes (no longer). Use a skimmer or slotted spoon to remove from pot, and while still warm, peel the skins off.
- To peel a tomato easily, place in boiling water for 1 minute. Skin will then easily come off. To seed; cut in half and gently squeeze the juice and seeds out.
- To cook asparagus; place a rubber band around the bunch of asparagus and stand them up in a tall coffee pot with water.
- If a recipe calls for water chestnuts, peel and slice heavy stalks of fresh broccoli and use as a substitute.
- Lemon peel steamed with cauliflower will keep it white.
- Use leftover mushroom stems in mushroom soup, mushroom omelettes, or sauté with onions and use to stuff baked potatoes.
- To keep vegetables warm and crisp, place in oven on a low temperature and keep door slightly open.

ARTICHOKE MARGOT

Serves: 4

1 (10-ounce) package frozen chopped spinach, cooked according to package directions and thoroughly drained
¼ pound mushrooms; at least 6 large size
3 tablespoons butter
½ tablespoon flour
¼ cup milk
¼ teaspoon salt
1 (8½-ounce) can artichoke bottoms

Sour Cream Hollandaise

½ cup sour cream
½ cup mayonnaise
⅛ cup lemon juice

- Combine and blend all ingredients in a saucepan. Heat slowly over low heat. Set aside.

- Preheat oven to 375 degrees. Use a buttered casserole large enough to hold artichokes in one layer.
- In a skillet sauté the mushroom tops in 1 tablespoon butter, set aside.
- Chop the mushroom stems and sauté in 1 tablespoon butter.
- In a saucepan make a cream sauce by combining 1 tablespoon melted butter and adding the flour, stirring with a wooden spoon until smooth. Remove from heat and add milk slowly stirring until smooth. Add salt, chopped mushrooms and spinach to the cream sauce.
- Drain artichoke bottoms, rinse well, drain again. Top each artichoke bottom with a mound of the spinach mixture and then a generous spoonful of Hollandaise. Top with a mushroom cap. Place in the casserole and bake for 20 minutes until heated through.

Note: This dish can be made ahead of time, refrigerated and then heated before serving.

Margot Sider
Boca Raton, Florida

ASPARAGUS RAVIGOTTE

Serves: Count on ½ pound (6 to 8 spears) per person

2½ to 3 pounds asparagus

Sauce

3 tablespoons white wine vinegar
1 tablespoon lemon juice
1 teaspoon minced flat parsley
1 teaspoon minced chives
Pinch each of dry tarragon and dry chervil
1 teaspoon capers, squeezed dry and then chopped
1½ teaspoons grated onion
8 tablespoons olive oil
1 hard-boiled egg, chopped fine
Salt and freshly ground pepper to taste

- Stand asparagus, tips up, in two inches of slightly salted water and steam, covered, about 3 or 5 minutes until slightly "al dente". Remove to serving platter.
- For the sauce, blend all ingredients together, except the oil and egg. When it is well mixed, blend in the oil and finally the chopped egg. Just before serving, spoon over the room-temperature or slightly chilled asparagus.

Gen Vergari
Yonkers, New York

AUDREY'S BAKED SQUASH

A wonderful way to serve squash.

Serves: 6 to 8

3 pounds yellow summer squash, halved, seeded and coarsely chopped
½ cup onions, chopped
½ cup butter
2 eggs, beaten
1 tablespoon sugar
1 teaspoon salt
½ teaspoon pepper
½ cup bread crumbs

- Preheat oven to 375 degrees. Use a 1½-quart baking dish.
- In a saucepan, boil the squash in a small amount of water until tender. Drain and mash.
- Sauté onions in 1 tablespoon of butter. Add to squash. Add eggs, ½ the remaining butter, sugar, salt and pepper. Mix thoroughly.
- Pour mixture into dish. Spread remainder of butter over the top. Sprinkle with bread crumbs. Bake for about 1 hour or until brown on top.

Audrey Mann
Boca Raton, Florida

BROCCOLI PIE

A delightful blending of flavors.

Serves: 4 to 6

1 medium onion, grated
3 tablespoons butter
1 (10-ounce) package frozen chopped broccoli
2 tablespoons flour
½ cup milk, room temperature
2 tablespoons sherry
½ cup mayonnaise
3 eggs, beaten
Salt and pepper to taste
2 to 3 tablespoons grated cheese, your choice
Paprika to taste

- Preheat oven to 350 degrees. Grease a 9-inch pie plate.
- Sauté onion in 1 tablespoon butter until soft. Set aside.
- Cook broccoli according to package directions and drain.
- In a saucepan, melt 2 tablespoons butter. Stir in flour with a wooden spoon. Add milk slowly, stirring constantly over low heat until thickened. Remove from heat and cool. Blend in sherry, mayonnaise and eggs. Stir and combine this mixture with onions and broccoli. Season with salt and pepper. Turn into a pie plate. Sprinkle with cheese and paprika. Bake for 30 minutes or until firm in center.

Ruth Rosenthal
New York, New York

Editor's note: This freezes well after being baked and cooled.

BUTTERNUT SQUASH

Serves: 4

1 butternut squash
1 small Bermuda onion, chopped
Butter or margarine
1 (8-ounce) can crushed pineapple
1 (4-ounce) package slivered almonds
½ cup orange juice
2 tablespoons sour cream
⅛ teaspoon nutmeg, or less
Small amount of granulated brown sugar

- Preheat oven to 350 degrees. Grease a casserole or 8-inch x 10-inch Pyrex dish.
- Bake the squash for a short time to soften and remove skin. Slice, then steam in a covered saucepan until soft. Drain and mash. Transfer to a large mixing bowl.
- Sauté onion in margarine until soft and add to squash.
- Add remaining ingredients, mixing thoroughly. Bake in casserole until heated through, 10 to 15 minutes.

Florence L. Greenberg
Great Neck, New York

CARROTS IN ORANGE MARMALADE

Serves: 4

3 cups carrots, thinly sliced
3 tablespoons margarine
½ cup chicken broth; jelled consommé has less fat
½ cup orange marmalade
Dash of Grand Marnier, optional

- In a heavy saucepan, combine carrots, butter and broth; cook covered 5 to 7 minutes. Add remaining ingredients. Cook uncovered until carrots are tender and sauce has become a thick glaze. Stir often as sauce thickens.

Marilyn Katz
Purchase, New York

CARROT PUDDING

Invite guests for this one.

Serves: 10

1 cup brown sugar, firmly packed
2 cups shortening (1 cup butter and 1 cup vegetable shortening)
2 eggs, beaten
3¼ cups grated carrots
2½ cups flour
2 teaspoons baking powder
2 teaspoons lemon juice
1 teaspoon baking soda dissolved in 1 tablespoon cold water

- Preheat oven to 350 degrees. Butter a 10-cup ring mold.
- In a large bowl, cream sugar and shortening. Add eggs and carrots, mixing well.
- Sift flour and baking powder together and add to carrots. Stir in lemon juice. Add baking soda to water and stir into mixture immediately.
- Pour into mold and bake for 50 to 60 minutes.

Note: After pudding is unmolded, fill center with fresh or frozen peas and fresh mushrooms or snow peas with water chestnuts or toasted slivered almonds.

Hope Hirschhorn
Harrison, New York

CORN PUDDING

Serves: 4 to 6

3 eggs, separated
1 tablespoon flour
1 tablespoon cornmeal
Salt and pepper to taste
½ cup milk
2 tablespoons melted butter
1 (16-ounce) can cream-style corn

- Preheat oven to 325 degrees. Use a 1½-quart ungreased casserole.
- Beat the egg yolks in a bowl. Add flour, cornmeal, salt, pepper, milk and melted butter. Mix well. Add corn and blend.
- Beat egg whites until stiff and fold into mixture. Pour into casserole.
- Bake at 325 degrees for 10 minutes, raise temperature to 350 degrees and bake for 30 minutes longer, or until well browned.

Estelle Silverstone
Harrison, New York

CREAMED KALE
(Without the cream)

Serves: 4 to 5

2 onions, red or white, coarsely chopped
4 to 5 shallots, chopped
2 tablespoons oil or butter
2 bunches kale, well-washed, coarse stems removed
½ pound butter
6 ounces cream cheese
1 hefty pinch cayenne pepper

- Sauté the onions and shallots in 2 tablespoons oil or butter until somewhat limp.
- Add well-washed kale; do this in two batches unless you have an enormous pan! Cook very briefly; should be bright green.
- In a food processor, process half of the butter and cream cheese until well blended. Add cayenne.
- Add half of the kale and process well. Remove from work bowl and repeat with remaining butter, cream cheese and kale. Return all to pan and warm when ready to serve.

Len Feiman
White Plains, New York

EGGPLANT Á LA PROVENÇAL

Serves: 8

2 medium-size eggplants, peeled and sliced ½-inch thick
6 medium-size tomatoes, peeled and quartered
Salt, pepper and paprika to taste
Vegetable shortening for frying
3 cloves garlic, minced
1 cup chopped fresh parsley
½ to 1 cup bread crumbs, as needed

- Preheat oven to 375 degrees. Grease a 9-inch x 13-inch baking dish.
- Sprinkle eggplant with salt and let stand for ½ hour. Rinse and pat dry. Fry slices until brown and drain on paper towel.
- In a saucepan, place tomatoes, salt, pepper and paprika. Simmer slowly until liquid evaporates.
- Mix garlic and parsley together.
- Spoon a layer of tomatoes into bottom of baking dish, add slices of eggplant, and sprinkle with garlic and parsley. Repeat twice, if necessary. Add salt and pepper after each layer.
- Top with bread crumbs and bake for ½ hour.

Judy Rosenberg
Brooklyn, New York

EGGPLANT CASSEROLE

Serves: 4

1 eggplant, peeled and diced
Salted water to cover
½ medium onion, diced
½ cup green pepper, diced
2 tablespoons butter
1 egg, beaten
⅔ cup grated American cheese
1 clove garlic, minced
¼ cup black olives, diced
1 cup bread crumbs

- Preheat oven to 325 degrees. Butter a 1-quart casserole.
- Cook the eggplant in salted water until tender. Drain.
- Sauté the onion and green pepper in butter.
- Mix the beaten egg with the eggplant. Add remaining ingredients and mix. Pour into casserole. Top with bread crumbs.
- Bake for 30 minutes.

Susan Kaskel
Harrison, New York

GINGERED PEAS AND WATER CHESTNUTS

Serves: 6 to 8

2 (10-ounce) packages frozen peas (petit pois)
2 tablespoons margarine
1 (5-ounce) can water chestnuts, retain liquid
1 cube or packet of chicken stock
½ teaspoon ginger, ground
¼ teaspoon nutmeg, ground
1 teaspoon arrowroot
1 tablespoon water

- In a saucepan put peas, margarine, liquid from water chestnuts, stock base, ginger and nutmeg. Heat covered until peas are hot.
- Blend arrowroot with 1 tablespoon water and stir into peas. Cook, stirring constantly, until liquid thickens. Add water chestnuts, which have been sliced thin, and cook until hot.

Note: This may be used as a vegetable or to fill the center of a carrot ring.

Carol Solomon
New York, New York

HERBED GREEN BEANS

Serves: 4

1 pound fresh green beans
Boiling water
¼ cup butter
½ cup minced onion
½ clove garlic, minced
¼ cup minced celery
½ cup minced fresh parsley
1 teaspoon fresh rosemary or ¼ teaspoon dried rosemary
1 teaspoon fresh basil or ¼ teaspoon dried basil
¾ teaspoon salt

- Snip ends from beans, cut diagonally into 2-inch pieces. Cook in about 1-inch boiling water in a covered pan 15 to 20 minutes, or just until tender. Drain.
- In a small pan melt the butter; add onion, garlic and celery and cook about 5 minutes. Add parsley, rosemary, basil and salt. Cover and simmer for 10 minutes.
- Just before serving, toss the herb-flavored butter with the drained beans.

Carolyn Davis
Armonk, New York

HERBED SPINACH BAKE

Serves: 4

1 (10-ounce) package frozen chopped spinach, cooked and drained.
1 cup cottage cheese
½ cup grated Parmesan cheese
2 slightly beaten eggs
1 tablespoon butter, softened
½ teaspoon Worcestershire sauce
Pinch onion powder
Salt and pepper to taste
¼ teaspoon rosemary

- Preheat oven to 350 degrees. Grease a 2-quart baking dish, or an 8½-inch or 9-inch square baking dish.
- Combine all ingredients well and pour into prepared dish. Bake for 20 to 30 minutes.

Susan Abrams
Katonah, New York

ITALIAN ZUCCHINI CRESCENT PIE

Millicent Kaplan's prize winning recipe.

Serves: 8

4 cups thinly sliced zucchini, unpeeled
1 cup coarsely chopped onion
½ cup margarine or butter
½ cup chopped parsley or 2 tablespoons parsley flakes
½ teaspoon salt
½ teaspoon pepper
¼ teaspoon garlic powder
¼ teaspoon sweet basil
¼ teaspoon oregano leaves
2 eggs, well beaten
8 ounces (2 cups) muenster or mozzarella cheese, shredded
1 (8-ounce) tube refrigerated crescent dinner rolls
2 teaspoons Dijon-style or prepared mustard

- Preheat oven to 375 degrees. Use an ungreased 11-inch quiche pan, a 10-inch pie pan or an 8-inch x 12-inch baking dish.
- In a large skillet cook zucchini and onion in margarine until tender about 10 minutes. Stir in parsley and seasonings.
- In a large bowl, blend eggs and cheese; stir in the vegetable mixture.
- Separate the dough into 8 triangles. Place in bottom of baking pan, press over bottom and up the sides to form a crust. Spread mustard on crust then pour vegetable mixture evenly on the crust. Bake for 30 to 35 minutes. Let stand 10 minutes before serving.

Note: This recipe may be prepared the day before using. Assemble recipe as written and bake partially for 15 minutes. Cool slightly and refrigerate. On day crescent pie is to be served, remove from refrigerator and bring to room temperature. Preheat oven to 375 degrees and bake the remaining 15 to 20 minutes. If using a 9-inch x 13-inch Pyrex dish, increase the zucchini amount by 1 to 2 cups, leaving rest of ingredients as written.

Ann Jacobson
Purchase, New York

LA BATTUE AUX OIGNONS
(Onion Custard)

Serves: 6 to 8

5 tablespoons butter
1 to 1½ pounds onions, peeled and thinly sliced
¼ cup flour
1½ teaspoons salt, or to taste
2 eggs
⅔ cup milk

- Preheat oven to 450 degrees. Butter a 9-inch or 10-inch gratin dish generously.
- Melt the butter in a heavy skillet and sauté onions gently for 15 minutes or until translucent.
- Sift flour and salt into mixing bowl, add eggs and milk. Mix well until smooth. Add cooled onions.
- Pour mixture into gratin dish and bake for 15 to 20 minutes or until golden. Wait 5 minutes before serving as onions keep hot for a long time and flavor will improve.

Janet Bernstein
Chappaqua, New York

LAYERED CHEESE VEGETABLE BAKE

Serves: 4 entrées or
8 as a side dish

1 pound zucchini, thinly sliced
3 potatoes, peeled and thinly sliced
1 cup grated sharp Cheddar cheese
1 cup grated Monterey Jack cheese
1 cup seasoned bread crumbs
½ cup chopped parsley
2 large cloves garlic, minced
Salt and pepper to taste
3 tablespoons olive oil
3 tablespoons butter
¼ cup water

- Preheat oven to 350 degrees. Butter a 1½-quart casserole or baking dish.
- Layer with ⅓ zucchini, and ⅓ potato slices. Sprinkle with ⅓ of cheeses, bread crumbs, parsley, garlic, salt and pepper. Drizzle with 1 tablespoon oil.
- Repeat each layer twice drizzling each layer with 1 tablespoon oil. Dot top with butter. Pour water over top. Cover and bake for 1 hour.

Debbie Simon
Scarsdale, New York

MEATLESS MOUSSAKA

Prepare ahead

Serves: 8

2 large eggplants, unpeeled, sliced ½-inch thick
Salt
16 ounces tomato sauce, bottled or homemade
4 tablespoons olive oil
⅔ cup Parmesan cheese, grated

- Sprinkle both sides of each eggplant slice with salt; place between several layers of paper towels, weigh down and let stand for 1 hour.
- Prepare or heat tomato sauce.
- Brush both sides of each slice eggplant with olive oil and broil quickly on each side until brown.

Cheese Filling

1 pound cream style cottage cheese
1 egg
2 tablespoons Parmesan cheese, grated
⅛ teaspoon crumbled rosemary
⅛ teaspoon mace
¼ teaspoon salt
⅛ teaspoon pepper

- Mix together all ingredients. Set aside.

To Assemble Moussaka

- Preheat oven to 375 degrees. Use a 9-inch x 13-inch baking pan.
- Spoon one half the tomato sauce over bottom of baking pan; sprinkle generously with grated Parmesan; arrange half the browned eggplant slices on top. Spread cheese filling over eggplant and sprinkle with Parmesan. Arrange remaining eggplant on top, sprinkle with cheese. Cover with remaining tomato sauce and one last sprinkling of cheese.
- Bake uncovered for 45 to 50 minutes until bubbling and browned. Remove from oven and let stand 15 minutes before serving.

Note Dish can be prepared up to several hours ahead of time and refrigerated until about 1 hour before baking.

Susan Abrams
Katonah, New York

OBERLIN VEGETABLE CHILI

A wonderful blending of spices, ingredients and flavor.

Serves: 6 to 8

Prepare ahead

2 cups kidney beans
1 large eggplant, peeled and cut into cubes
2 tablespoons olive oil
1 cup onions, chopped
4 cloves garlic, minced
1 cup chopped green pepper
1 cup chopped celery
1 cup corn, removed from cob
2 teaspoons chili powder
2 teaspoons cumin
1 teaspoon cinnamon
1 teaspoon allspice
Dash cayenne pepper
2 cups chopped fresh tomatoes or 1 (1 pound, 12-ounce) can
3 tablespoons tomato paste
4 ounces white Vermont Cheddar cheese, grated
4 to 6 scallions, chopped

- Soak kidney beans overnight. Rinse well and cook covered, in 6 cups water for about 1 hour, until tender. Watch water level, and add more water if necessary. Meanwhile, steam cubed eggplant for about 20 minutes or until tender.
- In large saucepot, sauté onions and garlic in olive oil for several minutes. Add green pepper, celery, and corn, and cook until tender. Add all spices and stir. Add tomatoes, tomato paste, drained beans and eggplant. Bring to a simmer and cook for 30 minutes, stirring occasionally. Taste and correct seasonings, if desired.
- Serve hot and garnish with grated Cheddar cheese and chopped scallions.

Note: Almost any vegetable can be used either in addition or as a substitute for one of the above.

Cynthia Hogan
Chevy Chase, Maryland

PARSLEY CARROTS AND POTATOES

Serves: 8 to 10

8 medium-size potatoes
4 large carrots
¼ cup butter, melted
Salt and pepper to taste
½ teaspoon sugar
¼ cup minced fresh parsley
Grated rind of 1 lemon

- Peel potatoes, rinse and pat dry. Using a melon scoop, scoop out balls of potatoes and place in a bowl of cold water. Drain potatoes and place in a bowl of boiling water for 15 to 20 minutes. Drain well.
- Cut carrots diagonally and cook until crisp tender. Set aside.
- Melt butter and sauté potatoes in a large skillet, over low heat, until tender. Add carrots and stir until hot. Sprinkle with salt, pepper and sugar. Add minced parsley and stir to coat potatoes and carrots. Add lemon rind and stir again. Continue to cook until heated through.

Amy Berk Kurtzman
New York, New York

SPINACH PIE

Serves: 8

3 tablespoons olive oil
2 large onions, finely chopped
1½ to 2 pounds fresh spinach, or 2 (10-ounce) packages frozen chopped spinach, well drained
1½ cups fresh ground Parmesan cheese
1 cup ricotta cheese
Salt and pepper to taste
4 eggs, slightly beaten
1 small package mozzarella cheese, shredded or cubed

- Preheat oven to 425 degrees. Grease a 10-inch pie plate or quiche pan.
- In a large skillet, heat oil and sauté onions until tender. Do not brown.
- In a large saucepan place washed spinach leaves, stems removed. Cover tightly and steam until wilted. Drain well; chop (if fresh) and squeeze dry with paper toweling.
- Combine spinach with onions and let cool. Add the Parmesan cheese, ricotta cheese, salt, pepper and eggs to the spinach mixture. Pour into a pie plate or quiche pan. Sprinkle with mozzarella cheese and bake for 40 minutes or until golden brown. Let stand 10 to 15 minutes before cutting.

Marsha Pollack
Short Hills, New Jersey

TURNIP PURÉE

Serves: 6

1 medium size turnip, peeled and cut into large cubes
1 very large Idaho potato, peeled and cut into quarters
¼ pound unsalted margarine, room temperature
Scant ⅛ teaspoon nutmeg
Salt and pepper, if desired

- Place turnip and potato into a large pot with enough water to slightly cover. Boil until fork tender (about 25 minutes). Do not overcook.
- Purée in a blender or food processor in batches using some turnips, potatoes and margarine each time. Add nutmeg to the last batch.
- Put mixture back into saucepan and heat through, stirring often.

Note: You can also use this purée to fill the center of fresh tomatoes or zucchini boats.

Corrine Katz
White Plains, New York

VEGETABLE AND RICE CASSEROLE

Serves: 8

1 box Uncle Ben's ® Long Grain and Wild Rice Blend, prepared as directed
2 (6-ounce) jars marinated artichokes
1 small onion, chopped
½ pound fresh mushrooms, sliced
1 (8-ounce) can water chestnuts, drained and sliced
1 (16-ounce) can peeled tomatoes, drained; reserve liquid
1 cup frozen peas, thawed
Salt and pepper to taste
Chicken broth, as needed
Paprika

- Preheat oven to 350 degrees. Grease a 2-quart casserole.
- Prepare rice and set aside.
- Empty artichokes into a saucepan, add chopped onion and sauté; add the mushrooms. When the onions are golden brown and mushrooms soft, add water chestnuts. Add tomatoes. Stir in the prepared rice and mix well, adding liquid from the tomatoes if mixture becomes too dry. Add peas and season with salt and pepper. Add 1 tablespoon chicken broth, stirring into mixture, and adjust seasonings again.
- Pour into the casserole and sprinkle with paprika. Bake for 20 to 25 minutes.

Linda Berk
Greensburg, Pennsylvania

ZUCCHINI CASSEROLE

Serves: 8 to 10

1 cup celery, diced
3 onions, sliced
2 tablespoons oil
6 to 8 zucchini (depending on size), cut diagonally into 2-inch slices, unpeeled
1 (16-ounce) can stewed tomatoes
2 tablespoons bouquet garni
1 teaspoon seasoned salt
¼ teaspoon pepper
¼ cup Parmesan cheese, grated

- Preheat oven to 325 degrees. Butter a 9-inch x 13-inch casserole.
- Sauté celery and onion in oil. Sauté zucchini, but keep it firm. Combine with remaining ingredients except cheese. Place in casserole and bake for 20 minutes, covered. Uncover, add cheese and brown.

Hope Hirschhorn
Harrison, New York

BAKED ZUCCHINI

Serves: 4 to 6

4 medium zucchini, washed and peeled
2 tablespoons oil
Salt to taste
1 onion, minced
2 cloves garlic, finely chopped
2 tablespoons oil
1 (15½-ounce) can marinara sauce
1 teaspoon basil
½ teaspoon salt
¼ teaspoon oregano
Dash pepper
½ pound Meunster cheese, sliced

- Preheat oven to 350 degrees. Use an 8-inch x 10-inch baking dish or 2-quart casserole.
- Cut zucchini into four lengthwise pieces. Brush each side with oil and sprinkle lightly with salt. Broil each side until golden brown.
- Sauté onion and garlic in oil until wilted. Do not let brown. Add marinara sauce, basil, salt, pepper and oregano. Simmer 10 minutes.
- Pour thin layer of sauce mixture into baking dish. Place half the zucchini slices over sauce, top with half the cheese slices. Add additional sauce and remainder of zucchini and cheese. Top with remaining sauce. Bake about 35 minutes.

Betty Laboz
Brooklyn, New York

ZUCCHINI PUFFS

These are fabulous!

Yield: 18 to 20 muffins or 36 tiny muffins

2 cups (1-pound) zucchini, unpeeled and shredded
6 slices Swiss cheese, broken into pieces
3 tablespoons onion, chopped
½ to 1 cup Italian seasoned bread crumbs or plain crumbs
2 eggs
¼ teaspoon salt
¼ teaspoon baking powder

- Preheat oven to 375 degrees. Heavily grease muffin tins with vegetable shortening.
- Combine all ingredients with a fork until mixed thoroughly. Fill muffin tins ⅔ to ¾ full. Bake for 30 minutes. Remove from oven and run a thin knife blade around each puff. Remove puffs before they cool. Serve hot.

Note: This recipe can be made ahead and frozen. Pack in aluminum foil or freezer bags. When ready to serve, defrost before placing in a preheated 350 degree oven and heat for 10 to 15 minutes or until just hot enough to serve. Can be used as an hors d'oeuvre if baked in tiny size muffin tins.

Susan Katz
Teaneck, New York

VARIATIONS FOR USING LEFT-OVER CRUDITÉS

- Purée all vegetables (that have been briefly steamed) in a food processor or blender. Add ½ cup to 1 cup chicken stock (this will depend on amount of vegetables) and you have soup. Correct seasoning with salt and pepper. Put mixture in a soup pot and heat through.
- Purée all steamed vegetables in a food processor or blender; add 1 stick of butter or margarine (cut into 8 pieces), 2 to 3 tablespoons Crème Fraîche (optional). Do this process in batches. Add salt and pepper to taste. Transfer to a saucepan and heat over low heat until heated through. Serve as a vegetable purée.

Len Feiman
White Plains, New York

CUISINARTS
Bay
Basil
Savory
Coriander
Sage
Rosemary
Parsley
Mint
Coriander
Sage
Sage
Rosemary
Parsley
Mint
Cinnamon
Marjoram
Thyme
Juniper
Bay
Bay
Basil
Savory
Coriander
Sage
Rosemary
Parsley
Mint
Cinnamon
Parsley
Sage
Rosemary
Parsley
Mint
Cinnamon
Marjoram
Thyme
Juniper
Coriander
Sage
Marjoram
Thyme
Juniper
Bay
Basil
Savory
Coriander
Bay
Basil

Cuisinarts®

Dear Fellow Cook:

We hope the food processor recipes in this chapter will add to your cooking pleasure.

Some of the recipes appeared previously in our bimonthly magazine, *The Pleasures of Cooking,* or our monthly newsletter, *The Cuisinart Cook.* Others are favorites developed by our food processing experts.

All the recipes have been tested many times to assure success and easy preparation.

Cordially,

CUISINARTS, INC.

Carl Sontheimer

Carl G. Sontheimer
President

CHEESE DIP

No one would guess how low in calories this delicious cheese dip is-only about 17 calories per tablespoon.

Yield: about 1¾ cups

4 ounces blue cheese or sharp Cheddar cheese, cut into 1-inch pieces
1 small scallion, cut into 1-inch pieces
12 ounces dry curd cottage cheese or pot cheese
6 drops hot pepper sauce, or to taste
2 tablespoons cold water, about
Salt, optional

- Insert the metal blade in a food processor. With motor running, add the blue or Cheddar cheese pieces through small feed tube. Chop until pasty, about 40 seconds. Add scallion. Pulse 5 times.
- Add the cottage cheese and hot pepper sauce. Process until smooth, stopping to scrape down side of bowl as necessary. With motor running, slowly add cold water until mixture is light and fluffy. Season with salt, if desired. Pulse twice. For smoothest consistency process for 90 seconds more.

RED PEPPER CAVIAR

Yield: about 2½ cups

A vibrant dip for raw or steamed vegetables. Also good on toast, sprinkled with Gruyere cheese and baked in a 400 degree oven until the cheese is browned.

5 pounds large sweet red peppers
1 cup olive oil
1 teaspoon salt
Pinch cayenne pepper
½ teaspoon dried thyme leaves
2 large egg yolks
Freshly ground black pepper

- Place a pepper stem-side up on a cutting board. With a sharp knife, cut 3 or 4 vertical slices from the sides, leaving only the core and stem. Remove seeds and ribs from slices. Repeat with all peppers.
- Insert the slicing disc, pack the pepper slices in the feed tube and process. Repeat until all peppers are sliced, emptying the work bowl as necessary.
- Heat ½ cup of olive oil in a 5-quart stockpot over moderate heat. Stir in the pepper slices, ½ teaspoon of salt, the cayenne and the thyme. Cover and simmer until very soft, about 1 hour.
- Drain the peppers in a colander for 10 minutes, stirring occasionally. Insert the metal blade and purée the peppers in 2 batches, stopping to scrape the bowl as necessary. Pass the purée through a fine sieve and discard bits of skin. Place the purée in a fine strainer and allow to stand for 30 minutes.
- Insert the metal blade and process the purée and egg yolks until combined, about 10 seconds. With the machine running, pour the remaining ½ cup of olive oil through the feed tube in a slow, steady stream. The mixture should have the consistency of thin mayonnasie. Season with remaining salt and pepper to taste.
- The mixture may be refrigerated, tightly covered, for up to a week.

COLD BEET SOUP WITH VEGETABLES

Serves: 6

1 pound fresh medium beets, with stems and 1-inch stalk left on
2 medium cucumbers (8-ounces each) peeled, halved and seeded
6 medium scallions (3-ounces), including 2 inches of green top, washed and trimmed
1 medium orange (6-ounces), scored and cut flat at ends
5 cups cold water
2 tablespoons red wine vinegar
2 teaspoons salt
1 cup plain yogurt
3 tablespoons orange juice
4 tablespoons finely chopped fresh dill
¼ teaspoon freshly ground pepper
Pinch of sugar, optional

- Wash the beets gently, put them in boiling water to cover and boil for 8 to 10 minutes. Drain and cover with cold water. When they are cool enough to handle, remove the stalks and stems and peel them.
- Insert the 6 x 6 mm French-fry cut disc. Cut the cucumbers in lengths to fit the feed tube vertically and wedge them in. Process, using light pressure, to obtain ¼-inch dice. Remove and spread them on paper towels to dry.
- Insert the 2 mm slicing disc. Cut the scallions into lengths to fit the small feed tube vertically. Insert them and process, using light pressure. Remove and reserve. Insert the orange in the large feed tube, flat side down, and process with the 2 mm slicing disc, using medium pressure. Remove and reserve for garnish.
- Insert the 2 x 2 mm julienne disc and process the beets, using medium pressure. Put them in a non-aluminum 3- or 4-quart saucepan, add the water and bring to a boil over high heat. Reduce the heat, add the vinegar and 1½ teaspoons salt. Partially cover and simmer for 30 minutes. Drain the beets in a stainless steel sieve over a large bowl and allow both the solids and liquid to cool to room temperature.
- When the liquid is completely cool, whisk it into the yogurt in a soup tureen or a large bowl. Add the beets, cucumbers, scallions, orange juice, 2 tablespoons of dill, ½ teaspoon of salt and the pepper. Taste carefully for seasoning and add more salt, pepper and a pinch of sugar if necessary. (Remember that cold foods need to be highly seasoned).
- Cover the bowl tightly with plastic wrap and refrigerate at least 2 hours or overnight.
- Ladle the soup into chilled soup bowls and garnish each bowl with a slice of orange and a sprinkling of chopped dill.

COPELAND MARKS' TOMATO SOUP WITH RICE

Yields: 6 servings

1 whole chicken (about 3 pounds), quartered, with excess skin and fat removed
6 cups water
1 teaspoon salt
1 large garlic clove (1/6-ounce), peeled
1 piece fresh ginger (about 1 by ¾-inch), peeled
1 medium onion (about 6-ounces), peeled and quartered
2 teaspoons vegetable oil
½ teaspoon ground cumin
½ teaspoon dry hot pepper flakes
½ cup tomato purée
2 cups hot, cooked rice (13-ounces)

- Place the chicken in a large saucepot. Add the water and salt and bring to the boil. Partially cover the pot and simmer the chicken for 25 minutes, skimming often, or until almost tender. Remove the chicken and, when it is cool enough to handle, remove and discard the skin and bones and cut the meat into ½-inch pieces. Reserve.
- Strain the broth into a large bowl. Cool for 15 to 20 minutes, then remove the surface fat.
- Drop the garlic and ginger through the feed tube of a food processor with the metal blade in place and the motor running and process for 10 seconds or until finely chopped. Drop the onion through the feed tube and process for 30 seconds or until finely chopped.
- Heat the oil in a large saucepan over moderate heat. Add the garlic mixture and cook, stirring, for 2 minutes. Add the cumin and pepper flakes and cook, stirring, for 2 minutes longer.
- Stir in the reserved broth, tomato purée and reserved chicken pieces and simmer, uncovered, for 15 minutes. Taste for seasoning. Serve with a bowl of cooked rice.

* Copeland Marks is a textile importer who lives in Brooklyn Heights and travels extensively, searching for handicrafts, and studying the native cuisine. His writing about the food of Burma, Guatemala, India and Indonesia appears frequently in *The Pleasures of Cooking* and other magazines.

APPLE WALNUT MUFFINS

Yield: 18 muffins

2 medium apples (10-ounces) cored but not peeled, preferably Greening or Granny Smith
2 cups unbleached, all-purpose flour (10-ounces)
2 teaspoons baking powder
½ teaspoon baking soda
1 teaspoon salt
½ teaspoon cinnamon
½ cup (2-ounces) walnut pieces
⅔ cup (5-ounces) sugar
One 2 x ½-inch strip of lemon peel, removed with a vegetable peeler, divided in 4 pieces
2 large eggs
¼ cup milk
¼ pound unsalted butter (4-ounces), at room temperature, in 8 pieces

- Preheat oven to 350 degrees. Butter 18 large muffin cups well.
- Insert the fine shredding disc and process the apples, using medium pressure. Remove and reserve them. (They will probably discolor, but that has no effect on the final product). Wipe the processor dry with a paper towel. Insert the metal blade and put the flour, baking powder, baking soda, salt, cinnamon and nuts in the work bowl. Pulse just until the nuts are coarsely chopped, about 5 or 6 times. Transfer the dry ingredients to a mixing bowl. Add the sugar and lemon peel to the work bowl and process until the lemon is coarsely chopped. Add the eggs and milk and process for 1 minute. Add the butter and process for an additional minute. Leave the mixture in the bowl. Add the reserved apples and pulse 3 times. Add the reserved dry ingredients and pulse 3 or 4 times, or until they just disappear into the batter. Do not overprocess or the muffins will be tough.
- Fill the muffin cups ¾ full and smooth the tops. Bake until the tops are dry and nicely browned and a cake tester inserted in the center comes out clean, about 25 to 28 minutes, then transfer to a wire rack.

BASIC WHITE BREAD

Yields: 2 loaves, each about 1½ pounds

1 package active dry yeast
2 teaspoons sugar
⅓ cup warm water
6 cups (30-ounces) unbleached all-purpose flour
4 tablespoons (½ stick) unsalted butter or margarine at room temperature, cut into pieces
2 teaspoons salt
1⅔ cups very cold water

- Dissolve yeast with sugar in warm water; let stand until foamy, about 5 minutes.
- Insert dough kneading blade in bowl of food processor. Add flour, butter and salt to work bowl. Process until butter is cut into mixture, about 20 seconds.
- Pour yeast mixture followed by cold water through feed tube in a steady stream as fast as flour mixture absorbs the liquid (should take 20 to 25 seconds). After dough leaves side of bowl and forms a ball, continue processing for 60 seconds to knead dough.
- With lightly floured hands, carefully lift dough from bowl and shape it into a smooth ball. Place dough in a lightly floured 1-gallon plastic bag. Squeeze out air and close end with a wire twist, allowing space for dough to rise. Let rise in a warm place (80 degrees) until dough has doubled, about 1 to 1½ hours.
- Remove wire twist and punch dough down in bag. Shape dough into two loaves and place each in a greased 8-inch x 4-inch loaf pan. Cover with oiled plastic wrap and let rise in a warm place until dough rises just above top of pans, about 45 minutes. Bake on middle rack in a preheated 375 degrees oven for 35 to 40 minutes. Remove from pans and cool on wire racks.

Variations

Herbed Whole Wheat Bread:

Substitute 2 cups whole wheat flour for 2 cups of all-purpose flour. Add 1½ teaspoons dried Italian herbs (mixture of basil, marjoram, oregano, rosemary, sage and savory) to flour mixture.

Cinnamon Raisin Oatmeal Bread:

Substitute 1 cup whole wheat flour and 1 cup old fashioned oats for 2 cups of the all-purpose flour. Add 1 teaspoon ground cinnamon to flour mixture. After first rising, sprinkle 1 cup dark seedless raisins over dough and knead briefly to distribute raisins evenly.

Fennel Orange Rye:

Substitute 2 cups rye flour for 2 cups all-purpose flour. Add 2 teaspoons fennel seed and 1½ teaspoons grated orange zest to flour mixture.

BLUEBERRY STREUSEL MUFFINS

Yield: 12 (2½-ounce) muffins

Streusel Topping

1 cup all-purpose flour (5-ounces)
½ cup whole wheat flour (2½-ounces)
2 teaspoons baking powder
½ teaspoons baking soda
¼ teaspoon salt
¾ cup sugar (5⅔-ounces)
⅔ cup buttermilk
1 stick unsalted butter (4-ounces), melted and cooled
2 large eggs
1 teaspoon pure vanilla extract
1½ cups frozen, unthawed blueberries (7½-ounces)

- Preheat the oven to 375 degrees. Oil twelve (½-cup) muffin cups. Set aside. Make the Streusel Topping and reserve. Process all the ingredients except the blueberries with the metal blade of a food processor for 3 seconds. Scrape down the work bowl and pulse 2 times more. Transfer the batter to a medium mixing bowl and stir in the blueberries.
- Fill each muffin cup two-thirds full with batter. Sprinkle each muffin with 1 tablespoon of the Streusel Topping. Bake in the center of the preheated oven for 25 to 28 minutes or until the muffins are firm to the touch and the tops are golden brown. Cool in the muffin cups for about 8 minutes, then remove to a wire rack. Serve warm.

Streusel Topping

Yield: ¾ cup (2½-ounces)

¼ cup sugar (1¾-ounces)
3 tablespoons all-purpose flour
1 tablespoon unsalted butter, chilled and cut in half
½ teaspoon cinnamon
Pinch salt

- Process all the ingredients with the metal blade of a food processor until coarsely crumbled, 10 to 15 seconds.

Variations

Cranberry Streusel Muffins:

Process 1½ cups frozen, unthawed cranberries with the medium (3mm) slicing disc and reserve. Follow the Blueberry Streusel Muffin recipe, using the sliced cranberries instead of the blueberries.

Currant Nut Streusel Muffins:

Coarsely chop ⅔ cup (2⅔-ounces) walnuts with the metal blade, about 5 pulses. Reserve. Follow the Blueberry Streusel Muffin recipe, using the chopped walnuts and ⅔ cup (3⅓-ounces) dried currants instead of the blueberries.

BRIOCHE

Yield: 1 pound brioche

1 package active dry yeast
3 tablespoons sugar
¼ cup warm water (105 to 115 degrees)
1¾ cups (8¾-ounces) unbleached all-purpose flour
¼ teaspoon salt
2 large eggs
6 tablespoons (¾ stick) unsalted butter, melted
Glaze (1 egg beaten with pinch of salt)

- Dissolve yeast with sugar in warm water; let stand until foamy, about 5 minutes.
- Insert metal blade in bowl of food processor. Add flour and salt. Turn machine on and off several times to aerate. Add yeast mixture and eggs. Process until mixed, about 5 seconds.
- Start processor and pour melted butter through feed tube in a steady stream. Stop processing after 20 seconds. Dough will be very sticky, like a batter. With a spatula, scrape it into a buttered mixing bowl. Cover tightly with oiled plastic wrap and let rise in a warm place (80 degrees) until almost tripled, about 3 hours.
- Generously flour your hands and top of dough. Punch dough down in bowl (it will be very sticky). Cover tightly with oiled plastic wrap and refrigerate overnight.
- Butter a 6-cup ring mold or tube pan. With floured hands, flatten dough into a 6- or 7-inch disc. Poke your thumb through the center and work around the dough with your hand until it resembles a doughnut the size of your mold. Place dough in mold, cover with oiled plastic wrap and let rise in a warm place until the dough reaches the top of the mold, about 2½ hours.
- With a sharp knife, make a circular cut along top of risen dough 1 inch deep and 1 inch from edge of pan. Make a second circular cut 1 inch from center of pan.
- Brush dough with egg glaze. Bake on lower rack in a preheated 425 degree oven for 10 minutes, then reduce heat to 350 degrees and bake for 5 to 8 minutes more or until lightly browned.

Variation

Individual Brioches:

- Lightly butter 8 individual 3-inch brioche molds or 3-inch muffin-pan cups. With hands and pastry board well floured, roll chilled dough into a cylinder about 8 inches long. Cut dough into 8 1-inch slices.
- To shape a single brioche, pinch off ⅓ of the dough from one of the slices. With floured hands, roll it into a ball, then into a pear shape. Roll remaining ⅔ of dough into a ball. Place the ball into a buttered mold or muffin-pan cup. Pole a floured finger into the center of the ball, then insert the point of the pear-shaped dough into the indentation. Repeat with remaining slices. Cover loosely with oiled plastic wrap and let rise in a warm place until double in size, about 2 hours.
- With a feather brush, glaze tops with egg-salt mixture. Bake on middle rack in a preheated 425 degree oven for 10 minutes. Reduce heat to 350 degrees and bake for an additional 5 to 8 minutes or until lightly browned. Makes 8 individual brioches.

HONEY WALNUT ROLLS

Yield: 36 rolls

1 package active dry yeast
⅓ cup warm water (105 to 115 degrees)
2 tablespoons honey
1 cup walnut pieces
7 cups (35-ounces) unbleached all-purpose flour
1½ teaspoons salt
4 tablespoons (½ stick) unsalted butter or margarine at room temperature, cut into 4 pieces
2 cups very cold water

- Dissolve yeast with honey in warm water; let stand until foamy, about 5 minutes.
- Insert metal blade in bowl of food processor and add walnut pieces. Process, pulsing on and off, until nuts are coarsely chopped. Remove and set aside.
- Insert dough kneading blade and add flour, salt and butter. Process for 20 seconds. Add yeast mixture. Start processor and add cold water through feed tube as fast as flour absorbs it (should take 20 to 25 seconds). Continue processing until dough forms a ball, then let machine run for 30 seconds to knead dough. Add reserved walnuts and process until they are evenly distributed, about 15 seconds.
- With lightly floured hands, carefully remove dough from bowl. Shape it into a smooth ball and place it in a lightly floured 1-gallon plastic bag. Squeeze out air and close end with a wire twist, allowing space for dough to rise.
- Let rise in a warm place (80 degrees) until double in bulk, about 1 hour. Remove wire twist and punch dough down in bag. Divide dough into 36 equal portions. Roll each portion into a 7-inch rope and tie loosely into a knot.
- Place rolls on greased baking sheets. Cover with oiled plastic wrap and let rise in a warm place until double in bulk, about 30 to 40 minutes. If desired, glaze rolls with a mixture of 1 beaten egg and ¼ teaspoon salt.
- Bake in a preheated 375 degree oven for 20 to 25 minutes or until nicely browned. Remove from baking sheets and cool on wire racks.

SWEET POTATO BREAD

Yield: 1½ pound loaf or 12 pan rolls

1 package active dry yeast
⅓ cup warm water (105 to 115 degrees)
2 tablespoons dark brown sugar
1 medium (8-ounces) sweet potato, cooked and peeled
6 cups (30-ounces) unbleached all-purpose flour
2 teaspoons salt
1 teaspoon ground cinnamon
4 tablespoons (½ stick) unsalted butter or margarine at room temperature, cut into 4 pieces
1 cup orange juice
⅓ cup very cold water

- Dissolve yeast with sugar in warm water; let stand until foamy, about 5 minutes.
- Insert medium shredding disc in bowl of food processor. Cut potato to fit feed tube and process, using light pressure on pusher. Remove potato from work bowl and set aside.
- Insert dough kneading blade and add flour, salt, cinnamon and butter to work bowl. Process for 20 seconds. Add shredded potato and yeast mixture. Process until mixed, about 5 seconds.
- Combine orange juice and water. Start processor and pour juice mixture through feed tube as fast as flour absorbs it (should take 20 to 25 seconds). Continue processing until dough begins to form a ball, then let machine run for 45 seconds to knead dough
- Remove dough from work bowl, shape it into a ball and place it in a lightly floured 1-gallon plastic bag. Squeeze out air and close end with a wire twist, allowing space for dough to rise.
- Let rise in a warm place (80 degrees) until double in bulk, about 1 hour. Remove wire twist and punch dough down in bag. Divide dough in half. Shape one half into a loaf and place it in a greased 8 x 4-inch loaf pan. Shape other half into 12 equal portions. Shape each piece into a smooth ball and place in a greased 9-inch cake pan. Cover the loaf and rolls with oiled plastic wrap. Let rise in a warm place until double in size.
- If desired, glaze top with a mixture of 1 beaten egg and ½ teaspoon salt. Bake on middle shelf in a preheated 375 degree oven, allowing 30 to 35 minutes for the loaf and 20 to 25 minutes for the rolls. Remove from pans and cool on wire racks.

DANISH CUCUMBER SALAD

Serves: 6

The Danes traditionally serve this tart salad with salmon or other fish, or use it as a garnish for smørrebrød, their spectacular open-faced sandwiches. It is equally good on its own as a salad, or as an accompaniment to meat or poultry.

3 large cucumbers (1½-pounds)
1 tablespoon salt
½ cup white vinegar
2 tablespoons sugar
¼ teaspoon freshly ground white pepper
2 tablespoons chopped fresh dill or parsley

- Wash the cucumbers, scrub off any wax, and score them lengthwise with fork. Divide into sections of equal length to fit the feed tube vertically.
- Insert the 1 mm slicing disc, put the cucumbers in the feed tube and slice them, using firm pressure. Lay the slices in a shallow non-metallic dish and sprinkle them with the salt. To press out excess moisture, put a plate on top of the cucumbers and put one or two heavy objects on it. Allow the cucumbers to rest at room temperature for about two hours.
- Remove the plate, drain all the liquid from the cucumbers, spread them out on paper towels and gently pat dry. Mix the vinegar, sugar and pepper in a measuring cup and taste for seasoning, adjusting as necessary. (This is important. The Danes like this salad very tart; you may want to add more sugar). Return the cucumber slices to their dish, pour the vinegar mixture over them and sprinkle with dill. Refrigerate for 2 or 3 hours and drain the liquid before serving.

MONKFISH AND POTATOES MAXINE WITH SHALLOT SAUCE

Serves: 4

6 small all-purpose potatoes (21-ounces total), peeled, halved crosswise
Salt and freshly ground black pepper
¾ cup clarified unsalted butter
1 stick unsalted butter (4-ounces)
1¾ pounds trimmed monkfish, cut into 12 1-inch thick pieces
½ cup Vegetable Stock (recipe follows)
8 cooked shallots reserved from Vegetable Stock
1 teaspoon fresh lemon juice

- Lightly butter a 15½-inch x 10½-inch jelly roll pan. Set aside. Preheat the oven to 400 degrees.
- Process the potatoes, flat sides down, with the ultra-thin (1 mm) slicing disc of a food processor. Rinse the potatoes in several changes of cold water until the water is clear.
- If you have a salad spinner, spin the potatoes gently to remove most of the water, or drain the potatoes in a colander, then dry them thoroughly on kitchen towels.
- Place the potatoes in a large mixing bowl, sprinkle with salt and pepper and pour ½ cup clarified butter over them. Mix the potatoes with your hands so that all the slices are covered with butter.
- Arrange the potato slices in overlapping rows on the prepared jelly roll pan. Dot with half of the solid butter. Bake in the oven until the potatoes are very soft, about 25 minutes; then place under the broiler until crisp and brown, about 2 minutes. Keep warm until ready to serve.
- Meanwhile, heat the remaining clarified butter in a large skillet over medium-high heat. Cook the monkfish in a single layer without crowding for 1 minute. Sprinkle with salt and pepper. Add the cooked shallots and continue cooking, shaking the pan, until the fish is almost cooked through and browned on one side, about 3 minutes. Turn the fish, sprinkle with salt and pepper and cook for 1 minute more. Remove the fish and 4 of the shallots to a heated dish and keep warm. Remove the remaining shallots, squeeze out the soft flesh, discard the skins, and process the flesh with the metal blade, until pureed, about 10 seconds.
- Pour out the remaining grease from the skillet and stir in the Vegetable Stock. Cook over medium-high heat, stirring to scrape up any browned bits, until reduced to ⅓ cup. Whisk in the shallot purée and the remaining butter, 1 tablespoon at a time. Stir in lemon juice and taste for seasoning.
- To serve, arrange a circle of potato slices on each of 4 warmed serving plates. Place 5 monkfish pieces and a whole shallot in the center of the potatoes and spoon some sauce over each portion. If necessary, reheat briefly in the oven before serving.

Vegetable Stock

Yield: 3 cups

8 medium shallots (about ½-ounce each), unpeeled, root end trimmed
1 medium garlic clove (1 10-ounce), peeled and halved
1 small carrot (3-ounces), trimmed, cut into 1-inch pieces
1 small leek (3-ounces), cleaned, cut into 1-inch pieces
1 sprig fresh thyme or ⅛ teaspoon dried
½ cup dry white wine vinegar
3 cups water

- Bring all the ingredients to the boil in a large saucepan. Cook gently, uncovered, until shallots are very tender, about 8 minutes. Strain. Reserve the stock and shallots and discard the remaining vegetables

Recipe provided by *Jean Louis Gerin,* Chef at the Restaurant Guy Savoy in Greenwich, Connecticut.

FLEMISH BEEF CARBONNADE

This classic recipe demonstrates the unique character of beer as a cooking ingredient. Any beer will work: flat or fresh, dark or light.

Serves: 6 to 8

2¼ pounds boneless beef (top or bottom round)
6 medium onions (2¼-pound total) peeled
3 tablespoons safflower oil
1 tablespoon sugar
2½ tablespoons flour
1¼ cups beer
1 cup beef broth
1 teaspoon dried thyme
Bouquet garni (1 sprig parsley, leafy tops of 2 celery stalks and 1 whole bay leaf, wrapped in cheesecloth)
Salt to taste
Freshly ground pepper
1½ tablespoons red-wine vinegar

- Cut meat to fit feed tube with grain perpendicular to slicing disc. Place on baking sheet lined with waxed paper. Freeze until firm to touch, but not frozen solid; you should be able to pierce it through with tip of sharp knife. Meat can be frozen up to two months. When it is firm, wrap each piece individually and seal in airtight bag. When ready to use, thaw to firmness described above.
- Insert medium slicing disc (3 mm) stand onions in feed tube and use firm pressure to slice.
- Heat oil in Oval Roasting Pan over medium heat. Add onions, cover and cook until very soft-about 15 minutes. Add sugar, reduce heat and cook gently, uncovered, until onions are golden brown-about 40 minutes. Watch carefully so onions do not burn. Add flour and cook, stirring often, for 2 minutes. Add beer, broth, thyme and bouquet garni and cook until slightly thickened - about 10 minutes.
- Fifteen minutes before baking, place rack in center of oven and preheat to 350 degrees.
- Insert thick slicing disc (6 mm) stand semi-frozen meat in feed tube and use firm pressure to slice.
- Season sliced meat with salt and pepper. Spoon ⅓ of onions into casserole. Add ½ of sliced meat, then continue making layers of onions and meat, finishing with onions. Cover tightly and bake until meat is tender - about 2 to 2½ hours. Remove bouquet garni, add vinegar and stir gently. Adjust seasoning.

Note: The dish freezes and reheats well.

CHICKEN, ZUCCHINI AND RED PEPPER STIR-FRY

Serves: 8 (6-ounces each)

4 whole boneless chicken breasts (1½-pounds) trimmed, skinned and split into 8 cutlets
1 large garlic clove peeled
2 large zucchini (about 1¼-pounds total) trimmed to fit feed tube horizontally
2 medium red peppers (about 11 ounces total), cored, seeded, cut into 2½ by 3½-inch rectangles
6 large scallions (5-ounces total), cut to fit the feed tube vertically
5 tablespoons vegetable oil
½ teaspoon salt
¼ cup light soy sauce
¼ to ½ teaspoon Oriental sesame oil

- Cut each chicken breast in half horizontally and arrange the pieces in one layer on a foil-lined baking sheet. Freeze partially until firm, but not frozen solid. The meat should feel firm to the touch, but it should be easily pierced with the tip of a sharp knife.
- Insert the medium (4 mm) slicing disc and stand the chicken pieces vertically in the feed tube so the slicing disc will cut against the grain. Process the chicken and reserve.
- Drop the garlic through the feed tube with the motor running and the metal blade in place and process until finely chopped, about 15 seconds. Leave the garlic in the work bowl.
- Insert the French fry disc (6 x 6 mm) and process the zucchini. If you do not have a french fry disc, process the zucchini with the medium (4 mm) slicing disc. Remove the slices from the bowl and insert them back into the feed tube side by side, so they will fit tightly. Process them again to produce julienne strips.
- Insert the medium (4 mm) slicing disc. Place the red pepper pieces vertically in the feed tube and process. Process the scallions. Reserve.
- Heat 2 tablespoons of oil in a wok or skillet. Divide the chicken slices into 3 batches and cook each batch just until opaque. Remove the chicken when it is cooked and set aside. Add additional oil if necessary, but use as little as possible. After removing the last batch of chicken, add more oil to the pan. Add the zucchini, garlic and salt and cook for 2 minutes. Add the cooked chicken, red pepper, scallion, soy sauce, and sesame oil. Heat the mixture only until it is warm, stirring thoroughly. Adjust the seasoning and serve immediately with rice.

JANSSON'S TEMPTATION

Serves: 6

1 slice good quality white bread, crusts removed, in 4 pieces
2 large yellow onions (1-pound) peeled and cut flat at ends
6 medium baking potatoes (2¼-pounds) peeled and cut flat on opposite ends
1 (2-ounce) can flat anchovy filets, drained, with juices reserved
3 tablespoons unsalted butter
Freshly ground pepper
1½ cups cream

- Preheat the oven to 350 degrees.
- Insert the metal blade and process the bread into crumbs. Remove and reserve them.
- Insert the 2 mm slicing disc and process the onions. Remove and reserve.
- Put 2 cups of cold water in the work bowl and insert the 6 x 6 mm French-fry cut disc. Process the potatoes, using firm pressure. Leave them in the work bowl; the water will prevent the strips from discoloring.
- Spread a 1½ to 2-quart baking dish with 1 tablespoon of the butter. Drain the potatoes, pat them dry on paper towels and spread ⅓ of them on the bottom of the baking dish. Cover with half the onion slices, followed by half the anchovies, another ⅓ of the potatoes, the remaining onions, anchovies, and potatoes. Sprinkle each layer with a little pepper.
- Sprinkle the reserved anchovy juices over the top, then the reserved bread crumbs. Dot with the remaining butter, cut into bits. Pour the cream over and bake until the potatoes are tender, about 50 minutes.

MEXICAN-STYLE POTATOES AND CHEESE

Green chiles and cheese are combined with thinly sliced potatoes in this side dish. Use mild or hot chiles, according to your taste.

Serves: 6 to 8

1½ ounces Parmesan cheese, in 2 pieces
6 ounces sharp Cheddar cheese, chilled (see NOTE)
4 medium boiling potatoes (1½-pounds) peeled
1 medium onion (5-ounces) peeled
1 (4-ounce) can diced green chiles, drained
¼ teaspoon salt, if desired
¼ teaspoon freshly ground black pepper
2 tablespoons butter, chilled and cut into small pieces
½ cup heavy cream

- Adjust oven rack to center position and preheat oven to 375 degrees.
- Lightly butter oval roasting pan.
- Insert metal blade. With machine running, drop Parmesan cheese through feed tube and process until it is finely chopped, about 20 seconds. Remove and set aside.
- Insert medium shredding disc, put Cheddar cheese in feed tube and use light pressure to process. Remove and set aside.
- Insert 2 mm slicing disc, put potatoes in feed tube, and use firm pressure to process. Remove and set aside.
- With 2 mm slicing disc in place, put onion in feed tube, and use medium pressure to process. Transfer to bowl and add chiles; mix to combine them well.
- Arrange ⅓ of potato slices in pan, overlapping them slightly. Sprinkle with ½ the salt and pepper, spread with ½ the onion and chile mixture, and sprinkle with ½ the Cheddar cheese. Arrange ½ the remaining potatoes on top, sprinkle with remaining salt and pepper, spread with remaining onion and chile mixture, and sprinkle with remaining Cheddar cheese. Arrange remaining potatoes on top and sprinkle with Parmesan cheese. Dot top with butter and pour cream evenly over all.
- Bake until potatoes are tender and top begins to brown, about 40 minutes. Check after 30 minutes; if top is brown enough, cover with foil for last 10 minutes of cooking. Let stand for 5 to 10 minutes before serving.

Note: For Cheddar, you may substitute Swiss, Fontina, Monterey Jack, or a mixture of Cheddar and Monterey Jack.

BAKED EGGPLANT AND SPINACH WITH FRESH TOMATO SAUCE

Serves: 8

Eggplant

2 medium eggplants (1 pound each), unpeeled, cut in half vertically and horizontally
2 teaspoons salt
3 tablespoons oil
1 large garlic clove, peeled (optional)
Freshly ground black pepper

- Grease a 1½-quart ovenproof dish, preferably a glass one. Insert the 4 mm slicing disc in the food processor and slice the eggplant, using medium pressure. Place the slices in a colander and sprinkle with salt. Toss carefully, being careful not to break the slices. Allow the eggplant to drain in the colander for 30 minutes. (You can prepare the other ingredients while it is draining). Dry the slices with paper towels. Add the oil to a large sauté pan.
- Insert the metal blade in the food processor and mince the garlic by dropping it through the feed tube while the machine is running. Add the minced garlic to the sauté pan and soften it over medium heat. Add the eggplant to the pan and cover it. Cook for 5 minutes, shaking the pan occasionally to prevent sticking. Be sure the eggplant is steamed through.

Spinach

1¼ pounds fresh spinach including stems, roots trimmed off
¼ cup fresh parsley leaves
2 large scallions (1 ounce total), cut into 1-inch pieces
3 tablespoons unsalted butter, at room temperature
1 teaspoon salt
Freshly ground black pepper
Freshly grated nutmeg
2 large egg whites

- Wash the spinach thoroughly and place it in a large pot with only the water clinging to its leaves. Cook over high heat, stirring once or twice. As soon as the spinach wilts, transfer it to a colander and place under cold running water until the spinach is cold to the touch. Drain it and wring "dry" in a dish towel. It is essential to remove as much liquid as possible.
- In the food processor fitted with metal blade, mince the parsley and scallions for 3 seconds. Add the spinach and the remaining ingredients and process for 10 seconds. Set the mixture aside.

Mornay Sauce

1½ tablespoons unsalted butter
1½ tablespoons unbleached, all-purpose flour
¾ cup milk
¼ to ½ teaspoon salt
Freshly ground white pepper
Freshly ground nutmeg
4 ounces Parmesan cheese, at room temperature

- Melt the butter in a saucepan, stir in the flour and cook for about 5 minutes. Add the milk slowly, stirring constantly until the mixture is thick. Remove the pan from the heat and add the salt, pepper and nutmeg.
- Insert the shredding disc in the food processor and shred the Parmesan cheese. Mix the shredded cheese into the cooled cream sauce and adjust the seasoning, if desired.
- Fifteen minutes before baking, preheat the oven to 375 degrees. Adjust the rack to the middle of the oven.
- Layer cooked eggplant slices, skin side out, in the prepared dish. Spread the spinach mixture over the eggplant slices and cover with Mornay Sauce. This dish can be prepared in advance up to this point and kept in the refrigerator, covered.
- Uncover, bake in preheated oven for 30 minutes until the top is lightly browned.
- Serve with the Fresh Tomato Sauce (see recipe)

Fresh Tomato Sauce

Yield: 1¼ cups

2 tablespoons fresh parsley leaves
4 large shallots (4-ounces) peeled
1 small clove garlic, peeled
4 large tomatoes (1½-pounds) peeled, seeded and quartered
3 tablespoons tomato paste
2 teaspoons sugar
1 teaspoon dry mustard
1 teaspoon dried basil
1 teaspoon dried oregano
½ teaspoon salt
Freshly ground black pepper
¼ pound plus 2 tablespoons unsalted butter (5-ounces), chilled and cut into 10 pieces
3 tablespoons snipped chives

- In the food processor fitted with the metal blade, mince the parsley using on/off pulses. Finely mince the shallots and garlic by dropping them through the feed tube with the machine running. Add the tomatoes and chop them coarsely, using on/off pulses. Transfer this mixture to a 1-quart saucepan. Add the tomato paste, sugar, mustard, basil, oregano, salt and pepper. Cook over high heat for 8 to 10 minutes until the excess liquid has evaporated and the tomato mixture is like a soft marmalade.
- Just before serving, bring the tomato sauce to a boil and add 2 tablespoons of the butter. Whisk thoroughly and when the butter is just melted and incorporated, add 2 more tablespoons. Repeat until all the butter is added and melted. Do not boil. Adjust the seasoning as desired and place in a sauce dish. Stir in the chives and sprinkle with a little minced parsley.

VEGETARIAN CHILI

Yield: 5 cups

Prepare ahead

¼ cup loosely packed parsley leaves
8 ounces dry red kidney beans, washed and drained
1 teaspoon salt
1 can (14-ounce) Italian peeled tomatoes
½ cup bulgur (2½-ounces)
2 large garlic cloves (⅓-ounce total), peeled
1 small onion (2-ounces), peeled and quartered
1 medium celery rib (3-ounces), cut into 1-inch pieces
1 medium carrot (3-ounces), cut into 1-inch pieces
1 small green pepper (5½-ounces), cored, seeded and quartered
2 tablespoons vegetable oil
2 tablespoons dry red wine
1 tablespoon tomato paste
1 tablespoon lemon juice
1 teaspoon chili powder
½ teaspoon ground cumin
3 drops red pepper sauce
Freshly ground black pepper
3 ounces sharp Cheddar cheese

- Drop the parsley through the feed tube of a food processor with the metal blade in place and the motor running and process until finely chopped, about 15 seconds. Reserve.
- Put the kidney beans in a large saucepan, add 3 cups of water and soak the beans for 3 hours. Add 1 cup more water and salt and bring to the boil. Reduce heat, cover and cook until beans are tender, about 1 hour. Set aside.
- Strain the tomatoes into a small saucepan. Reserve the tomatoes and bring the tomato liquid to the boil. Add the bulgur, remove from heat, cover and soak for at least 15 minutes.
- Drop the garlic through the feed tube with the motor running and process until finely chopped, about 15 seconds. Add the onion and process until coarsely chopped, about 5 pulses. Reserve.
- Process the celery, carrot and green pepper until coarsely chopped, 6 to 8 pulses. Reserve.
- Process the reserved tomatoes until puréed, about 15 seconds.
- Heat the oil in a large skillet over moderate heat. Add the garlic and onion mixture and cook, stirring, until the onion is tender, about 3 minutes. Add the chopped vegetables, puréed tomatoes, 1 tablespoon of the chopped parsley, red wine, tomato paste, lemon juice, chili powder, cumin, red pepper sauce, salt and black pepper to taste. Cook for another 5 minutes, stirring often, or until the vegetables are barely tender.
- Stir the vegetable mixture and soaked bulgur into the undrained kidney beans and reheat if necessary.
- Insert the fine shredding disc and process the cheese. Sprinkle the cheese and remaining parsley over the chili and serve.

VEGETABLE STUFFED ZUCCHINI

An attractive and delicious combination. May be made in advance and refrigerated for 24 hours, lightly covered with plastic wrap. Reheat for 25 minutes in a preheated 325 degree oven.

Serves: 6

3 small zucchini (about 4-ounces)
½ teaspoon salt
3 medium carrots (11-ounces total), peeled and cut into 1-inch pieces
1 small all-purpose potato (4-ounces), peeled and quartered
½ medium Granny Smith apple (3-ounces), peeled, seeded and quartered
2 tablespoons unsalted butter, room temperature
⅛ teaspoon freshly grated nutmeg
Freshly ground white pepper

- Preheat oven to 375 degrees. Butter a baking dish large enough to hold the zucchini in a single layer.
- Trim off the stem ends and cut the zucchini in half lengthwise. Use a melon baller to remove the pulp, leaving a ¼-inch shell. Sprinkle the interior of the shells with half the salt and drain them on paper towels for 20 minutes. Rinse the zucchini under cold water to remove the salt.
- Bring 2 quarts of water to the boil in a large saucepot. Cook the zucchini for about 5 minutes or until barely tender. Remove with a slotted spoon to paper towels to drain.
- Meanwhile bring 1½ quarts of water to the boil in a medium saucepan. Cook the carrots for 10 minutes, add the potatoes and cook ten minutes more. Add the apple and continue cooking until all the ingredients are very tender, about 15 minutes. Drain well and cool for 10 minutes.
- Process the cooked mixture and the butter, nutmeg, remaining salt and white pepper with the metal blade until smooth, about 1 minute. Scrape the bowl as necessary.
- Butter baking dish and arrange the shells skin-side down in the dish. Blot the insides of the shells with a paper towel.
- Fill a pastry bag fitted with a No. 5 star tip with the puréed mixture and pipe it into the zucchini shells. Bake for 15 to 20 minutes until the zucchini is tender and the tops feel dry. Transfer to a serving dish with a spatula.

ZUCCHINI PRIMAVERA

Serves: 6

1 medium carrot (3-ounces), peeled and cut in half crosswise
6 medium firm zucchini (6-ounces each), unpeeled and cut in half crosswise
1 garlic clove, peeled
1 cup parsley leaves
6 tablespoons unsalted butter, at room temperature
¾ cup tiny frozen peas, thawed
2 teaspoons fresh lemon juice
½ teaspoon dried oregano
½ teaspoon dried basil
1 teaspoon salt
Freshly ground black pepper

- Insert the 4 mm slicing disc and cut the carrots into julienne strips using the double-slicing technique of food processor. Use medium pressure on the pusher. Remove the strips from the bowl and set them aside. Slice the zucchini into julienne strips, using the same technique, and set aside.
- Insert the metal blade and mince the garlic by dropping it through the small feed tube while the machine is running. Add the parsley leaves and process for about 20 seconds, or until the parsley is finely chopped. Add the butter and process for about 5 seconds.
- Place the butter mixture in a large sauté pan and melt it over medium high heat. Add the zucchini and cook for 3 to 5 minutes, or until the zucchini is barely heated through. Shake the pan occasionally to prevent it from sticking. Add the carrot strips and peas, lemon juice, oregano, basil, salt and pepper. Toss gently with two rubber spatulas and cook 2 minutes longer. Place in a serving dish and serve immediately.

PIZZA

30-Minutes (From food processor to table)

Basic Thin Crust (recipe follows)
4 ounces Parmesan cheese, room temperature, cut into 4 pieces
½ pound mushrooms, sliced and sautéed in butter until soft
12 ounces mozzarella cheese, chilled
1 small onion (about 2-ounces), peeled, ends cut flat
1 medium green pepper, (about 5½-ounces), cored, seeded, ends cut flat
1 medium tomato (about 6-ounces), cored, ends cut flat
1 cup Fresh Tomato Pizza Sauce (recipe follows)
Pinch sugar
Freshly ground black pepper
½ teaspoon dried basil or 1 teaspoon fresh basil
½ teaspoon dried oregano or 1 teaspoon fresh oregano

- Preheat the oven to 425 degrees. Bake the prepared pizza crust in the lower third of the preheated oven for 6 minutes. If the crust puffs up during baking, press it down gently with a kitchen towel.
- While the crust is baking, prepare the toppings for the pizza. Process the Parmesan cheese with the metal blade of a food processor until coarsely chopped, 15 to 20 pulses. Reserve.
- Insert the medium shredding disc and process the mozzarella cheese. Reserve.
- Insert the thin (2 mm) slicing disc and process the onion, flat end down. Reserve.
- Insert the medium (3 mm) slicing disc and process the green pepper, stem end down. Reserve. Process the tomato, flat end down and drain onto paper towel. Reserve.
- With a rubber spatula, spread the tomato sauce evenly over the baked crust, leaving the rim exposed. Separate each sliced onion into rings and distribute them over the sauce. Top evenly with the mozzarella cheese. Arrange the tomato slices evenly over the cheese and sprinkle with sugar and black pepper to taste. Top with the Parmesan-mushroom mixture and arrange the pepper rings evenly over the pizza. Sprinkle with basil and oregano.
- Bake the pizza in the preheated oven for 18 minutes or until the rim of the crust is golden brown.

Basic Thin Crust

Yield: One 14-inch or two 9-inch crusts

1 package active dry yeast
1 teaspoon sugar
½ cup plus 2 tablespoons warm water (105 to 115 degrees)
1½ cups plus 2 tablespoons all purpose flour (8-ounces)
¾ teaspoon salt
2 teaspoons vegetable oil
1½ tablespoons white or yellow cornmeal, for pan

Mixing and Kneading the Dough

- Stir the yeast and sugar into the warm water in a 1-cup liquid measure. Process the flour and salt with the metal blade of a food processor for 20 seconds. With the motor running, pour the yeast mixture through the feed tube in a steady stream and process until the dough pulls away from the side of the bowl, about 45 seconds. Pour the oil through the feed tube and process for 60 seconds more.
- If the dough sticks to the side of the bowl, add more flour, 1 tablespoon at a time, processing for 10 seconds after each addition, until the dough leaves the side of the bowl but remains soft.
- The dough may be used directly from the food processor. The texture of the dough will improve and it will be easier to roll if it rests in the refrigerator for 1 hour, sealed in a lightly floured 1-gallon (4L) plastic bag.
- The dough may be refrigerated for up to a day.

Rolling the Dough

- Roll the dough on a floured surface into a circle, rotating and turning the dough often and using enough flour so that it doesn't stick to the surface. If the dough resists rolling, let it rest for a few minutes and try again.
- For a flat pan the dough should be 1 inch bigger than the pan all the way around. For a deep-dish pan, roll the dough so that it is 2½ inches bigger than the bottom of the pan all the way around.

Preparing the Crust for Filling and Shaping the Rim

- Oil the pan or pans lightly and sprinkle with the cornmeal, dividing it if you are using two 9-inch pans.
- Fold the rolled dough in half loosely and then in half again. Position the point at the center of the pan and gently unfold. Press it into place from the center outward.
- For a flat pan turn under the 1-inch overhang of the dough and shape it into a rim. The crust is now ready to fill.
- For a deep-dish pan, press the dough against the side. There should be a ½-inch overhang. Trim the overhang if necessary. The rim is shaped after the filling is added. To shape the rim, fold it toward the inside of the pan so that the edge is about ¼ inch below the top of the filling. Press firmly into place. Shape a decorative rim at the top.

Fresh Tomato Pizza Sauce

Yield: 2 cups

2 large tomatoes (about 12-ounces total), juiced, seeded and quartered
1 cup canned tomato sauce
¼ cup tomato paste
¾ teaspoon dried oregano or 1½ teaspoons fresh oregano
¾ teaspoon dried basil or 1½ teaspoons fresh basil
1 teaspoon sugar
Salt and freshly ground black pepper

- Process the tomatoes with the metal blade of a food processor until coarsely chopped, about 6 pulses. Add the remaining ingredients and pulse 4 times to combine.
- When this sauce stands, some watery liquid may accumulate on its surface. Pour off all but 1 or 2 tablespoons of it and then stir well before using.

ALMOND DELIGHTS

Yield: 4 dozen cookies

¼ cup blanched almonds (1½-ounces)
2 sticks unsalted butter (8-ounces), room temperature cut into 16 pats
½ cup confectioners sugar (2-ounces)
2 cups all-purpose flour (10-ounces)
⅛ teaspoon salt
⅛ teaspoon pure almond extract
Cookie Sheets
1 recipe Chocolate-Almond Filling (recipe follows)

- Preheat the oven to 350 degrees.
- Toast the almonds on a baking sheet in the preheated oven until lightly browned, 8 to 10 minutes. Cool to room temperature.
- Process the almonds with the metal blade of a food processor, until finely chopped, 6 to 8 pulses. Set aside.
- Process the butter and sugar until smooth and creamy, about 20 seconds, stopping to scrape down the work bowl as necessary. Add the flour, salt and almond extract and pulse 8 to 10 times or until well mixed, stopping to scrape down the work bowl as necessary.
- Roll a rounded half teaspoon of dough into a ball. Place 1½ inches apart on ungreased baking sheets.
- Bake the cookies in the center of the preheated oven until firm, but not brown, 10 to 12 minutes. Cool on a wire rack.
- Spread about ½ teaspoon of the filling on the bottom of one cookie. Place another cookie bottom side down over the filling and press lightly. Roll the chocolate edge in the chopped almonds.

Chocolate-Almond Filling

Yield: 1 cup

3 ounces semisweet chocolate such as Tobler or Lindt, broken into 1-inch pieces
2 tablespoons unsalted butter
2 tablespoons heavy cream
½ teaspoon pure almond extract
Pinch salt
1 cup confectioners sugar (4-ounces)

- Process the chocolate with the metal blade of a food processor until finely chopped, about 1 minute.
- Bring the butter and cream to the boil in a small saucepan.
- With the motor running, pour the hot butter-cream mixture through the feed tube and process for 15 seconds or until the chocolate is smooth. Add the remaining ingredients and pulse 4 to 6 times to combine, stopping to scrape down the bowl as necessary.

CHOCOLATE CHIP POUND CAKE

Yield: One cake (about 3 pounds)

8 ounces cream cheese, room temperature, cut into 1-inch dice
2 sticks unsalted butter (8-ounces), cut into 8 pieces, room temperature
1½ cups sugar (11¼-ounces)
4 large eggs
2 tablespoons sour cream
2 teaspoons pure vanilla extract
2¼ cups cake flour (9-ounces)
2 teaspoons baking powder
¼ teaspoon salt
1 cup semi-sweet chocolate chips (6-ounces)
Confectioners sugar

- Preheat the oven to 325 degrees. Butter and flour a 10-cup tube pan.
- Pulse the cream cheese, butter and sugar with the metal blade of a food processor 3 times, then process until smooth, about 30 seconds, scraping down the work bowl as necessary. With the motor running, add the eggs through the feed tube and process for 40 seconds, scraping down the work bowl as necessary. Add the sour cream and vanilla and process 10 seconds. Add the flour, baking powder, salt and chocolate chips and pulse just until the flour is incorporated, 8 to 10 times. (If some flour remains on the surface of the batter, fold it in with a spatula).
- Spoon the batter into the prepared pan. Tap the pan on the counter twice to smooth the batter and bake in the center of the preheated oven until a cake tester inserted in the cake comes out clean, about 1 hour.
- Remove the cake to a wire rack and cool for 10 minutes. Remove the cake from the pan and cool completely. Dust with confectioners sugar, if desired.

FRUIT ICES

Basic Method

- At least 5 hours before serving, prepare the fruit (see individual recipes for specific ingredients). Cut the fruit into 1-inch pieces. For Fruit Ices, freeze ¾ of the fruit in a single layer on a baking sheet and place the remaining ¼ in the refrigerator. For Frozen Fruit yogurt, freeze all of the fruit in a single layer on a baking sheet.
- A few minutes before serving, process the frozen fruit with the metal blade of a food processor until finely chopped, pulsing 8 times then processing continuously. Scrape down the work bowl and cover as necessary.
- Add the refrigerated fruit pieces (or the plain yogurt) and any additional ingredients called for in each recipe. Process just until smooth and creamy, scraping down the work bowl as necessary. Taste for sweetness; add more sugar if needed.
- The ices and yogurts are at their best when served immediately, but they may also be frozen for later use. To prepare for serving, cut the Frozen Yogurt or Fruit Ice into 1-inch chunks. Process with the metal blade just until smooth and creamy.
- Ascorbic acid (Vitamin C powder) maintains the bright, fresh color of many fruits. You can buy it in the health food stores and drugstores.

Pear Ice

3 large pears (about 23-ounces total) halved, cored and peeled
⅓ cup confectioners powder sugar (1¼-ounces)
1½ teaspoons pear brandy
¼ teaspoon Vitamin C powder

Frozen Pear Yogurt

3 large pears (about 23-ounces total), halved, cored and peeled
½ cup plain yogurt
1 tablespoon plus 1 teaspoon fresh lemon juice
¼ cup confectioners sugar

Nectarine Ice

5 small nectarines (about 18-ounces total), peeled and pitted
1½ teaspoons fresh lemon juice
¼ cup confectioners sugar (1-ounce)
¼ teaspoon Vitamin C powder

Frozen Nectarine Yogurt

5 small nectarines (about 18-ounces total), peeled and pitted
½ cup plain yogurt
⅓ cup confectioners sugar (1⅓-ounces)
¼ teaspoon Vitamin C powder

Red Plum Ice

8 medium red plums (about 17-ounces total), blanched until skins split, about 30 seconds, cooled, unpeeled and pitted

¼ cup plus 2 tablespoons confectioners sugar (1½-ounces)

Frozen Plum Yogurt

8 medium red plums (about 17-ounces total), blanched until skins split, about 30 seconds, cooled, unpeeled and pitted

½ cup plain yogurt

½ cup confectioners sugar (2-ounces)

Banana-Apple Ice

3 small bananas (about 13-ounces total), peeled

2 medium Golden Delicious apples (about 10-ounces total), halved, cored and peeled

1½ tablespoons fresh lemon juice

1½ teaspoons confectioners sugar

Frozen Banana-Apple Yogurt

3 small bananas (about 13-ounces total) peeled

2 medium Golden Delicious apples (about 10-ounces total), halved, cored and peeled

½ cup plain yogurt

1 tablespoon plus 1 teaspoon fresh lemon juice

1¼ teaspoons confectioners sugar

Strawberry Ice

1½ pints small strawberries (about 17-ounces total), washed and hulled

¼ cup confectioners sugar

1½ teaspoons fruit brandy, such as Framboise or Kirsch

Frozen Strawberry Yogurt

1½ pints small strawberries (about 17-ounces total), washed and hulled

½ cup plain yogurt

1 tablespoon fresh lemon juice

⅓ cup confectioners sugar

PEAR SAUCE "TATIN"

Yield: About 2 cups

6 ounces (1½ sticks) unsalted butter
2 pounds firm, ripe Anjou or Comice pears, peeled, cored and cut into eighths
⅔ cup sugar

- Melt the butter in a heavy 12-inch skillet over moderately high heat. Add the pears and sauté them, turning often, until very soft and lightly browned, about 30 minutes. Use the metal blade of a food processor to process the pear mixture until smooth, about 45 seconds, stopping twice to scrape down the bowl. Leave the mixture in the bowl.
- Put the sugar in an even layer in a 1½-quart saucepan over moderately low heat. When the sugar has melted and just begun to color, reduce the heat to low and begin to stir with a wooden spoon. Stir constantly until the sugar has turned a deep caramel color, taking care not to let it burn. Immediately remove the saucepan from the heat. This procedure can take up to 10 minutes.
- Turn on the processor and carefully pour the caramelized sugar through the center of the feed tube. Do not worry if any of the hot syrup touches the inside of the feed tube and hardens. After you have finished pouring, simply loosen these globs with a knife and let them drop into the still-running machine. Process for 15 seconds, stopping once to scrape down the bowl.
- Serve warm or at room temperature. The sauce will keep for several weeks, stored covered in the refrigerator. It freezes well.

PEAR SOUFFLÉ "TATIN"

Serves: 6

1 cup Pear Sauce "Tatin" (see recipe)
4 large egg yolks
2 tablespoons pear brandy
1½ teaspoons lemon juice
5 large egg whites
2 tablespoons granulated sugar plus extra for coating soufflé dish
Confectioners sugar

- Cut a length of aluminum foil long enough to fit around the side of a 6-cup soufflé dish. Fold it along its length so that it will be about 1½-inches wider than the height of the soufflé dish. Butter a 2-inch-wide strip along one side of the length. Tie the foil about the soufflé dish with the buttered side facing in along the rim. Sprinkle the dish and the buttered strip of foil with sugar. Preheat the oven to 375 degrees.
- In a 1-quart saucepan, warm the Pear Sauce "Tatin" to lukewarm (about 100 degrees). Put the metal blade in a processor and add the egg yolks, brandy, and lemon juice to the bowl. Turn the machine on and pour in the warmed pears through the feed tube. Stop the machine and scrape down the bowl.
- In a 3-quart mixing bowl, beat the egg whites to soft peaks with an electric mixer. Add the sugar and continue to beat until the whites are shiny and form stiff peaks. Add a quarter of the egg whites to the fruit mixture and turn the machine on and off about 4 times or until the egg whites just disappear.
- Pour the fruit mixture over the remaining egg whites and fold it in quickly but gently. Don't worry if a few blobs of white still show. Gently scrape into the prepared soufflé dish. Run your finger through the mixture in a circle, about 1 inch from the edge of the dish to a depth of about ½ inch. This helps it to rise properly. Bake for 35 to 40 minutes or until well browned and slightly firm. Sprinkle with confectioners sugar.

RESTAURANTS
& CELEBRITIES
Bay Basil Savory Coriander Sage Rosemary Parsley Mint Coriander Sage Rosemary
Sage Rosemary Parsley Cinnamon Marjoram
Marjoram Thyme Juniper Bay
Bay Basil Savory Coriander Sage Rosemary Parsley Mint Cinnamon Parsley
Sage Rosemary Parsley Mint Cinnamon Marjoram Thyme Juniper Coriander Sage Rosemary
Marjoram Thyme Juniper Bay Basil Savory Coriander Bay Basil

Culinary Productions Ltd.
Bedford Hills, New York

MOCHA MOUSSE CAKE

Serves: 10 to 12

½ pound cream cheese, room temperature *
3 eggs, separated, room temperature *
2 packages (12 to a package) lady fingers
6 ounces dark, sweet chocolate
1 tablespoon gelatin
2 tablespoons cold water
Pinch salt
1 cup light brown sugar, firmly packed
1 teaspoon vanilla
2 cups heavy cream, whipped
1 teaspoon powdered coffee or coffee flavored liqueur
Grated chocolate for garnish

- * Let the cream cheese stand at room temperature for at least half an hour. Separate 3 eggs and let stand at room temperature for the same time. Eggs are easier to separate when cold, and beaten whites produce more volume at room temperature.
- Line bottom and sides of 9-inch spring form pan with waxed paper, then line pan with split lady fingers.
- Melt chocolate, let cool.
- Soften gelatin in water in a measuring cup. Place cup in a skillet of simmering water until gelatin is dissolved.
- Beat egg whites until they form soft peaks. Add a pinch of salt. Beat in ½ cup of sugar, a little at a time. Add vanilla. Continue beating until very stiff and glossy.
- Whip 1½ cups cream. Beat the cream cheese until fluffy, add remaining ½ cup sugar, a little at a time. Add coffee or liqueur. Add egg yolks, one at a time, beating well after each addition. Beat in the chocolate and gelatin. Fold in egg whites and 1½ cups cream into the chocolate mixture. Place in prepared pan.
- Chill in refrigerator until set, at least 2 hours or overnight if you wish.
- Whip remaining ½ cup cream and garnish the top with rosettes of whipped cream and a little grated chocolate.

Abigail Kirsch
Culinary Productions Ltd.
Bedford Hills, New York

STUFFED GOUDA CHEESE

Serves: 8

14 ounce baby Gouda cheese
½ cup beer
1 teaspoon Dijon mustard
⅛ teaspoon nutmeg
¼ cup butter, room temperature
2 cloves garlic, crushed
4 ounces cream cheese, room temperature
1 tablespoon caraway seeds

- Cut out a circle from center of top of the Gouda cheese. Carefully scoop out the cheese inside, leaving the shell intact. Use a small curved knife such as a grapefruit knife. Avoid puncturing the casing. Cut the cheese into very small pieces.
- Place ¼ cup beer in a blender, add the cheese, mustard, nutmeg, butter and garlic and blend until smooth, adding remaining beer gradually with motor running. (You may find that the blender does not blend cheese to the desired smooth consistency. In that case, pour the contents into a Foley mill and finish the blending process). Add the softened cream cheese at end of blending. Fold in the caraway seeds and fill the shell with this mixture. Sprinkle more caraway seeds on top.

Note: Cheese mixture can be made 24 hours ahead of serving and refrigerated. The flavor, however, does not improve if held longer. It is delicious served on thin slices of Westphalian pumpernickel bread.

AMERICA

New York, New York

MEDALLIONS OF LONDON BROIL WITH WILD MUSHROOMS AND HERBS

Serves: 4

1½ pounds london broil, deveined and sliced paper thin
Salt and pepper to taste
6 shallots, peeled and minced
¼ cup olive oil or cooking oil
½ pound fresh shitakes, chanterelles, morelles, or other wild mushrooms, sliced (standard white mushrooms may also be used)
½ cup beef broth or stock
¼ cup dry red wine
1 tablespoon tomato paste
1 teaspoon tarragon

- Season meat with salt, pepper and minced shallots.
- Heat a sauté pan until very hot and add the oil. Add meat and stir fry for 2 minutes or until the meat looses its redness. Add the sliced mushrooms and sauté for 2 minutes. Add broth, wine, tomato paste and tarragon and cook until the sauce has thickened.

TARTE TATIN

Serves: 6 to 8

6 to 7 baking apples
4 tablespoons butter
8 tablespoons granulated sugar
½ ounce calvados or applejack
1 pound puff pastry

- Preheat oven to 350 degrees. Use a 10-inch skillet.
- Peel, core and cut apples into ¼-inch thick slices.
- Melt butter in a 10-inch skillet and cover the butter evenly with 6 tablespoons of the sugar. Arrange the apples over the butter and sugar in a circular fashion starting at the rim of the pan and working to the center. Sprinkle the remaining sugar over apples, then sprinkle with the liqueur.
- Roll out the pastry into a circle about ⅛-inch thick and cut it to fit over the apples but not overlapping the rim of the pan. Cut 5 to 6 holes about ⅛-inch long into the top of the pastry to allow the steam to escape.
- Bake for 35 to 40 minutes. If pastry begins to brown too much, cover with aluminum foil. The tart is done when the light colored liquid has turned into a thick, light brown syrup.
- Place a serving plate over the top of the pan and quickly invert the tart. Cool before serving.

Brae Burn Country Club
Purchase, New York

GLAZED ORANGES Á LA BRAE BURN

Serves: 6

6 navel oranges
8 cups sugar
10 cups cold water
4 ounces Grand Marnier
2 ounces brown sugar

- You will need a pot large enough to hold oranges in a single layer.
- Peel the zest from the oranges. Cut the strips into very fine julienne pieces. Set aside.
- Remove the membrane from the oranges. Discard the membrane; leave oranges whole.
- In an uncovered pot, add sugar and water. Bring to a boil. Add the oranges. Reduce heat and poach them in the liquid for 15 to 20 minutes, then remove the oranges from the stock (liquid). Set aside.
- In the same stock bring the orange strips to a boil, simmer for 25 minutes. Remove and drain.
- In a separate pan melt the brown sugar and Grand Marnier over low heat. Add 15 ounces of stock and bring to a boil; this will make the sauce.
- When ready to serve, place orange in dessert bowl, and garnish heavily with peel and sauce. Add a sprig of mint for color.

THE CAFE BUDAPEST
Boston, Massachusetts

CHILLED CHERRY SOUP Á LA BUDAPEST

Serves: 12

4 (16-ounce) cans pitted tart cherries
3 pieces of cinnamon stick
20 pieces of clove
20 pieces of allspice
1 slice of lemon
1 cup sugar
Pinch of salt
1 tablespoon flour
1 pint heavy cream
½ bottle red Burgundy wine
Additional whipping cream for topping

- Combine in a large pot, two whole cans of tart cherries. Use only the juice from the other two cans. Add spices, lemon, sugar and a pinch of salt. Bring to a boiling point. Add flour to cream and blend using a wire whisk. Add cream and wine to cherry mixture. Bring to boiling point again.
- Remove from heat, let cool and then refrigerate.
- Add a tablespoon of whipped cream on top of each serving.

Note: Will keep at least two weeks under refrigeration.

RESTAURANTS BY CHUCK MUER

Palm Beach, Florida

NACHOS

Serves: 6 to 8

Garnish of 80's

1/4 cup chopped parsley
4 green onions, chopped
1 teaspoon lemon juice
3 dashes (1 shake) Tabasco
2 dashes Worcestershire sauce

- Mix all ingredients together.

Nachos

3 ounces corn tortilla chips
3 ounces mild taco sauce (Old El Paso)
6 ounces Monterey Jack cheese with jalapeño pepper, grated
2 tablespoons grated Parmesan cheese
2 ounces fresh tomato, chopped medium
1 ounce onion, chopped very fine
2 ripe avocados, peeled and mashed
Salt and pepper to taste
1 teaspoon sour cream

- Preheat oven to 400 degrees. Use a large oval, ovenproof, serving platter (approximately 15½-inches).
- Line the chips around the edges of plate. Sprinkle taco sauce over chips; spread as evenly as possible.
- Combine the Monterey Jack cheese with the Parmesan and sprinkle over the chips evenly. Be sure *not* to get the cheese on the plate as it will burn. Cover all chips completely.
- Sprinkle tomatoes over chips evenly. Sprinkle onion over chips and tomatoes.
- Place in oven for about 7 minutes or until cheese is completely melted.
- Remove from oven and add the mashed avocado (mixed with salt and pepper) and sour cream to center of plate.
- Sprinkle with "garnish of 80's" over the entire dish and serve hot immediately.

Note: This dish must be served with the chips crisp. This is the reason for leaving in the oven longer - to get the chips crisp.

Houston, Texas

LIME MOUSSE IN ALMOND CUP WITH FRESH FRUIT ON RASPBERRY SAUCE

Serves: 10 to 12

Lime Mousse

14 eggs
1½ cups sugar
¾ cup lime juice
2 lime zests
1⅔ cups heavy cream
1½ tablespoons unflavored gelatin
5 tablespoons cold water

- Separate the eggs. Beat yolks with ½ cup sugar, lime juice and zest. Boil the cream and pour a little at a time into yolk mixture, whisking all the time. Place mixture over low heat and whisk until thick. Remove from heat.
- Dissolve gelatin in cold water and add to cream mixture.
- Beat egg whites until frothy. Gradually add remaining sugar, beating continuously until very stiff. Fold egg whites into warm cream mixture.
- Refrigerate for 3 hours.

Raspberry Sauce

10 ounces of fresh or frozen raspberries
2 tablespoons superfine sugar
1 teaspoon lemon juice or 1 tablespoon raspberry liqueur

- Purée raspberries and sugar together in a food processor or blender.
- Strain through a wire sieve to remove the seeds.
- Add lemon juice or liqueur and mix thoroughly. Set aside.

Almond Cups

1½ cups flour, sifted
1½ cups confectioners sugar
6 egg whites
½ teaspoon almond extract
½ cup butter, melted

- Preheat oven to 475 degrees. Lightly grease a cookie sheet.
- Using a whisk, add sugar, egg whites and extract to the flour. Work batter as little as possible. Whisk in melted butter to form a smooth paste.
- Make 12 thin crêpe-like circles onto cookie sheet.
- Bake for 5 to 10 minutes until edges begin to brown. Remove from oven and shape each pastry by placing it over a glass or bowl while hot and cover with a slightly larger glass. It only takes a few minutes to harden.

Assembly

- Spoon mousse into almond cups to cover the bottom. Garnish with fresh fruit and place on a plate in a pool of raspberry sauce.

Houston, Texas

STEAMED ATLANTIC HALIBUT ON MIXED GREENS WITH SAFFRON DRESSING

Serves: 4

Fish Stock

2 cups white wine
1 cup water
Fish bones
2 carrots, sliced
1 onion, sliced
1 bay leaf
3 peppercorns
½ teaspoon dried dill or 1 teaspoon fresh dill
½ teaspoon salt
¼ teaspoon black pepper

- Simmer all ingredients until liquid is reduced to 2 cups.

Steamed Halibut

4 (4-ounces each) slices Halibut

- Place halibut in a steamer and steam for approximately 10 minutes or until "white" in the center of the fish. Remove and set aside to cool to room temperature.

Saffron Dressing

2 egg yolks
2 ounces steaming liquid (fish stock)
½ ounce champagne vinegar
½ teaspoon dry mustard
½ teaspoon saffron threads
Salt, pepper and lemon juice to taste
6 ounces extra virgin olive oil

- Combine all ingredients except oil in a blender and blend thoroughly. Slowly add oil and blend.

Mixed Greens

1 head bibb lettuce
1 bunch watercress
2 Belgian endives
1 small head radicchio lettuce
1 ounce extra virgin olive oil
½ teaspoon vinegar
½ teaspoon chopped dill
1 teaspoon salmon roe caviar

- Combine "greens" and toss lightly in oil, vinegar and dill.
- Arrange ¼ of "greens" neatly on a plate, place a slice of fish on the "greens", spoon saffron dressing over all and top with salmon roe.
- Serve at room temperature.

Wine Suggestion: Chablis Les Clos, Moreau 1983

Houston, Texas

WINTER SQUASH RAVIOLI WITH GOAT CHEESE AND BASIL

Yield:30

Squash Purée Filling

1 pound butternut, hubbard or acorn squash peeled, seeded, cooked and squeezed dry
⅓ pound unsalted butter, room temperature
1 tablespoon garlic purée
¼ teaspoon nutmeg
⅛ teaspoon ground allspice
⅛ teaspoon ground ginger
⅛ teaspoon dry mustard
1/6 teaspoon cayenne pepper
Salt and pepper to taste

- Purée squash pulp in processor until smooth. Add rest of ingredients and process until combined.

Ravioli

3 large eggs
1 (6-ounce) can tomato paste
1 tablespoon salt
1 tablespoon olive oil
1¼ pounds unbleached flour
Cornmeal as needed
1 pound squash purée, recipe above
2 cups basil goat cheese sauce, recipe follows

- Combine eggs, tomato paste and salt in a food processor until well combined. Add flour in ¼'s until dough is formed. It should be moist but not tacky. Add more flour if needed.
- Form into fist-sized balls and pass through pasta machine on 2nd thinnest setting. Lay pasta on surface dusted with cornmeal.

To Assemble

- Spoon squash on pasta about 1½ inches apart; brush pasta with egg wash and cover with one more sheet pushing out air around squash.
- Cut into 2½ inch squares. Freeze immediately if not to be cooked until later.
- Cook raviolis in boiling, salted water for about 3 minutes Coat with sauce and garnish with tomato and pine nuts.

Basil Goat Cheese Sauce

2 cups heavy cream
1 tablespoon chopped basil
2 ounces domestic goat cheese
2 ounces butter
Salt, pepper and nutmeg to taste

- Reduce first three ingredients by ⅓. Remove from heat; whisk in butter and seasonings. Keep in warm place until ready to use. *Do not re-boil.*

Wine Suggestion: Long Chardonnay 1983

"EMPRESS SUBARU"
Chef Abbie Treat Boody

FRUIT TART

Yield: One 12-inch tart

Tart Dough

2½ cups flour
¾ cup sugar
1¼ cups butter or margarine, room temperature or cut into small pieces
1 teaspoon vanilla
1 egg
¼ cup finely chopped toasted almonds (optional)

- Preheat oven to 350 degrees. Use a 12-inch tart pan with removable bottom.
- In a large mixing bowl, combine all ingredients with your hands until thoroughly blended. Chill.
- Before rolling out, knead and rework the dough with your hands like a bread dough. Form into a smooth ball. Roll out on a well-floured board, and place into the tart pan.
- Bake in oven for 10 minutes or until golden.

Cream Cheese Filling

8 ounces cream cheese, room temperature
½ pint heavy cream
2 cups sugar
2 tablespoons vanilla
2 tablespoons liqueur such as Amaretto, Kaluah, * Frangelico (optional)

- Fold in all ingredients and whisk until sugar dissolves. Pour filling into a baked tart crust and top with fresh fruit. Arrange in a decorative manner. Chill and serve.

Note: Blueberries, strawberries, kiwis, hazelnuts, or champagne grapes may be used. * Chef Boody prefers to use Frangelico liqueur.

Mamaroneck, New York

SNAPPER POSILLIPO

Serves: 4

2 cups cooking oil
4 fillets of snapper (10-ounces each)
1 cup flour
1 teaspoon minced garlic
1 cup white wine
2 cups marinara sauce
4 cups chicken stock
½ teaspoon finely ground pepper
¼ teaspoon oregano
½ teaspoon seasoning powder
1 tablespoon margarine

- In a 12-inch skillet, pour all but 2 tablespoons of oil and heat.
- Flour the fillets lightly, make 3 to 4 incisions on the skin, place them in the pan skin side up, until lightly browned. Turn and cook for 2 to 3 more minutes. Remove from pan and drain the oil. Pour remaining 2 tablespoons of oil into the pan, heat, and add the garlic sautéeing until light brown. Add wine and remaining ingredients. Bring to boil, reduce heat, and place fillets back in pan skin side down. Cook to desired doneness.

New York, New York

DEATH BY CHOCOLATE

A layered chocolate torte.

Serves: 16

Crust

1 cup all purpose flour
⅓ cup granulated sugar
⅓ cup cocoa powder
1½ teaspoons baking powder
1 egg beaten lightly
4 tablespoons (½ stick) butter, room temperature
1½ teaspoons baking soda

- Preheat oven to 350 degrees. One 10-inch springform pan.
- Soften butter in a food processor or mixer. Add all the dry ingredients and blend thoroughly. Add beaten egg slowly.
- Form the crust mixture by hand to the bottom of the springform pan. Bake for 5 minutes. Let cool.

Filling: First Layer

2 pounds semisweet chocolate
2 cups heavy cream
2 tablespoons pure vanilla extract
¼ cup Grand Marnier

- Melt chocolate, cream and vanilla in a double boiler, stirring well and making sure not to boil. When chocolate is melted, add Grand Marnier and put mixture in a mixer bowl and blend at high speed for 15 to 20 minutes until color lightens and mixture thickens. Pour on top of crust and refrigerate until set.

Topping

1 pound semisweet chocolate
1 cup heavy cream
1½ teaspoons vanilla extract

- Melt ingredients together in double boiler stirring well. Do not boil. Remove from heat and let mixture rest until just warm. Stir once again then pour over set filling in springform pan. Return to refrigerator for 4 hours, until firm.
- To serve, remove ring from pan and slice with a thin warm knife. Garnish with fresh berries and whipped cream.

Suzanne Farrel
New York City Ballet, State Theater
Lincoln Center
New York, New York

APPLESAUCE BEEF LOAF

Serves: 4 to 5

1 cup soft bread crumbs
½ cup applesauce
1 pound ground beef
1 egg, slightly beaten
2 tablespoons chopped onion
1 teaspoon celery flakes
1 teaspoon Dijon mustard
Salt and pepper to taste

- Preheat oven to 350 degrees. Use a 9-inch x 9-inch x 2-inch baking pan.
- Combine all ingredients and blend thoroughly. Shape into a round loaf and place in the baking pan. With a spoon, make a crater-like depression in top of loaf.

Combine and pour into depression:

½ cup applesauce
1 tablespoon tarragon vinegar
1 teaspoon Dijon mustard

- Bake for 1 hour.

Note: Quick to make. Also good cold with rice.

SCARSDALE, NEW YORK

CHICKEN CURRY

Serves: 6

3 (2-pound) chickens, cut into serving pieces
1 cup oil
1 cup finely chopped celery
1 cup finely chopped onions
4 medium-size apples, pared and chopped
1/8 teaspoon cayenne pepper
2 teaspoons salt
Freshly ground black pepper to taste
3 tablespoons curry powder
2 cups boiling water

- In a large skillet, sauté chicken in oil for ten minutes or until brown. Remove chicken and keep hot. Add celery and onions to oil remaining in skillet and sauté for 5 minutes. Add all other ingredients. Cover and simmer for 30 minutes. Add chicken and 2 cups boiling water. Cover and simmer for 30 minutes.

Note: Turkey, duck or capon may be substituted for chicken, but may take longer to cook.

Fenway Golf Club
Scarsdale, New York

Diane Von Furstenberg
New York, New York

DIANE VON FURSTENBERG'S GAZPACHO SOUP

Delicious and Nutritious!

Serves: 4

3 very ripe medium tomatoes, peeled
1 large onion, cut in half
1 large green pepper, quartered
1 large cucumber, cut into small cubes
1 canned pimiento, drained
24 ounces tomato juice, natural, no additives
⅓ cup olive oil, more if needed
⅓ cup red wine vinegar
¼ teaspoon Tabasco sauce
¼ teaspoon black pepper, freshly ground
1¼ teaspoons salt
Chives, for garnish
Toasted white bread or croutons
1 clove garlic, minced

- Peel tomatoes (place in boiling water for one minute and skin will come off easily), and slice.
- In a large bowl combine half the onion, green pepper and cucumber with 2 of the tomatoes, the pimiento and ½ cup of tomato juice. Toss.
- Place this mixture, half at a time, in blender and blend for 1 minute.
- Add to this mixture the olive oil, remaining tomato juice, red wine vinegar, Tabasco, black pepper and salt.
- Refrigerate overnight or a minimum of 6 hours.
- Dice the remaining onion, green pepper, cucumber and tomato and serve as a garnish with soup.
- Just before serving heat olive oil and garlic and gently brown croutons or white bread cut into cubes. Garnish with chives.

GREGORY'S
White Plains, New York

CHICKEN SCARPARELLO

Serves: 2

¾ cup vegetable oil
4 cloves garlic, crushed
4 boneless chicken breasts, cubed
1 cup dry white wine
Juice of 2 large lemons
1 teaspoon rosemary, fresh or dried
1 cup sliced fresh mushrooms
¼ cup chopped parsley
1½ cups chicken stock
Salt and pepper to taste

- Heat oil in a large iron skillet, almost to smoking point. Add crushed garlic, stir until edges begin to brown. Add cubed chicken breast, stir and cook until lightly browned. Drain oil from skillet. Add wine, lemon juice and rosemary. Add mushrooms. Cook and reduce liquid for approximately 8 minutes. Reduce heat to avoid burning. Add parsley and chicken stock. Lower heat and simmer for 10 minutes, uncovered, then add salt and pepper to taste. Stir occasionally. Sauce should have a creamy consistency when done.

Greenwich, Connecticut

BROWN RICE SALAD

Serves: 6 to 8

1¾ cups water
½ cup brown rice
½ teaspoon salt
½ bunch scallions, greens included, diced
2 medium tomatoes, seeded and chopped
1 bunch curley parsley, chopped
½ bunch celery, diced
1 cup currant raisins
1 cup walnuts, coarsely chopped
*** Safflower oil dressing, recipe follows**

- In a pot, bring water to a boil. Stir in rice and salt. Cover and simmer until water is absorbed, about 30 minutes. Pour rice into a colander and rinse with cold water. Drain thoroughly.
- Place rice in a large bowl, add scallions, tomatoes, parsley, celery and dressing. Mix thoroughly. Fold in raisins and walnuts.
- Rice dish can be made a day ahead; omit the tomatoes until ready to serve. Serve chilled or at room temperature. This is a wonderful side-dish and works well with the "Curry Chicken" recipe.

***Safflower Oil Dressing**

Yield: 1½ cups

1 cup safflower oil
½ cup imported red wine vinegar
Salt and pepper to taste

- In a medium bowl, add oil, vinegar, salt and pepper. With a wire whisk, mix the ingredients thoroughly, until well blended. Correct seasoning and set aside.

Note: Dressing can be made ahead of time and stored in refrigerator for 1 week. Whisk before stirring into Brown Rice Salad.

Greenwich, Connecticut

HAY DAY CURRY CHICKEN

Serves: 8 to 10

3½ to 4 pounds boned, skinned chicken breasts: to yield 2½ pounds cooked; steamed approximately 12 to 15 minutes, cut into strips
3 cups celery, sliced thin, about ½ bunch
1½ cups scallions, diced, including the greens
1 green pepper, sliced into thin strips
2 tomatoes seeded and cubed
1 cup unsalted peanuts
⅓ cup currant raisins
*** 2 cups Curried Mayonnaise, recipe follows**

- In a large bowl, place chicken, celery, scallions, green pepper and tomatoes. Toss gently until mixed. Add curried mayonnaise dressing. Mix carefully until blended. Fold in peanuts and raisins.
- This can be served chilled or at room temperature.

*** *Curried Mayonnaise***

Yield: 2 cups

1 large egg
¼ cup lemon juice
1 tablespoon curry powder, medium or hot
1 teaspoon Dijon mustard
1 teaspoon salt
½ teaspoon white pepper
1½ cups safflower oil

- In a blender or food processor, place all ingredients except oil. Blend until mixed. With the motor running, add the oil slowly. Mix thoroughly. Adjust seasoning to taste and set aside.

Note: Curried mayonnaise can be made ahead of time and will keep in the refrigerator for 1 week. Whisk before adding to Curry Chicken.

Mark Filippi
Harrison, New York

GRILLED TUNA WITH WARM RADICCHIO, ARUGULA AND ENOCK MUSHROOMS

This recipe was created to meet the current demand for eating light.

Serves: 4

2 pounds blue fin tuna cut into 4 steaks (8-ounces each)
1 large head Radicchio
1 bunch Arugula
1 (3.5-ounce) pack of Enok mushrooms
1 ounce hazelnut oil
⅓ ounce balsamic vinegar
Salt, pepper to taste
1 bunch chopped chives

Marinade

3 ounces olive oil
1 ounce soy sauce

- Marinate tuna in olive oil and soy sauce for ½ hour. Turn several times.
- While tuna is marinating, light outdoor grill and allow coals to get very hot.
- Clean radicchio by separating the leaves and rinsing in cold water. Cut the stems from the arugula with just the leaves remaining and rinse in cold water. Cut Enok mushrooms ½-inch above the root end.
- Spray grill with a non-stick aerosol product and coat with oil. Place tuna on grill and cook medium rare (don't over-cook). Time depends on the thickness of fish.
- While tuna is cooking, mix salad in a bowl with oil, vinegar, salt, pepper and chives. Heat salad until just warm. Place neatly on 4 dinner plates. Place tuna in center of each plate and serve. Bon Repas!

Jorge's Uptown Enchilada Bar, Inc.
Austin, Texas

BILLIE'S CHILI

Serves: 8

1½ pounds Chili Grind meat (large grind) if you cannot get this, purchase 1 pound boneless beef and ½ pound ground beef
1 to 2 tablespoons oil
1 medium onion, chopped
1 clove garlic, crushed
2 tablespoons chili powder, or to taste
½ teaspoon oregano
½ teaspoon ground cumin
1 teaspoon salt
1½ teaspoons garlic powder
1 (16-ounce) can tomatoes
1 (16-ounce) can water
1 beef bouillon cube
Cornstarch Paste: 1 tablespoon cornstarch and 2 tablespoons water

- Dice beef into ¼-inch pieces (easier to cut if meat is partially frozen).
- Place in a Dutch oven or heavy kettle with oil. Cook, stirring frequently, until meat loses its red color. Add all other ingredients and bring to a boil, then reduce heat to simmer, about 2 hours. Thicken juice of chili with cornstarch paste.

Hotel Inter-Continental
New York, New York

SOLE SALAD WITH VEGETABLE VINAIGRETTE

Serves: 4

Assorted greens (e.g. radishes, red leaf, arugula)
½ medium carrot, diced
12 French green beans, diced
10 cauliflower flowerets
2 tablespoons water
2 tablespoons Dijon mustard
1 tablespoon champagne vinegar
1 cup sunflower oil
Salt and pepper to taste
12 Dover sole or grey sole fillets

- Preheat oven to 360 degrees.
- Clean greens, spin dry in a salad spinner. Set aside.
- Cook the carrot, green beans and cauliflower separately in salted boiling water until al dente. Reserve some vegetables for garnish. Purée each vegetable separately.
- Place water, mustard and vinegar in a stainless steel bowl. Slowly add oil and whisk vigorously so the oil emulsifies in the mustard mixture. When completely mixed, add equal amounts of each vegetable purée until balanced to taste. Season with salt and pepper.
- Arrange fillets on a broiler plate. Season with salt and pepper. Cook for 3 to 4 minutes.
- Arrange greens on a plate and place 3 fillets on top. Sprinkle vinaigrette on top and garnish with reserved vegetables.

Marion and Robert Merrill
Metropolitan Opera
New York, New York

FISH NEWBURG

Serves: 6 to 8

4 tablespoons butter or margarine
4 tablespoons flour
1 teaspoon onion powder
2 cups Half 'n Half or light cream
½ teaspoon salt
¼ teaspoon paprika
½ cup dry cooking sherry
2 pounds fish, cooked, cooled and flaked

- Melt the butter in saucepan; blend in flour. Add onion powder and blend. Add cream and stir constantly over medium heat until thickened and smooth. Add salt, paprika and sherry. Heat, stirring, to serving temperature but do not boil. Add cooked fish and again heat to serving temperature.

Note: Can be served with hot, fluffy rice or in baked patty shells or over toast points.

White Plains, New York

EGGPLANT SORRENTINA

Serves: 4 to 6

2 medium-size eggplants, peeled
3 eggs, beaten
Pinch salt and pepper
2 tablespoons Parmesan cheese, grated
1/8 cup parsley, chopped
Flour, as needed
Bread crumbs, as needed
Vegetable oil for frying

- Slice eggplants into rounds approximately 1/4-inch thick.
- Season eggs with salt, pepper, Parmesan cheese and parsley.
- Dip eggplant slices in flour, then eggs, then in bread crumbs. Fry until golden brown. Drain on paper towels to remove excess oil.

Filling

1 pint ricotta cheese
1 cup Mozzarella cheese, shredded
Pinch black pepper
Salt to taste
Chopped parsley
1 egg, beaten

- Blend all ingredients in a bowl, with a wooden spoon, then set aside.

To Assemble

- Preheat oven to 350 degrees. Use a 9-inch x 13-inch baking pan.

2 cups plain tomato sauce
1/4 pound Mozzarella cheese, sliced and squared off

- Layer a full tablespoon of filling mixture between two slices of eggplant. Top with plain tomato sauce and a slice of Mozzarella cheese. Repeat. Bake in oven until cheese is completely melted. Serve with pasta or any vegetable.

OLD·DROVERS·INN

Dover Plains, New York

OLD DROVERS INN KEY LIME PIE

As presented on Channel 7's Eyewitness News; Bob Lape, Gourmet Reporter.

Serves: 6

5 egg yolks
19 ounces sweetened condensed milk
4 ounces freshly squeezed lime juice
Grated rind of 1 lime
1 (8-inch) graham cracker crust

- Beat egg yolks with wire whisk. Blend in condensed milk; add lime juice and grated lime rind. Pour into crust and refrigerate for two hours.

Roberta Peters
Metropolitan Opera
New York, New York

MEATLOAF ROSSINI

Serves: 6

3 pounds ground beef
1 large onion, chopped
1 teaspoon salt
1 teaspoon fresh pepper
1 teaspoon mustard
3 teaspoons green pepper, chopped
2 eggs
½ cup bread crumbs
1 teaspoon oregano

- Preheat oven to 325 degrees.
- Mix all ingredients until blended. Form into a loaf and place in a baking pan. Bake for 1½ hours, basting occasionally.

New York, New York
Chef Pascal Dirringer

SALMON Á LA MOUTARDE

Serves: 4

Small amount of butter
2 shallots, finely chopped
2 sprigs parsley, finely chopped
4 slices fresh salmon, 8 ounces each
Salt and pepper to taste
1½ cups dry white wine
1 cup heavy cream
2 tablespoons Dijon mustard
1 bunch fresh chives, chopped

- Brush the bottom of a casserole with butter and add finely chopped shallots and parsley.
- Arrange salmon in casserole, add salt, pepper and wine. Cover with water. Cook over medium heat for 10 minutes. Remove salmon to a warm platter. Reduce liquid almost to ⅓, add cream and mustard to remaining contents of casserole and allow to reduce to smooth consistency. Add salt and pepper to taste. Strain and pour sauce over the salmon. Sprinkle with chopped chives.

New York, New York
Chef Pascal Dirringer

TRUFFLES Á LA CRÉME DE GRAND MARNIER

Yield: 36

1 pound Swiss bittersweet chocolate
1 cup crème de Grand Marnier
1 cup bitter chocolate
½ cup confectioners sugar

- Mix the bittersweet chocolate with Créme de Grand Marnier in a bowl and heat in waterbath (double boiler) until chocolate is completely melted and mixed. Chill mixture for ½ hour.
- Melt the bitter chocolate in another bowl, using same method as before. Keep in a warm place.
- Shape the bittersweet chocolate mixture into small balls 1-inch in size. Place on a tray and refrigerate for 1 hour.
- Pierce each truffle with a toothpick and dip in the liquid bitter chocolate. Return to tray and keep refrigerated. After 15 minutes roll them in confectioners sugar; return to refrigerator to preserve the truffles.

New York, New York

GATEAU PARADISE

Serves: 8 to 10

6 egg whites
2 cups sugar
⅓ cup finely ground almonds
2 tablespoons sweet cocoa
1 cup sweet butter, softened
¼ pound sweet chocolate, melted
Confectioners sugar

- Preheat oven to 250 degrees. Cut 4 rounds of parchment paper about 8 inches in diameter.
- Whip 4 egg whites until frothy. Gradually add 1½ cups sugar and ⅓ cup finely ground almonds and beat until stiff.
- Spread each round of paper with meringue. Bake on a baking sheet in a slow oven for about 15 minutes, or until the meringue is dry. Turn layers over and continue to dry for about 5 minutes.
- In the top of a double boiler, over hot but not boiling water, beat 2 egg whites until foamy. Beat in gradually ½ cup sugar, sweet cocoa, butter and melted sweet chocolate. Beat well and remove from heat. Allow to cool.
- When the filling is firm, spread it on 3 meringue layers, put them together, place 4th layer on top. Dust with confectioners sugar. Chill until serving time.

New York, New York

EGGPLANT SALAD

"Sammy's Style"

Serves: 4 as an appetizer
2 as an entrée

2 large eggplants
1 large cucumber, peeled, sliced in half lengthwise, seeded and diced
2 large tomatoes, diced
1 large green pepper, seeded and diced
1 large Spanish onion, peeled and diced
3 tablespoons cotton seed, soy, or vegetable oil
Juice of 1 lemon
Freshly minced garlic to taste
Salt and freshly ground pepper to taste

- Use tongs to turn the eggplants (to avoid piercing them).
- Roast the eggplants over a medium to high flame, turning frequently, until the outer skin is charred on all sides. The eggplant may be roasted directly on a gas burner or on a metal rack which has been placed over the burner.
- When all sides are evenly charred, remove the eggplants and allow them to cool.
- Peel the eggplants, from top to bottom, and then dice finely. Place the eggplants in a large bowl.
- Add the cucumber, tomatoes, green pepper, onion, oil and lemon juice and mix well.
- Season with garlic, salt and pepper and serve at room temperature.

New York, New York

"MEDAGLIONI AL BAROLO"

Serves: 4

½ cup vegetable oil
8 Medallions of beef, cut ¾ to 1-inch thick
½ cup flour
2 cloves of garlic (optional)
3 tablespoons margarine
¼ cup shallots, finely chopped
1½ cups Barolo wine
Salt and freshly ground pepper to taste
¼ cup brown gravy

- Heat the oil in a large sauté pan over medium heat.
- Sprinkle medallions on both sides with flour. As soon as the oil is hot place the medallions and garlic in the pan, and cook briefly for about one minute per side. Remove the meat from the pan and dispose of the oil and the garlic. Lower the heat.
- Using the same pan, rapidly melt 2 tablespoons of margarine and sauté the shallots. Add ½ cup of Barolo wine, raise the heat to high, letting it evaporate rapidly.
- Return the meat to the pan, season with salt and pepper, and add the rest of the wine. Let it evaporate again, turning the meat from time to time. By the time the wine has evaporated, the heat should be high enough so that the meat will be done at the medium-rare stage.
- Transfer the medallions to a warm plate. To the sauce in the pan, add one tablespoon of margarine and the brown gravy. Stir rapidly over high heat with a wooden spoon.
- Pour all the sauce from the pan over the medallions and serve at once.

New York, New York

"RISOTTO CON PUNTE DI ASPARAGI"

Serves: 6

1 onion, chopped
1 teaspoon parsley, finely chopped
2 cloves of garlic
1 tablespoon of olive oil and 3 tablespoons of margarine
6 cups of chicken bouillon or more as needed
½ cup of white wine
Salt and freshly ground pepper to taste
2 cups "Arborio" Italian rice
18 green asparagus tips, steamed and cut in pieces

- Heavy ¾-inch saucepan.
- In a saucepan over medium heat, brown the chopped onion, parsley and the cloves of garlic in 3 tablespoons of margarine and olive oil. Add ½ cup of bouillon, ½ cup of white wine, salt and pepper. Cook for 10 to 12 minutes, then remove the garlic.
- Add rice and bring to a boil. Start adding the bouillon a little at a time as is needed keeping the rice very moist and stirring occasionally.
- Cook for about 20 minutes until the rice is "al dente". A few minutes before the rice is done, add the asparagus and stir for the last time.
- Remove from heat and turn into a hot serving platter.

THE "21" CLUB

New York, New York

MUSHROOMS Á LA DAUM

Serves: 4

2 cups sliced mushrooms
1 cup minced onions
1 cup cooked tongue, cut into julienne strips or any tasty meat diced fine
Salt and freshly ground pepper to taste
8 tablespoons (½ cup) unsalted margarine
* ¼ cup Brown Sauce, recipe follows
Fresh parsley

- In a mixing bowl, combine the mushrooms, onions, tongue and seasonings.
- Melt the margarine in a skillet and sauté the mushroom mixture over medium heat for about 5 minutes, until the mushrooms and onions are soft. Stirring in the brown sauce, heat for 1 more minute. Serve over toast or prepared artichoke bottoms. Garnish with parsley.

* ***Brown Sauce***

Yield: 1 quart

5 cups strong beef stock
4 tablespoons unsalted margarine
4 tablespoons all-purpose flour
1 clove garlic, peeled
1 bay leaf
½ teaspoon dried chopped thyme
1 small onion, chopped
¼ teaspoon Worcestershire sauce
Madeira wine to taste
Salt and freshly ground pepper to taste

- Preheat oven to 350 degrees.
- Bring the stock to a boil. In a small heavy-bottomed saucepan, melt the margarine and add the flour, blending thoroughly with a whisk. Allow to cook for a few minutes until the mixture is slightly browned. Pour the stock into a casserole dish and stir in the roux (butter-flour mixture). Simmer over low heat until the stock is slightly thickened. Add the garlic, bay leaf, thyme, onion and Worcestershire sauce. Place the casserole in the oven, "roasting" for about 1½ hours. Strain the sauce into a bowl or pan, add the wine, and season to taste with salt and pepper.

New York, New York
Stefan Kopf, Executive Chef

FILLET OF SALMON WITH LEMON BUTTER SAUCE AND BABY ASPARAGUS

Serves: 2

Lemon Butter Sauce

Juice from 2 lemons
1 cup heavy cream
½ pound sweet butter, room temperature
Salt to taste
Cayenne pepper

- Pour lemon juice into pan, place on stove and reduce by one half.
- Add heavy cream and reduce until thickened. Remove from heat; whip in butter a little at a time. Season with salt and cayenne pepper.

2 salmon fillets
12 baby asparagus

- Steam salmon fillets, place on a plate. Pour sauce over them and garnish with asparagus.

New York, New York

BLUEFISH WITH GINGER AND SCALLIONS

Serves: 2

1 (10-ounce) piece fillet bluefish
1 tablespoon scallion, sliced
½ tablespoon ginger, shredded
Fresh ground pepper to taste
½ tablespoon soy sauce
1 tablespoon sherry wine
½ cup water

- Preheat oven to 400 degrees.
- Lay bluefish in a flat pan. Sprinkle with scallion, ginger and pepper. Pour soy sauce, wine and water over the fish.
- Cover with aluminum foil and bake for 30 minutes.

The Point
Saranac Lake, New York

ANTHONY'S FLOURLESS CHOCOLATE RUM CAKE

Serves: 8

2 ounces unsweetened chocolate
14 ounces semisweet chocolate
5 tablespoons Myers Dark Rum
4 tablespoons strong coffee
1 teaspoon vanilla extract
½ cup granulated sugar
6 whole eggs, extra large
1 cup heavy cream, whipped

- Preheat oven to 350 degrees. Prepare a 12-inch spring form greased with shortening and lightly sugared.
- In a double boiler, melt the chocolates with rum, coffee and vanilla. Be careful not to burn chocolate.
- Beat the eggs and sugar in mixer until 5 times the volume.
- Incorporate whipped cream with chocolate. Fold in beaten eggs and sugar. Be careful not to overmix, this will lessen the volume.
- Bake for 1 hour. Let cake rest for ½ hour before removing from form.

Note: Be sure spring form does not leak because cake must be baked in a water bath.

New York, New York

FRESH TUNA GRILLED ON CHARCOAL WITH GARLIC, HERBS AND ANCHO CHILI BUTTER

Serves: 4

Sauce

8 ancho chili peppers, or other dry red chili pods
1 gallon very hot water
½ cup warm water
3 tablespoons olive oil
2 cloves fresh garlic, minced
1 small onion, minced
1 teaspoon ground cumin
1½ teaspoons oregano
4 tablespoons butter or margarine cut into very small cubes

- Soak ancho chilies in very hot water for 20 minutes to reconstitute. Remove from water and split, remove tops and all seeds from inside. Place in food processor or blender and purée with ½ cup warm water into a fine, smooth paste.
- In a medium saucepan, heat oil and add onion and garlic, cooking until onion is clear. Add chili purée and remaining seasonings and bring to a boil. Reduce heat and simmer for 10 minutes. Take pan off heat and whisk in butter cubes very slowly. Serve chili butter on side of cooked tuna and garnish with sliced fresh limes.

Grilled Tuna

2 pounds fresh tuna steaks, ⅔-inch thick
4 cloves fresh garlic, minced
1 teaspoon oregano
1 teaspoon fresh coriander leaves, chopped
2 tablespoons olive oil
Salt and pepper to taste
2 limes, sliced
Sauce, preceding recipe

- Start a charcoal fire outdoors. (It is preferable to use an electric starter rather than fluid as fluid tends to flavor food.) Let charcoal burn down to hot coals. Five minutes prior to cooking, the addition of mesquite chips to fire will add a very rich smoke flavor.
- Rub tuna steaks with garlic and sprinkle with olive oil, herbs, salt and pepper. Grill over charcoal for approximately 4 to 5 minutes on each side.

Note: Tuna should be cooked over very high heat to lock in flavor.

Houston, Texas

FILLETS OF TROUT WITH TOMATOES AND PESTO SAUCE

Serves: 6

Pesto Sauce

1 cup coarsely chopped fresh basil, moderately packed
½ cup olive oil
Salt and pepper to taste
4 ripe tomatoes, peeled and seeded
¼ cup pignolias (pine nuts)
⅓ cup grated Parmesan cheese

- Combine the ingredients in a blender, process until fairly smooth.

6 ripe tomatoes, peeled, seeded and sliced
Butter, as needed
Salt and pepper to taste
6 fillets of trout
½ cup pesto sauce
3 tablespoons butter, cut into bits

- Preheat oven to 300 degrees. Butter a shallow casserole or gratin dish.
- Cover the bottom of baking dish with half the tomato slices. Season with salt and pepper. Bake 15 minutes.
- Place the fillets of trout on top of the tomatoes, each fillet folded in half with a tablespoon of heated pesto sauce inside. Cover with the remaining tomato slices. Season again and dot with butter.
- Grill 5 to 10 minutes or until fish is pure white and flaky. Serve hot or cold.

Houston, Texas

OSSOBUCO MILANESE

(The classic veal shank Milan-style)

Serves: 6

6 to 8 pieces (about 5½-pounds) meaty slices of veal shank cut across the marrowbone, each slice about 2-inches thick
Salt and freshly ground pepper to taste
Flour for dredging
3 tablespoons olive oil or margarine
1½ cups finely chopped onions
½ cup chopped celery
1 cup chopped carrots
2 tablespoons plus 1 teaspoon finely minced garlic
1 teaspoon crushed marjoram
1½ cups dry white wine
3 cups peeled, crushed tomatoes
1 teaspoon finely grated lemon rind
2 teaspoons finely grated orange rind
¼ cup finely chopped parsley

- Sprinkle the veal with salt and pepper to taste and dredge in flour. Shake off excess.
- Heat the oil or margarine in a heavy skillet large enough to hold the veal shanks, bone upright, in one layer. Brown the veal all over, about 30 minutes. Add the onion, celery and carrots. Cook, stirring, about 5 minutes. Add two tablespoons garlic and the marjoram. Stir and add the wine. Cook about one minute and add tomatoes, salt and pepper to taste. Cover and cook about one and one-quarter hours.
- Blend the lemon and orange rinds and remaining teaspoon minced garlic. Sprinkle over the veal and stir to blend. Cover and cook fifteen minutes longer. Sprinkle with chopped parsley.
- Serve with Risotto.

UMBERTO RISTORANTE

Exquisite Italian Cuisine

Rye, New york

ZUCCHINI Á LA UMBERTO

Serves: 4

6 small zucchinis unpeeled
1 tablespoon butter
½ cup heavy cream
½ cup grated Parmesan cheese
Pinch of fresh ground black pepper

- Wash and trim the ends off the zucchini. Cut each zucchini into 4 quarters lengthwise. Remove a little of the center core (seed section) of each piece. Cut each quarter into 2-inch pieces.
- Place zucchini into a pot of slightly salted boiling water. Parboil for 2 minutes. Drain and pat dry.
- In a large skillet melt butter and cook lightly (do not burn). Add zucchini, stirring slightly and making sure it is hot and dry. Add cream and stir to mix. Add half the Parmesan cheese, stirring carefully until cheese melts.
- Sprinkle with the remaining cheese. Remove from skillet and place in a Au Gratin or casserole dish.
- Place under broiler for a minute or two, until golden in color. Do not burn. Serve immediately.

New York, New York
Christian Marteau, Chef de Cuisine 1984

ESCALOPE OF SALMON IN FRESH HERBS SAUCE

Serves: 6

4 small shallots, thinly sliced
4 medium (button) mushrooms, thinly sliced
1 pound of butter, room temperature
1½ cups dry white wine
2½ cups fish stock
2 cups Crème Fraîche (or heavy cream)
Salt and black pepper to taste
1 teaspoon fresh chervil, chopped very fine, reserve some leaves for decoration
1 teaspoon fresh Italian parsley, chopped very fine, reserve some leaves for decoration
1 teaspoon fresh basil, chopped very fine
1 teaspoon fresh tarragon, chopped very fine
8 ounces of salmon (1 large escalope per person)
2 teaspoons olive oil

- In a saucepan, melt about 1 tablespoon of butter. Add shallots and mushrooms. Cook over low heat (slowly) for 5 minutes.
- Add the wine. Over moderate heat, reduce by half, then add the fish stock and again reduce sauce by half.
- Pour in the Crème Fraîche (or heavy cream) and continue to reduce the sauce until it has thickened. When the sauce has a nice consistency, add salt and pepper. Strain sauce into a clean saucepan. Add the herbs to the sauce. Over low heat finish the sauce by whisking the rest of the butter (except for ½ teaspoon needed for salmon preparation). Strain and reserve.
- Sauté the escalopes of salmon for about 3 to 5 minutes in a teaspoon of olive oil and ½ teaspoon of butter. Sprinkle with a touch of salt and pepper.
- The dish is now ready to serve as follows:
  Nap the bottom of each plate with about ¼ cup sauce. Place the salmon escalope on top of the sauce (one for each plate). Add some leaves of chervil or Italian parsley around the salmon for decoration.

New York, New York
Christian Marteau, Chef de Cuisine 1984

TARTE AU CHOCOLAT

Serves: 8

Note: An electric mixer *is not* recommended. Please use whisk as instructed.

5 ounces butter
*** 7 ounces semisweet chocolate**
2 eggs
4 ounces sugar
1 ounce flour

- Preheat oven to 250 degrees. Use an 11-inch steel or "Tefal®" tart pan (circular).
- Combine the butter and chocolate in a double boiler. Melt over low heat; cool.
- In a mixing bowl, with whisk, beat the eggs until light. Add sugar; beat until fluffy. Add flour; beat for 8 minutes. Slowly add the cooled chocolate mixture and stir until just combined.
- Spread mixture into tart pan and bake for 20 minutes. Let cool.

Glaze (Topping)

*** 5 ounces semisweet chocolate**
¾ ounce sugar
4 ounces butter
1½ ounces milk

- Combine all ingredients for glaze in a double boiler, stir until melted. Then over direct heat, whisk until it just comes to a boil.
- Spread over top of the cooled baked portion of the tart. Serve at room temperature.

* *Note:* A European chocolate is recommended for best taste.

Vista International Hotel
New York, New York
Walter Plendner, Executive Chef

FILLET OF RED SNAPPER WITH ORANGE SLICES AND GINGER

Serves: 6

2 tablespoons margarine
6 (8-ounce) fillets of red snapper
2 tablespoons orange juice
2 tablespoons lemon juice
2 tablespoons dry kosher vermouth
Rind of 2 oranges, julienned
Salt to taste
Freshly ground white pepper to taste
½ ounce fresh ginger, julienned
2 oranges, sectioned

- Preheat oven to 350 degrees. Grease a baking dish with margarine.
- Place the fillets, skin side down, in a single layer in the prepared baking dish.
- Combine the orange and lemon juice, pour over fish, cover and place in refrigerator to marinate for 30 minutes.
- Bake for 15 to 20 minutes or until fish flakes easily.
- Reduce marinade in a skillet, add vermouth, orange rind, salt, pepper and ginger.
- Pour sauce over red snapper fillets and garnish with fresh orange sections.

Vista International Hotel
New York, New York
Walter Plendner, Executive Chef

ROAST RACK OF LAMB WITH MUSTARD SEEDS

Serves: 6

2 racks of lamb, fully trimmed
1 clove garlic
½ teaspoon salt
½ teaspoon thyme, dried
3 tablespoons English mustard, prepared
4 tablespoons light olive oil
4 tablespoons mustard seeds
¼ cup parsley or watercress

- Preheat oven to 500 degrees. Oil a roasting pan.
- Place oven rack at upper middle level.
- Score the tops of the racks of lamb lightly, making shallow crisscross knife cuts in the covering fat.
- Mash the garlic and salt together in a small mixing bowl. Mash in the thyme, then beat in the mustard and oil. Brush mixture over tops and meaty ends of lamb.
- Set racks, meat side up, on the roasting pan, and fold a strip of aluminum foil over the rib ends to keep them from burning.
- Place lamb in oven for 10 minutes. Turn oven down to 400 degrees. Cover the top of the racks of lamb with mustard seeds and roast for 15 more minutes. Remove from oven.
- Spoon sauce from pan juices around the lamb. Garnish with parsley or watercress.

New York, New York

CAPELLINI PRIMAVERA

Sirio Maccione of Le Cirque, originated Capellini Primavera. This is our popular version of this favorite dish.

Serves: 4

1 medium carrot, finely julienned
¼ pound fresh mushrooms
8 broccoli flowerets
¼ pound snow peas
2 cups consommé, chicken or clear vegetable broth
1 medium zucchini, finely julienned
1 small tomato, quartered
¼ pound lightly salted margarine
Salt and pepper to taste
¾ to 1 pound capellini spaghetti
8 quarts water

- Blanch all vegetables except tomato and zucchini. Drain. Vegetables should be CRISP.
- Bring consommé to a boil, add all vegetables, margarine, salt and pepper to taste. Cook for 2 or 3 minutes keeping emphasis on NOT overcooking vegetables. Set aside.

To prepare

- Fill a large pot with 8 quarts water. Add salt and bring to a rapid boil. Add capellini and STIR IMMEDIATELY. Remove before "al dente" (still firm to the bite). Drain.
- Place capellini into a heated serving bowl. Add all the hot liquid from the vegetables to the Capellini. Toss. Add remaining vegetables and serve promptly.

Note: Capellini is a very fine pasta and will continue to cook even after it has been removed from the boiling water. Therefore, it is very important that the timing between the pasta and the sauce be simultaneous. Enjoy!

Vivolo

New York, New York

CHICKEN FIORENTINA

Serves: 4

4 boneless chicken breasts
Flour, as needed
2 eggs, beaten
Peanut oil, for frying
¼ cup white wine
1 stick margarine, room temperature
2 lemons
Salt and pepper to taste
1 cup consommé
½ pound fresh spinach
Lemon wedges for garnish

- Use a 10-inch fry pan.
- Dredge chicken breasts in flour then in beaten egg. In a fry pan, add just enough oil to fill bottom of pan to ¼ inch depth. When hot (a drop of water must bounce), sauté chicken until golden brown on both sides. Do not crowd in pan when sautéing. Remove from pan; when finished discard all the oil.
- Deglaze pan by adding ¼ cup white wine (turn heat to high until all the alcohol has evaporated). Add ½ stick of margarine and lower heat. When margarine is melted, squeeze one whole lemon into pan, return all the chicken, add salt and pepper to taste, add the consommé and continue to cook thoroughly for about 5 to 7 minutes. Reduce sauce. It will thicken on its own. If too thick, add additional consommé. If too thin, remove chicken, and add additional margarine and turn heat on high.
- Steam spinach and then sauté in margarine.
- To serve, place spinach on a warm serving dish, top with chicken, add sauce and lemon wedges to garnish. Enjoy!!

Shelley Winters
New York, New York

CAESAR SALAD

My favorite recipe

Serves: 8 to 10

4 heads romaine lettuce, torn into bite size pieces
3 cloves garlic
1 teaspoon salt
1 teaspoon black pepper
1 raw egg
Juice of 3 lemons
½ cup salad oil
1 tablespoon Worcestershire sauce
1 cup croutons
6 tablespoons grated Italian cheese
Anchovies, as desired

- Chill lettuce in refrigerator until ready to use.
- Rub salad bowl with garlic; add salt and pepper. Break in raw egg; add lemon juice.
- Combine salad oil with Worcestershire sauce and add.
- Place chilled lettuce in bowl and mix lightly. Add croutons, cheese and anchovies (as desired) and toss all together.

SPA CUISINE
Bay Basil Savory Coriander Sage Rosemary Parsley Mint Coriander Sage Rosemary
Sage Rosemary Parsley Mint Cinnamon Marjoram
Marjoram Thyme Juniper Bay
Bay Basil Savory Coriander Sage Rosemary Parsley Mint Cinnamon Parsley
Sage Rosemary Parsley Mint Cinnamon Marjoram Thyme Juniper Coriander Sage
Marjoram Thyme Juniper Bay Basil Savory Coriander Bay Basil

BONAVENTURE®
RESORT & SPA

THE SPA OMELETTE WITH FRESH HERBS, SHALLOTS, DICED TOMATO AND PARMESAN CHEESE

Serves: 4

1 ripe tomato, diced
2 tablespoons minced shallots
2 teaspoons safflower oil
12 egg whites
1 tablespoon fresh chopped parsley
½ teaspoon oregano leaves (no more)
2 teaspoons chopped basil
2 tablespoons grated Parmesan cheese

- Mix tomato and shallots together. Drizzle safflower oil over them, taking care not to add too much oil.
- Heat a small non-stick skillet until very hot. Add ¼ of mixture to pan and stir until shallots are clear. Add three egg whites, slightly beaten.
- Mix all herbs and Parmesan cheese together in a small bowl. Sprinkle about 1 teaspoon of herb mixture over eggs, fold over and sprinkle about an additional ½ teaspoon of herb mixture over folded omelette. Cook just until firm throughout.
- Serve on clear glass plates, garnished with parsley and a thin slice of kiwi, orange, or melon.
- 80 calories per serving.

Andrew Adriance, R.D.
Bonaventure Resort & Spa
Fort Lauderdale, Florida

BONAVENTURE®
RESORT & SPA

GRILLED MARINATED CHICKEN BREAST WITH FRESH HERBS

Serves: 12

Prepare ahead

2 cups chicken stock
½ cup chablis
½ cup chopped shallots
½ cup safflower oil
2 tablespoons chopped fresh parsley
2 tablespoons chopped fresh rosemary
Rosemary sprigs
12 boneless chicken breasts, skin and fat removed, 4-ounces each

- Place all marinade ingredients in a ½ -inch deep shallow stainless steel pan. Marinade may be reused for up to 6 days. Cover boneless chicken breasts in mixture for at least 24 hours, up to 48 hours refrigerated.
- Grill chicken for about 5 minutes on each side over medium flame. Brush with marinade 2 to 3 times during cooking to avoid drying out.
- Serve hot, garnished with fresh rosemary sprig.
- 170 calories per serving.

Andrew Adriance, R.D.
Bonaventure Resort & Spa
Fort Lauderdale, Florida

BONAVENTURE®
RESORT & SPA

SZECHWAN RED SNAPPER

Serves: 4

4 fresh Red Snapper fillets, 6-ounces each
1 green chile, diced finely
1 teaspoon Tabasco sauce
1 tablespoon low sodium soy sauce
1 small purple onion, sliced very thinly
Juice of 2 lemons
1 cup dry white wine
4 black mushrooms, soaked, then sliced
1 cup celery hearts, sliced very thinly diagonally
2 tablespoons minced lemon grass or baby chives

- Use an 11-inch x 13-inch non-stick baking dish sprayed with a food release spray or oiled lightly.
- Arrange fillets in the prepared baking dish and refrigerate.
- In a medium bowl, combine remaining ingredients, except lemon grass. Allow to marinate at room temperature ½ to 1 hour.
- Preheat broiler to 375 degrees. Position rack in middle of oven, not close to heat source.
- Pour marinade with vegetables over fish. Arrange onion slices over top of fish.
- Broil 12 to 16 minutes depending on thickness of fillets. Fish is done when flesh is white throughout. Serve immediately over brown rice or cellophane noodles. Spoon sauce over top. Sprinkle with lemon grass.
- 210 calories per serving.
- 70 calories per ½ cup for rice or noodles.

Andrew Adriance, R.D.
Bonaventure Resort & Spa
Fort Lauderdale, Florida

BONAVENTURE®
RESORT & SPA

WHOLE WHEAT VEGETABLE LASAGNA

Serves: 12

1 pound whole wheat lasagna noodles, cooked according to package directions
2 tablespoons extra virgin olive oil
2 tablespoons diced garlic in oil
1 small white onion, diced
1 green pepper, diced
1 cup diced zucchini
1 cup diced cauliflower
2 #303 cans low sodium tomato sauce
1 teaspoon oregano leaves
3 tablespoons fresh basil, chopped
2 tablespoons fresh parsley, chopped
½ pound part-skim mozzarella cheese, grated
¾ cup fresh grated Parmesan cheese

- Preheat oven to 350 degrees. Oil an 11-inch x 14-inch baking pan.
- Drain noodles and hold in cold water with ice cubes.
- Heat oil in a large sauté pan. Add garlic and onion. Stir-fry for 2 minutes. Add green pepper, zucchini, broccoli and cauliflower. Stir-fry for 4 minutes. Add tomato sauce, oregano, basil and parsley. Reduce to simmer, cover and cook for 10 minutes.
- Line bottom of prepared baking pan with cooked noodles. Pour ⅓ of sauce mixture over noodles. Sprinkle ⅓ of each cheese over this. Repeat layering procedure twice so cheese is on top.
- Cover baking pan with foil. Bake for 45 minutes. Remove foil and bake an additional 15 minutes. Cut into 12 square portions. Serve in shallow glass bowl.
- This will hold well in 275 degree oven, covered, for about 1 hour.
- 270 calories per serving.

Andrew Adriance, R.D.
Bonaventure Resort & Spa
Fort Lauderdale, Florida

Acknowledgement is made to Sabino Health and Fitness Resort, Inc., d/b/a Canyon Ranch for permission to reprint the recipes for Bran Muffins, Canyon Ranch Bread, Canyon Ranch Stuft Spud, French Lamb Chops and Lasagna from Canyon Ranch Menus and Recipes by Jeanne Jones, Copyright© 1984 by Sabino Health and Fitness Resort, Inc., d/b/a Canyon Ranch. Reprinted by permission of the publisher, Sabino Health and Fitness Resort, Inc., d/b/a Canyon Ranch, Tucson, Arizona.

BRAN MUFFINS

Yield: 12 muffins

¼ cup orange juice
1 cup buttermilk
1 egg
¼ cup molasses
1 cup whole wheat flour
¾ cup bran
¼ teaspoon salt
¾ teaspoon baking soda
¼ teaspoon nutmeg
1½ teaspoons orange peel
½ cup apple, grated (optional)

- Preheat oven to 350 degrees. Use a 12-cup non-stick muffin pan.
- Combine the orange juice, buttermilk, egg and molasses and mix well.
- Add the flour, bran, salt, soda, nutmeg and orange peel and mix thoroughly. Add the apple if desired.
- Place in non-stick muffin pans and bake for approximately 15 minutes.
- Each muffin contains approximately 70 calories.

Canyon Ranch
Tucson, Arizona

CANYON RANCH BREAD

Yield: 18 slices

1½ cups whole wheat flour
1 cup unprocessed wheat bran
1 tablespoon baking powder
¼ teaspoon baking soda
3 tablespoons fructose
1 teaspoon ground cinnamon
⅓ cup raisins, finely chopped
1⅓ cups buttermilk
1 egg, lightly beaten
4 teaspoons vanilla extract

- Preheat oven to 350 degrees. Use a 9-inch x 5-inch x 3-inch non-stick bread pan.
- Combine the flour, wheat bran, baking powder, soda, fructose and cinnamon in a large mixing bowl and mix well. Add the raisins and again mix well.
- Combine the buttermilk, egg and vanilla in another bowl and mix well.
- Pour the liquid ingredients into the dry ingredients and again mix well.
- Pour the mixture into the bread pan and bake for 50 minutes. Place the bread on its side on a wire rack to cool.
- Each slice contains approximately 60 calories.

Canyon Ranch
Tucson, Arizona

LASAGNA

Yield: 18 (3-inch x 2¼-inch servings)

3 (16-ounce) cans Italian tomatoes, undrained
4 (6-ounce) cans Italian tomato paste
4 large onions, diced
3 garlic buds, finely chopped
1 cup finely chopped parsley
1 tablespoon oregano, crushed, using a mortar and pestle
1 teaspoon marjoram, crushed, using a mortar and pestle
1 teaspoon salt
½ teaspoon thyme, crushed, using a mortar and pestle
½ teaspoon freshly ground black pepper
½ pound lasagna noodles, cooked
1 (16-ounce) carton part skim ricotta cheese
2 cups (½-pound) grated part skim mozzarella cheese
¾ cup grated Parmesan or Romano cheese

- Preheat oven to 375 degrees. Use an 8¾ -inch x 13½-inch baking dish.
- Pour all of the juice from the canned tomatoes into a large pot. Chop the tomatoes and add to the juice. Add all other ingredients except the lasagna and cheeses and bring to a boil.
- Reduce the heat and simmer, uncovered, for 1½ hours, stirring occasionally.
- Pour ¼ of the sauce in the bottom of the baking dish. Add a layer of lasagna noodles and a layer of each of the cheeses. Repeat these layers, placing the last ¼ cup of the sauce over the top and sprinkling it with Parmesan or Romano cheese.
- Bake in oven for 1 hour. Remove from the oven and allow to stand for at least 10 minutes before slicing to serve.
- Each serving contains approximately 140 calories.

Canyon Ranch
Tucson, Arizona

FRENCH LAMB CHOPS

Serves: 8

8 small loin lamb chops, cut 1½-inch thick and all fat removed
Garlic powder
Freshly ground black pepper
3 cups finely chopped parsley
3 tablespoons unprocessed wheat bran
¾ cup Dijon mustard

- Preheat oven to 500 degrees.
- Lightly sprinkle both sides of the lamb chops with garlic powder and freshly ground black pepper and place them in a baking dish.
- Combine the parsley, wheat bran and mustard and mix thoroughly. Spread the mustard mixture evenly over the tops of the lamb chops. Place in the center of the oven for 4 minutes. Turn the oven off but do not open the door for 30 more minutes.
- Each serving contains approximately 110 calories.

CANYON RANCH STUFT SPUD

Serves: 2

2 small baking potatoes
1 medium onion, finely chopped
¼ cup buttermilk
½ cup low fat cottage cheese
3 tablespoons grated Parmesan or Romano cheese
2 tablespoons chopped green onions, including the tops

- Preheat oven to 400 degrees.
- Wash the potatoes well. Pierce with the tines of a fork and bake for 1 hour.
- Cut a very thin slice form the top of each potato. Remove the pulp from the potatoes, being careful not to tear the shells. Mash the potato pulp and set aside in a covered bowl. Keep the shells warm.
- Cook the onions, covered, over low heat until soft, stirring occasionally to prevent scorching. Add the mashed potatoes, cottage cheese and all other ingredients except the chopped green onions. Mix well and heat thoroughly. Stuff the potato mixture back into the warm shells. They will be heaping way over the top!
- To serve, sprinkle the top of each Stuft Spud with 1 tablespoon of chopped green onion. If you have prepared them in advance, heat in a 350 degree oven for 10 to 15 minutes, or until hot, before adding the chopped onions.
- Each serving contains approximately 180 calories.

ROSEMARY DRESSING

Yield: 1½ cups

¾ cup virgin olive oil
½ cup red wine vinegar
1 tablespoon balsamic vinegar
¼ cup water
1 tablespoon Dijon mustard
2 tablespoons fresh rosemary
1 teaspoon freshly ground black pepper

- Remove rosemary leaves from stem. Place in a small pot on medium heat with virgin olive oil. Simmer oil and rosemary until light brown. Do not burn rosemary. Cool to room temperature. Strain to remove rosemary.
- Combine vinegars, water, mustard and pepper in a medium mixing bowl. Whisk in rosemary flavored oil drop-by-drop unitl combined.
- Store in refrigerator.
- Serving Size: 1 tablespoon, Calories: 55, Fat Points: 6.

Michael McVay, Executive Chef
Carol Caldwell, R.D., M.S., Lead Nutritionist
Doral Saturnia International Spa Resort
Miami, Florida

BUCKWHEAT WAFFLES

Yield: 3 whole waffles

1 cup buckwheat flour
1 cup whole wheat flour
1 teaspoon baking powder
½ teaspoon baking soda
1 teaspoon molasses
1 medium egg, beaten
1 cup buttermilk

- Combine dry ingredients. Beat wet ingredients. Stir egg mixture into flour mixture.
- Cook in waffle iron, following manufacturer's guidelines.
- Serve each ½ waffle with 1-ounce blueberry sauce.

Note: Use 4-ounce ladle of mix for 1 waffle. (Calories per ½ waffle: 155, Fat Points per ½ waffle 2, Calories with 1-ounce blueberry sauce: 190, Fat points with 1-ounce blueberry sauce: 2).

BLUEBERRY SAUCE

Yield: 1 cup

2 cups fresh blueberries
1 teaspoon lemon juice
½ cup pear nectar
½ cup water
2 tablespoons cornstarch

- Place all ingredients in a small stainless steel sauce pan. Bring to a low boil, stirring constantly.
- Reduce heat and simmer for 10 minutes.
- Serving size: 1-ounce, Calories: 35, Fat points: 0.

Michael McVay, Executive Chef
Carol Caldwell, R.D., M.S., Lead Nutritionist
Doral Saturnia International Spa Resort
Miami, Florida

CANNELLONI WITH VEGETABLE FILLING

Serves: 6

12 (1-ounce) sheets of whole wheat pasta, approximately 6-inch x 6-inch, cooked
3 cups cannelloni vegetable filling, recipe follows
12-ounces red sauce, recipe follows

- Preheat oven to 325 degrees.
- On a 1-ounce sheet of pasta place ¼ cup of cannelloni filling across one end and roll to seal. Do the remaining sheets in the same fashion.
- Place in a glass casserole and cover with aluminum foil to form a tight seal.
- Place in oven and bake for 25 minutes.
- To serve: Place two rolled cannelloni on serving dish, top with 2-ounces of red sauce and serve.
- Calories: 280, Fat Points: 4.

Cannelloni Vegetable Filling

Yield: 3¼ cups

½ pound onions
½ pound carrots
½ pound celery
½ pound zucchini
2 tablespoons garlic, chopped
½ teaspoon salt
Pinch pepper
2 teaspoons fresh oregano
2 teaspoons fresh basil
1 teaspoon fresh thyme
½ pound cottage cheese, 1% low sodium
1-ounce Parmesan cheese, grated

- Shred all vegetables on the coarse side of a box grater or in a food processor.
- Place grated vegetables and seasonings in a heavy saucepan. Simmer until volume is reduced by half. Remove from heat.
- Fold in cottage cheese and Parmesan cheese.
- Serving Size: ¼ cup, Calories: 45, Fat Points: 1.

Red Sauce Yield: 5½ cups

1 (28-ounce) can crushed tomatoes
1 carrot, peeled and chopped
1 small onion, peeled and chopped
2 cups clear vegetable broth (no fat, low sodium)
4 cloves garlic, chopped
1 tablespoon fresh basil, chopped

- Simmer all ingredients in a heavy saucepan for 1 hour. Cool to room temperature.
- Place in food processor or blender and purée until smooth.
- Serving Size: ¼ cup, Calories: 20, Fat Points: 0.

Michael McVay, Executive Chef
Carol Caldwell, R.D., M.S., Lead Nutritionist
Doral Saturnia International Spa Resort
Miami, Florida

TOMATO MIX FOR PASTA PRIMAVERA

Serves: 2

1 anchovy filet
2 cups vine ripened tomatoes, diced
1 teaspoon virgin olive oil
1 tablespoon garlic, chopped
2 tablespoons fresh basil, chopped
¼ teaspoon salt

- Press anchovy filet with the side of a knife on cutting board, rubbing back and forth to form a paste. Place in a bowl with the rest of the ingredients.
- Cover and refrigerate for 2 hours.
- May be prepared the day before.

To Finish

- Place in a non-stick sauté pan on high heat. Stir and bring to a boil. Add 2-ounces cooked pasta, stir until heated and serve.
- For Sauce; Serving Size: 1 cup, Calories: 70, Fat Points: 3
- For Finished Dish: Calories: 240, Fat Points: 5.

Michael McVay, Executive Chef
Carol Caldwell, R.D., M.S., Lead Nutritionist
Doral Saturnia International Spa Resort
Miami, Florida

BAKED ACORN SQUASH WITH TURKEY AND WILD RICE STUFFING

3 (1½-pound) acorn squash
2 cups full-flavored turkey stock or canned chicken consommé
½ cup brown rice
½ cup wild rice
½ cup chopped celery
½ cup chopped onion
2 tablespoons walnut or olive oil
2 cups diced cooked turkey or chicken
¼ cup dry sherry or brandy
1 teaspoon rosemary
1 teaspoon chopped sage
2 tablespoons chopped parsley
¼ cup slivered toasted almonds (toast almonds in a 400 degree oven for about 10 minutes)
Salt and pepper to taste
Large red cabbage leaves
Fresh herb sprigs (parsley, sage, rosemary)

- Preheat oven to 400 degrees.
- Poke a few holes into acorn squash, place on a baking pan and bake for 1 hour and 15 minutes until tender to the touch; slice in half and remove seeds.
- Add stock, brown rice and wild rice to the saucepan, cover and cook on a low heat for about 50 minutes until rice has absorbed all the liquid.
- In a large skillet, sauté the celery and onion in oil until onion is translucent and slightly browned. Remove from heat; add rice, turkey, sherry, herbs and almonds. Mix and season to taste with salt and pepper.
- Portion out mixture into the cavity of each acorn squash. Before serving, heat squash in a covered casserole; remove from casserole and serve on a large platter or individual dinner plates lined with a bed of red cabbage leaves and garnished with fresh herbs.

Harris Golden, Executive Chef
Elizabeth Arden's Maine Chance
Phoenix, Arizona

CHEESE SOUFFLÉ

The cheese soufflé has been served at Maine Chance every Saturday afternoon for more than thirty-five years.

Serves: 6

Butter
Grated Parmesan cheese
1 cup skim milk
½ cup skim milk mixed with 3 tablespoons whole-wheat flour
1 cup grated Jarlsberg cheese (4-ounces)
1 cup grated mild Cheddar cheese (4-ounces)
¼ teaspoon cayenne pepper
5 egg yolks
8 egg whites
¼ teaspoon cream of tartar

- Preheat oven to 350 degrees. Prepare an 8-cup soufflé bowl by lightly buttering and sprinkling grated Parmesan cheese inside of bowl.
- In a saucepan, heat 1 cup milk until simmering. Add the well-blended mixture of ½ cup milk and 3 tablespoons flour to simmering milk and cook, stirring constantly, until mixture thickens. Remove from heat.
- Add cheese and cayenne pepper. Egg yolks may be added as soon as the mixture is cool enough to prevent them from cooking. Mix thoroughly to obtain a smooth, lump-free sauce.
- In a mixing bowl, beat the egg whites until foamy. Add cream of tartar and continue beating until egg whites are stiff and hold their shape, but still have a velvety appearance.
- Fold cheese mixture into egg whites.
- Pour mixture into the prepared soufflé bowl. Place in a pan of water and bake for 1 hour and 15 minutes.

Note: The major difference between this cheese soufflé and conventional ones is the amount of fat. In most cheese soufflé recipes, a roux made with a good quality of butter mixed with flour is used to thicken the milk. The cheese by itself has enough fat to make the soufflé tender and creamy. Therefore, skim milk substitutes perfectly well for whole milk without affecting quality. I think you will find this soufflé to be healthier, lighter and tastier than most butterfat-laden conventional cheese soufflés.

Harris Golden, Executive Chef
Elizabeth Arden's Maine Chance
Phoenix, Arizona

SPINACH SOUFFLÉ

Serves: 6

Softened butter
Whole-wheat bread crumbs
2½ tablespoons butter
2 tablespoons minced shallots or green onions
1½ cups milk
4½ tablespoons whole-wheat flour
2 heads spinach, cleaned and chopped
¼ cup toasted slivered almonds (toast almonds in 400-degree oven for 12 minutes)
½ teaspoon salt
¼ teaspoon black pepper
¼ teaspoon nutmeg
5 egg yolks
8 egg whites
¼ teaspoon cream of tartar

- Preheat oven to 350 degrees. Prepare an 8-cup soufflé bowl by buttering and sprinkling whole-wheat bread crumbs inside of bowl.
- Sauté the minced shallots or onions in butter until soft. Add 1 cup of milk and heat until simmering.
- Meanwhile, mix together the remaining ½ cup milk and whole-wheat flour. Make a smooth paste and add to simmering milk. Cook, stirring constantly, until mixture comes to a boil and thickens. Remove from heat.
- In a large kettle of boiling water, blanch the spinach for 1 minute, then drain well by pressing down on spinach with your hands in a colander. Add spinach, almonds, salt, pepper and nutmeg to milk mixture. Add egg yolks one at a time.
- In a mixing bowl, beat the egg whites until foamy. Add cream of tartar and continue beating until egg whites are stiff and hold their shape, but still have a velvety appearance.
- Fold egg whites into spinach mixture. Pour mixture into prepared soufflé bowl and sprinkle top with whole-wheat bread crumbs. Place bowl in a pan of water and bake for 1 hour and 15 minutes.

Harris Golden, Executive Chef
Elizabeth Arden's Maine Chance
Phoenix, Arizona

BULGUR WHEAT PILAF WITH SKEWERED VEGETABLES

Serves: 6

Ingredients for Bulgur Wheat Pilaf:

1 cup chopped onions
2 tablespoons safflower oil
1½ cups bulgur wheat (may be purchased in most health food stores)
3 cups water
⅓ cup dark raisins
⅓ cup golden raisins
½ cup shelled, unsalted, uncolored pistachio nuts
1 teaspoon cinnamon
½ teaspoon cayenne pepper
1 teaspoon salt

- In a skillet with a tight-fitting cover sauté the onions in the oil until soft and translucent.
- Add bulgur wheat, stir and cook until golden.
- Stir in remaining ingredients. Cover, bring to a boil, reduce heat and simmer for 15 minutes until all water is absorbed and the bulgur wheat is tender but still crunchy.

Note: One can dream up any combination of vegetables to put on the skewers. To give it the gourmet touch always try to vary shapes, colors and textures. Here is just one example:

Ingredients for Skewered Vegetables:

12 large mushroom caps
12 squares of cut red pepper about 2-inches x 2-inches
12 cauliflower buds about 2-inches in diameter
6 pieces of cut zucchini about 3-inches long
2 tablespoons honey
2 tablespoons melted butter
½ tablespoon lemon juice
½ cup cornmeal
1 teaspoon salt

- Cook vegetables until tender but somewhat crunchy. On 6 skewers thread the vegetables in the following order: a mushroom cap, a red pepper square, a cauliflower bud, a piece of zucchini, a cauliflower bud, a red pepper square and a mushroom cap. Place skewered vegetables on a lightly greased or nonstick baking pan.
- Mix honey, butter and lemon juice together and brush on vegetables.
- Mix cornmeal and salt together. Sprinkle over vegetables.
- Place prepared vegetables under a pre-heated broiler and broil until crumb topping is golden brown. Place over Bulgur Wheat Pilaf and serve.

Harris Golden, Executive Chef
Elizabeth Arden's Maine Chance
Phoenix, Arizona

HOT BLUEBERRY COBBLER WITH HONEY YOGURT

Serves: 6

2 pints blueberries
2 tablespoons granulated sugar
1 teaspoon grated lemon rind
⅓ cup water
4 tablespoons butter, room temperature
½ cup whole-wheat flour
½ cup rolled oats
¼ cup brown sugar
¼ teaspoon cinnamon
⅛ teaspoon almond extract
2 cups plain yogurt
Honey

- Preheat oven to 375 degrees. Use a large shallow heatproof casserole or individual casserole dishes.
- Combine the berries, granulated sugar, lemon rind and water in a saucepan. Bring ingredients to a boil and simmer for 2 minutes.
- Meanwhile, combine the butter, flour, oats, brown sugar, cinnamon and almond extract. Work with your hands until mixture is crumbly.
- Transfer blueberries to a large shallow heatproof casserole or individual casserole dishes. Sprinkle crumbs over berries. Bake about 30 minutes until browned.
- Mix yogurt with honey until desired sweetness. Serve on the side with the hot blueberry cobbler.

Harris Golden, Executive Chef
Elizabeth Arden's Maine Chance
Phoenix, Arizona

ANJOU PEARS WITH ORANGE ZABAGLIONE

Serves: 4

Gently poached Anjou pears are flavored with cinnamon, honey and vanilla and served with an extravagant Orange Zabaglione spiked with Grand Marnier. This elegant dessert is the perfect climax for a sumptuous Spa dinner party. If you're planning ahead, the poaching liquid can be made several days in advance and the pears can be cooked the day before, but the zabaglione must be whisked at the last minute, just before serving, to maintain its frothy finesse.

Poaching Liquid

1 quart water
1 tablespoon vanilla extract
2 tablespoons honey
¼ teaspoon barley malt sweetener (optional)
¼ cup white wine
1 cinnamon stick
⅛ teaspoon ground coriander
2 slightly underripe Anjou pears

Orange Zabaglione

2 egg yolks
¼ teaspoon vanilla extract
1½ teaspoons Grand Marnier
2 teaspoons grated orange rind
¼ cup fresh orange juice
1½ teaspoons honey
Pinch of barley malt sweetener (optional)

Garnish

Finely julienned orange rind
4 lemon leaf sprigs

- Combine all poaching liquid ingredients in a saucepan. Bring to a boil, then reduce heat and simmer for 10 minutes. Strain the mixture and let cool.
- Cut the pears in half lengthwise and core. Place in a wide saucepan, cut side down, and cover with the cooled poaching liquid. Bring to a boil, lower the heat, and simmer, uncovered, until the pears are tender but still somewhat firm, about 3 to 5 minutes, depending on the ripeness of your pears. Remove from the heat and let stand while you prepare the zabaglione.
- In the top of a double boiler or in a metal mixing bowl (copper is best), combine all the zabaglione ingredients. Whisk constantly over simmering water until the sauce is thickened and foamy, about 5 minutes. Remove the bowl from the water to keep the eggs from coagulating.
- Spoon 2 tablespoons of zabaglione on each of 4 serving plates and arrange the pears over the sauce, cut side down. Decorate with the orange rind and lemon sprigs and serve at once.

We acknowledge *Edward J. Safdie's* gracious permission to reprint this recipe from his book, SPA Food.

MINNESOTA WILD RICE SALAD

Serves:4

Prepare ahead

2⅔ cups raw wild rice
1 teaspoon chopped fresh tarragon or ½ teaspoon dried
1 garlic clove
6 ounces firm tofu
¼ cup chopped chives
2 tablespoons chopped Italian parsley
1 small red onion, minced
½ red or green pepper, minced
½ cup Spa Vinaigrette made with walnut oil, recipe follows
10 cherry tomatoes
2 large carrots
2 large zucchini
20 endive spears

- The night before you serve the salad, cover the wild rice in cold water to cover and soak in the refrigerator until morning. Drain the wild rice and put it in a large kettle. Cover with 2 quarts of cold water and add the tarragon and garlic. Bring to a boil and cook until tender but not mushy, about 15 to 20 minutes. (Start testing the wild rice after 15 minutes.) Do not allow the grains to "pop". When done, drain the wild rice, remove the garlic, and let cool in a large mixing bowl.
- Cut the tofu into small bite-size pieces and add to the cooled wild rice, together with the chives, parsley, onion and pepper. Pour on the vinaigrette, toss gently to mix, and let stand at room temperature for 2 hours.
- Just before serving, cut the cherry tomatoes in half. Shred the carrots and zucchini on a mandoline or with the fine shredder of food processor.
- Arrange 5 spears of endive in a star shape over two thirds of each serving plate. Spoon the wild rice-tofu mixture over the bottom of the leaves and mound the carrots and zucchini around the base of the rice, leaving the endive tips exposed. Place half a cherry tomato in each endive spear and serve.

Note: Originally created for the Spa, this spectacular salad has become one of the most popular dishes on the regular menu at the Sonoma Mission Inn. When planning, note that the wild rice preparation must begin the night before.
• 205 calories per serving.

Spa Vinaigrette Yield: ¾ cup

2 tablespoons cold-pressed safflower oil
2 tablespoons rice wine vinegar
2 tablespoons sparkling mineral water
1½ tablespoons fresh lime juice
1 tablespoon grainy mustard (Pommery or Moutarde de Meaux)
2 tablespoons minced shallots
1 tablespoon chopped fresh chives
8 grinds white pepper
Vegetable seasoning to taste

• Put all ingredients in a bowl and whisk to blend. Store in the refrigerator in a tightly covered container.

Note: In summer, add fresh basil, tarragon, savory, or oregano. Add chopped or pressed garlic (judiciously) or a drop or two of hot sauce for more piquancy. For a variation, you might wish to substitute cold-pressed walnut oil for a strong distinctive flavor or fruity extra-virgin olive oil, and blend with a simple red wine or champagne vinegar. Plan to make it a few days ahead; as it ages the flavors blend together and are enhanced.

We acknowledge *Edward J. Safdie's* gracious permission to reprint this recipe from his book, SPA FOOD.

HALIBUT STEAMED IN LETTUCE LEAVES WITH NEW POTATOES

Serves: 4

8 large leaves red leaf lettuce
4 (4-ounce) halibut fillets
2 tablespoons minced shallots
4 small new red potatoes, unpeeled
1 quart fish stock, recipe follows
1 tablespoon unsalted butter
1 medium leek (white part only), washed, patted dry, and cut into julienne strips
1 large celery stalk, cut into julienne strips
1 carrot, peeled and cut into julienne strips
½ zucchini, cut into julienne strips
¼ cup water
1 tablespoon each chopped fresh chives, parsley, basil and tarragon

- To prepare the halibut packages, have a bowl of ice water ready. Bring 3 quarts of water to a boil and blanch the lettuce leaves for 2 seconds. Immediately scoop up the leaves with a slotted spoon or wire strainer and plunge them into the ice water. Carefully spread the leaves on towels and pat dry.
- For each package, overlap 2 lettuce leaves and place a piece of fish in the center. Sprinkle 1½ teaspoons of shallots over each fillet and wrap the lettuce around it, completely enclosing it. If the packages are made in advance, cover them tightly with plastic wrap and refrigerate.
- About 25 minutes before serving, put the potatoes in a saucepan with cold water to cover, bring to a boil, reduce the heat, and cook at a fast simmer until they are fork-tender, about 15 to 20 minutes.
- Pour the stock into a steamer and bring to a boil. Place the halibut packages in the top of the steamer, lower into the pot, and steam for 5 to 8 minutes.
- Just before serving, melt the butter in a large sauté pan, add the leek, celery, carrot and zucchini and toss for 1 minute. Add the water and chopped herbs and bring to a boil, stirring and tossing to combine the ingredients. Remove from the heat and divide the vegetables and their juices among 4 heated dinner plates. Place the halibut over the vegetables. Drain and slice the potatoes and place 1 on each plate. Serve at once.

Note: After the fish has been steamed, cool and freeze the stock for future use, its flavor now further enriched by the halibut juices.

- 180 calories per serving.

Fish Stock

Yield: 3 quarts

5 pounds fish bones (gills removed) from white-fleshed fish
1 gallon water
1 onion, cut into wedges
1 celery stalk, sliced
1 sprig Italian parsley
¼ cup chopped mushrooms or mushroom trimmings
1 tablespoon white peppercorns
1 cup dry white wine (optional)

- Wash the fish bones under cold running water and remove any blood or entrails. Put in a large soup kettle with all the remaining ingredients and bring to a boil over high heat. Reduce the heat and simmer, uncovered, for 30 minutes. (Further cooking would make this stock bitter.) Strain through a fine sieve and discard the bones and vegetables. Unless the stock is to be used immediately let cool, uncovered, to room temperature.
- 12 calories per quart.

We acknowledge *Edward J. Safdie's* gracious permission to reprint this recipe from his book, SPA FOOD.

YELLOW AND GREEN VEGETABLES WITH HUMMUS DIP

Serves: 8

Prepare ahead

1 cup cooked chickpeas
¼ cup soft tofu
1 large garlic clove
2 tablespoons extra-virgin olive oil
2 tablespoons chopped Italian parsley
¼ cup minced scallions
Freshly ground white pepper to taste
Vegetable seasoning to taste
16 slender asparagus spears, tough ends trimmed
24 snow peas, ends trimmed and strings removed
8 broccoli flowerets
2 yellow bell peppers
½ pound zucchini

- Purée the chickpeas, tofu, garlic and oil in food processor. Scrape into a bowl, add all the remaining dip ingredients, and stir to combine. Cover and store in the refrigerator for at least 2 hours before serving.
- Bring a large pot of water to a boil; prepare a large bowl of cold water. Blanch the asparagus in the boiling water for 30 seconds. With tongs or a large skimmer, remove from the pot and place in the cold water. Put the snow peas in a strainer, dip into the boiling water for 10 seconds, then remove and add to the asparagus. Add the broccoli to the boiling water, cook for 30 seconds, and drain, discarding the water. Add the broccoli to the bowl of cold water. When the vegetables have cooled completely, drain and pat dry.
- Remove and discard the stem from the pepper, cut it into quarters, and cut away the seeds and membranes. Cut the quarters in half lengthwise. Scrub the zucchini, cut off the ends, and cut sticks about 2½ inches long by ¼ inch thick.
- Arrange the vegetables on a tray or platter and serve with the bowl of hummus.

Note: Make this thick creamy dip ahead of time, even the night before the party, to give the flavors time to blend. Use any seasonal vegetables that strike your fancy; carrots, blanched green beans, celery, and endive are good choices.
- 92 calories per serving.

We acknowledge *Edward J. Safdie's* gracious permission to reprint this recipe from his book, SPA FOOD.

SKINNY SALADE NICOISE

Serves: 4

1 (14-ounce) can packed-in-water tuna, drained
1/8 teaspoon Dijon mustard
1 tablespoon fresh lemon juice
1/2 onion, thinly sliced
1 clove garlic, minced
1 green pepper, chopped
2 tablespoons chopped parsley
1/4 cup chopped celery
6 stuffed olives, sliced
1 tomato, cut in chunks
Freshly ground pepper, rosemary and oregano

- Mix all ingredients together, seasoning to taste with pepper and crushed herbs.
- 130 calories per serving.

Rosalie Woodrow
Woodrow Weigh of Life
Rye Brook, New York
Weight Control Counsellor

EGG WHITE OMELETTE WITH FARMER CHEESE, COTTAGE CHEESE, OR FRESH MUSHROOMS

Serves: 1

3 egg whites - 45 calories
1/4 cup Farmer Cheese - 50 calories
1/2 cup sliced fresh mushrooms - 20 calories
1/2 cup diced peppers - 15 calories
1/2 cup diced onions - 10 calories

- Spray teflon pan with Pam and heat. Lighlty blend egg whites with fork. Cook egg whites slowly over low heat until bottom is set. Add Farmer cheese, mushrooms, peppers and onions. Put under broiler if desired.
  Omelette with Farmer Cheese - 95 calories
  Omelette with Fresh Mushrooms - 65 calories
  Omelette with Peppers and Onions - 70 calories

Rosalie Woodrow
Woodrow Weigh of Life
Rye Brook, New York
Weight Control Counselor

CHINESE CHICKEN WITH PLUM SAUCE

Serves: 4

4 large chicken breast halves, skin removed
6 very ripe purple plums, unpeeled, pitted and sliced thin
1 medium onion, sliced thin
1 clove garlic, crushed
2 tablespoons lemon juice
2 tablespoons lite soy sauce
⅓ cup water

- Spray medium frying pan with Pam. Brown chicken breasts on all sides. Discard any fat. Turn chicken skinned side up. Add remaining ingredients and cover.
- Simmer for 40 minutes, basting occasionally with sauce. Add more water, if necessary, or if sauce is too thin. Remove lid and simmer a few minutes longer. Serve.
- 210 calories per serving.

Rosalie Woodrow
Woodrow Weigh of Life
Rye Brook, New York
Weight Control Counsellor

ROASTED WHOLE CHICKEN

Juiciest and most delicious chicken you've ever eaten!

Serves: 2

1 whole chicken
1 to 2 cloves fresh garlic, chopped or garlic powder
Freshly ground pepper to taste
Lemon juice to taste
Fresh vegetables, (broccoli, green beans, onions, peppers and zucchini)
Lemon rinds

- Preheat oven to 450 degrees.
- Season chicken with garlic, pepper and lemon juice both inside and out.
- Stuff cavity with vegetables and lemon rinds.
- Roast for 1½ hours.

Rosalie Woodrow
Woodrow Weigh of Life
Rye Brook, New York
Weight Control Counselor

BAKED TUNA, BOSTON SCROD OR HALIBUT

Serves: 1

½ pound tuna, scrod or halibut
1 tablespoon Dijon mustard
1 teaspoon mustard seed
Freshly ground pepper to taste
Paprika to taste
¼ teaspoon dill
Sprinkling of lemon juice
½ cup white wine

- Preheat oven to 350 degrees.
- Spread tuna with mustard and mustard seed. Add freshly ground pepper, paprika, dill, lemon juice and wine.
- Bake for approximately 15 minutes and then brown under broiler for 1 minute.

Rosalie Woodrow
Woodrow Weigh of Life
Rye Brook, New York
Weight Control Counsellor

BROILED CORNISH GAME HEN WITH TOASTED COCONUT AND ORANGE WEDGES

Serves: 2 to 4

2 Cornish game hens
1 tablespoon low-sodium soy sauce
2 teaspoons toasted coconut
1 small orange, cut into wedges

- Preheat oven to 375 degrees.
- Cut hens in half and sprinkle with soy sauce. Broil to brown each side.
- Bake in oven about 35 minutes. Sprinkle with coconut and garnish with orange wedges.

Rosalie Woodrow
Woodrow Weigh of Life
Rye Brook, New York
Weight Control Counsellor

CRUNCHY HAWAIIAN TURKEY SALAD

Serves: 4

Prepare ahead

2½ cups cubed cooked turkey
½ cup low calorie dressing
½ cup sliced celery
½ cup pineapple chunks
¼ cup sliced water chestnuts
½ teaspoon sugar substitute
⅛ teaspoon ground ginger
3 cups finely shredded lettuce
Watercress
Poppy seeds

- Marinate turkey in dressing in refrigerator for several hours or overnight. Drain, reserving ¼ cup dressing.
- In a large bowl, toss marinated turkey, reserved dressing, celery, pineapple, water chestnuts and seasonings.
- Serve over lettuce. Garnish with watercress and sprinkle poppy seeds over all.

Rosalie Woodrow
Woodrow Weigh of Life
Rye Brook, New York
Weight Control Counsellor

DIET PIE

Unbelievably delicious!

Serves: 6 to 8

- Preheat oven to 375 degrees. Use a 9-inch or 10-inch pyrex pie plate. Fill pie plate with cut up fruit. You may use apples, pears, peaches, plums, strawberries, blueberries, nectarines, or pineapple in it's own juice.
- Add 2 packages gelatin mixed with 1 (16-ounce) bottle Black Cherry No Cal. Top with ½ cup dry milk powder and 2 teaspoons cinnamon.
- Bake for 45 minutes and refrigerate until firm.

Rosalie Woodrow
Woodrow Weigh of Life
Rye brook, New York
Weight Control Counsellor

SPA COFFEE MALTED

So thick and rich you won't believe you're dieting.

Yield: 2½ cups

8 ounces skim milk
1 heaping tablespoon instant powdered coffee or instant powdered espresso
1 (.035-ounce) package low-calorie sugar substitute
2 ice cubes

- Put all ingredients into a blender. Turn machine onto Frappe and blend until ice cubes have dissolved.
- Malted will be thick and frothy.

Corrine Katz
White Plains, New York

WILD RICE SOUP

Add this to your repertoire.

Serves: 8

1 tablespoon butter
2 ounces leeks, diced finely
1 ounce carrots, diced finely
1 ounce celery, diced finely
1 tablespoon flour
3½ cups clear vegetable broth
4 ounces wild rice
7 ounces evaporated skim milk
Salt to taste
1 tablespoon sherry
Chopped chives and parsley to garnish

- Sauté leeks, carrots and celery in butter until soft, but not brown. Add flour and stir over heat for 2 minutes. Add broth gradually, stirring continuously to avoid lumps. Add rice and skim milk once simmering. Simmer until rice is tender. Season to taste.
- When ready to serve, add sherry and garnish with chopped chives and parsley.
- 93 calories per serving.

Helen Campbell
New York, New York

MARINATED CHICKEN SLICES

A delicious combination of colors and flavors.

Serves: 2 to 4

1 pound boned and skinned chicken breasts, sliced very thin
¼ cup lemon juice
¼ teaspoon minced garlic
1 tablespoon oil
1 (8-ounce) can water chestnuts, drained and sliced
1 cup fresh mushrooms, thinly sliced
½ cup scallions with tops, chopped
½ cup green pepper, thinly sliced
½ cup red pepper, thinly sliced
¼ teaspoon black pepper
⅛ teaspoon crushed red pepper
1 tablespoon light soy sauce

- Marinate chicken in lemon juice and garlic for 15 minutes.
- While chicken is marinating, heat oil in wok or large skillet, and add water chestnuts, mushrooms, scallions, green and red peppers. Cook until scallions and peppers are tender, about 3 minutes. Remove vegetables from wok and keep warm.
- Drain chicken, reserving lemon juice marinade. Place chicken slices in wok (or skillet) and brown lightly. Return vegetables to wok, add reserved lemon juice, black pepper, crushed red pepepr, and soy sauce. Heat through and serve immediately over cooked rice.

Lisa Katz
White Plains, New York

CHICKEN YVONNE

No salt or oil-but delicious!

Serves: 6

2 medium or 1 large onion, sliced thin
¾ teaspoon white pepper
¾ teaspoon basil
¾ teaspoon thyme
1 tablespoon parsley, chopped
¾ teaspoon garlic powder
¼ cup lemon juice
2 chickens, cut into pieces
1 teaspoon paprika

- Preheat oven to 400 degrees. Use a large baking pan.
- Layer onions on bottom of baking pan. Mix seasonings together except paprika. Sprinkle on both sides of chicken pieces. Pour lemon juice over the chicken. Top with paprika.
- Bake for 25 minutes, then turn; baste with juices. After 1 hour turn again and bake until golden brown.

Yvonne Maxwell
Los Angeles, California

PITA PIZZA

A great new lunch idea.

Serves: 2

2 large pita pockets, split in half
½ to ¾ cup tomato sauce, homemade or jar
1¼ teaspoons dried minced garlic
Crushed red pepper, to taste
1 medium tomato, chopped
1 cup chopped onions
2 green Italian peppers, chopped
½ pound fresh water packed mozzarella cheese or 1 (6-ounce) package sliced low-sodium cheese of your choice

- Lightly toast each pita half. Remove from toaster.
- Spread tomato sauce evenly over each half. Divide the remaining ingredients onto each half and top with cheese.
- Place under broiler and broil until cheese has melted. Watch carefully so they do not burn.

Lisa Katz
White Plains, New York

DIET CHEESE CAKE

What a way to diet!

Serves: 8 to 10

Prepare ahead

15-ounces ricotta cheese
1 egg
6 envelopes Sweet-N-Low
1 teaspoon vanilla
1 (16-ounce) can crushed pineapple, unsweetened, drained, reserve ½ cup juice
Pinch salt
1 envelope gelatin, dissolved in ½ cup water or pineapple juice
Cinnamon

- Preheat oven to 350 degrees. Grease an 8-inch square pan or 9-inch pie plate.
- Mix all ingredients together and pour into pan or pie plate. Sprinkle with cinnamon.
- Bake for 35 minutes. Allow to stand until cool. Refrigerate for at least 4 to 5 minutes.

Note: ¼ of recipe is equivalent to a Weight Watchers lunch.

Ruth Turim
Brooklyn, New York

INDEX